BEYOND THE VEIL OF DELUSIONS

Understanding Relationships Through Homeopathy

SECOND REVISED EDITION

Mati H Fuller, DI Hom (pract)

Bigger Vision Books

BEYOND THE VEIL OF DELUSIONS

Understanding Relationships Through Homeopathy

SECOND REVISED EDITION

ISBN 978-0-6151-7138-8

Published by Bigger Vision Books
Cover design by Mati H Fuller and Nigell Fuller
Printed by http://www.lulu.com

Credits

New Comprehensive Homeopathic Materia Medica of Mind,
by Dr. H.L. Chitkara
B. Jain Publishers (P.) Ltd.
Email: bjain@vsnl.com
Website: http://www.bjainindia.com

There are Two Types of Relationships:

One is of Fight, Fear, Hatred –

This Creates Ego –

The other is of Love, Compassion, Sympathy.

These are the Two Types of Relationships.

Wherever Love is, Fight Ceases, Ego Drops.

This is Why You Cannot Love.

It is Difficult,

Because to Love Means to Drop the Ego,

To Drop Yourself.

Love Means Not to Be.

A Bird on the Wings

Bhagwan Shree Rajneesh

ACKNOWLEDGEMENTS

First I would like to thank my friend and editor Dianne Bairstow for patiently reading and editing this book. Her efforts to make the book easy to read and understand is much appreciated. I would also like to thank all the couples who volunteered their stories for the book so that we can all learn more about relationship dynamics. A big thanks to Maria T Bohle for writing the forword, and last, but not least, to Nigell, Holly and Taru for putting up with me while I was working on this project. Thanks to all of you who made it possible for me to write this book, I couldn't have done it without your help!

FOREWORD

"Beyond the Veil of Delusions - Understanding Relationships Through Homeopathy" by Mati H Fuller is a fascinating psychological and homeopathic study of human nature and its inner relationships.

Mati's understanding of psychology and her proficiency in homeopathic medicine merge together in this delightful, easy to read and easy to understand book.

We all have a need for water, food, and a hospitable climate where we can live and thrive comfortably. We all have a need for love, attention and affection, but our love relationships and interactions have always been a source of mystery to many of us. How often have we heard, "What does he see in her?" or "They seemed like such a nice couple, why did they split up?" Or, even, "Why do they stay together?" These questions have never been adequately explained, but Mati's insights remove the mystery. This book sheds light upon the motivations of many constitutional remedies and it enlightens the reader to the needs, desires and fears each remedy exhibits. Now we can understand the glue that holds relationships together or the repelling forces that might precipitate a separation.

Beyond the Veil of Delusions is fascinating reading, not just for the homeopath, but for anyone who is a student of human behavior, or for anyone who wants to achieve a better understanding of what makes relationships work or not work. Through Mati's understanding of human needs at the more elemental levels of security, image and delusions these remedy pictures come alive.

Mati Fuller brings a rich background to the homeopathic table. Her study of homeopathy and her clearness of vision and understanding of human behavior make this a unique but solid compilation of her knowledge. Although her book is more than 300 pages long, I do have one complaint: it was so good that Mati left me wanting more. I scoured the index hoping for just one more remedy, well maybe two more, or even three more would be nice...

Mati has opened a door for us, a door that many homeopaths can now pass through, she has brought our literature and understanding to a new, exciting dimension, and I look forward to her next book as time allows her to continue her project into the future.

This book is a classical piece of literature; it will take its place prominently on my book shelf right next to Catherine Coulter, Robin Murphy's Workbook, Gibbson and Bailey's Psychology. I am always delighted to have another reference book that I can use to refresh my knowledge in a particular area and Mati's book has done that – taught me more in an exciting, refreshing way.

Maria T. Bohle, CCH, RS Hom (NA), DHM, DCN, FBIH, Director, The British Institute of Homeopathy, USA

Table of Contents

PART THREE

RELATIONSHIPS

Predictable Patterns

PART FOUR

THE BIGGER PICTURE

Conclusions and Reflections

INTRODUCTION
What Inspired Me to Write This Book

Life isn't always fun. Good things happen, and bad things happen, too. We live in a dimension of duality, where good and bad are just two sides of the same coin. When good things happen, we are at ease, and when bad things happen, we become stressed and troubled. We often wish for only happiness and joy, but the fact is, it is often the more difficult times that allow us to "rise to the occasion" and expand to new levels of consciousness in order to find a way to move beyond the misery we are experiencing.

It was one of those difficult times that actually inspired me to write this book. As every woman knows, when we feel miserable, it always helps to talk to a girlfriend, so that is what I did. In fact, I talked to three different girlfriends that day, and every one of them had a different response to my story. After the first one heard what I had to say, she looked around and said: "Well, at least you still have a nice house." The second girlfriend listened to the exact same story and said: "I don't know why you are so miserable. You didn't even have to pay out any money!" And after I told the story, again, to the third girlfriend, she took my head in her hands and looked into my eyes and said: "Whatever happens, try not to be bitter about it!"

As I thought about their comments, I wondered why their responses were so totally different, when the story I told each one was exactly the same. All of a sudden, I could clearly see why. The first girlfriend was a Calcarea Carbonica, and in her perception of reality, life is extremely scary if you don't have a house. I still have a nice house, so she couldn't see any reason for me to be miserable. The second girlfriend was an Arsenicum Album, always worried about money issues, so in her perception of reality I was fine because nobody took my money. And the third girlfriend was, of course, a Natrum Muriaticum. She was feeling my pain, and she gave me the best advice she could, based on her own perception of reality: "Try not to get bitter about it!" I thought to myself, whoa! This is probably what we all do, but why do we do this? And why do different people perceive the same thing in so many different ways? I wondered if I could find more answers if I studied the mental and emotional symptoms associated with each remedy profile, and I also wondered how much these different perceptions of reality affect our lives and our relationships. As I delved into my books as deeply as I could, with great interest and determination, one thing led to another, and before long, I found myself in the middle of writing this book.

BACKGROUND

As far back as I can remember, I have always been interested in medicine and psychology, and I had a hard time deciding which one of the two I wanted to study. After looking into both, I decided not to study either. Each view was simply too limited and it wasn't until I learned about homeopathy that I really found what I was looking for. In homeopathy we don't just look at a small part of the picture. Homeopathy is a holistic form of healing that takes into consideration that true healing has to happen on every level, physically, mentally and emotionally, and this point of view made much more sense to me.

As a student of homeopathy, I started reading everything I could find about the psychological profiles of the remedies, since I was especially interested in how the mental state can affect our lives. However, many of the books that offer insight into the psychological profiles are mainly based on the homeopath's observations of their own clients. They don't necessarily offer any explanations as to why people act the way they do, or how they perceive their reality. While finding what I read interesting, I wanted to go deeper than that. My goal was to find a way to really understand where someone was coming from. I wanted to literally "get into their heads" and find out who the people of the Materia Medica really were. So my next step was to buy books that contained only mental and emotional symptoms so that I could study this issue more in depth by looking for the thread that ties all the symptoms together.

Finding the thread that ties the symptoms together was, however, much easier said than done! The amounts of mental and emotional symptoms collected in the books are enormous, page after page of symptoms under each remedy. The symptoms are listed alphabetically, which is nice if you are looking for a particular symptom, but nowhere do they show how the symptoms are connected to each other in such a way that the person, who needs the remedy, literally appears before you, and you can see how he perceives his reality. So the first thing I did was to rearrange all the symptoms in a more logical way to see if that would make a difference. First I grouped together the symptoms that describe the person in a balanced state. Then I looked at ailments, to see what kind of situations the person was affected by. I also looked at delusions and fears to see how the situations associated with this remedy profile changed the person's perception of reality over time, and at last I looked at how the person coped, or didn't cope, with the situation. The interesting thing that I found, by arranging the symptoms in this kind of order, is that there does, indeed, seem to be a core story, or a core situation, reflected in each remedy profile. Once we know what this core story is, and what remedy someone needs, we can easily explain, or even predict, what someone is going to do in a given situation since we can actually understand where they are coming from once we know what the story is. The story, or situation I am referring to, may be nothing but an old memory, past down through the generations, but nevertheless, it still affects us deeper than we could ever imagine! Therefore, the story, or situation, doesn't necessarily reflect something that has actually happened to someone in this lifetime, it simply reflects how he perceives his reality on a daily basis, and this perception of reality then affects everything he does. He lives and acts *as if* the core situation that goes with the remedy profile, actually, is the reality of his life, here and now, even though this perception is most likely just based on subconscious beliefs, or delusions, that he is not even aware of.

Here I would like to clarify why we are talking about delusions and not just illusions. Psychologists believe that you have to be almost psychotic to have delusions, and that what we may be dealing with are just illusions. An illusion is a false understanding, or erroneous perception of reality, that will change if there is proof that the illusion is wrong. An example is when you are walking in the forest and you see a stick on the ground and somehow think it is a snake. It may scare you at first, but as soon as you see that it isn't a real snake, the illusion disappears. If, however, you are dealing with a false perception of reality that you believe to be true, regardless of any evidence, we are dealing with delusion, and not just illusion.

Delusions are extremely hard to change because they don't respond to logical arguments or other types of evidence. Because the delusions always seem real to the person who suffers from them, they have the power to make us sick physically or mentally and often complicate our relationships to other people. The only way we can free ourselves from these delusions, is by slowly becoming more and more aware of what our subconscious beliefs, or delusions, really are. As our awareness grows and we are able to see these delusions in ourselves, we'll also be able to recognize old patterns in our lives that are caused by these delusions. Once recognition is there, we can then slowly start making a conscious effort to break these patterns.

As an example of this, we can look at how Nux Vomica perceives his reality. Nux acts as if he is on the battlefield, even if he isn't really on the battlefield in his present life, and he may have never been on any battlefield, ever. If we study the Nux remedy picture, we can see that Nux is a leader type who likes to make quick decisions without consulting anyone else, he likes confrontation, he is willing to take risks, and he loves being in charge. These are all qualities that would help him survive on a battlefield, where it is essential to have the ability to quickly assess a situation and make decisions on the spot, without having to ask for anyone's advice. In the Nux profile we also find ailments from deception, disappointment and wounded honor. This is often what happens to warriors after they have won a battle. They receive great honor from their victory, only to be betrayed by someone they trust after the battle has been won (like Cesar was betrayed by his stepson Brutus). The fear, that someone could betray him again, makes Nux tense and irritable, always on guard. He therefore prefers to work alone, relying only on himself.

All of Nux's qualities are essential for his survival on the battle field, or even in a competitive job situation, but it can be detrimental to his personal relationships, since he isn't able to just "switch off" his battle mode when it isn't needed any more. Because he perceives reality as if he were on a battlefield at all times, and the perception can't be changed by showing him that there is no battle, he is under *the delusion* that he is on a battle field. If he could be aware enough to "switch off" his battle mode when it wasn't needed any more, it would no longer be a delusion, but that is easier said than done, since most people are completely unaware of the delusions that create their realities.

While I am in the process of clarifying things, I would also like to clarify my use of he or she throughout the book. Some of the remedies are primarily female or male remedies. Because I didn't feel like writing s/he throughout the text, I used she in the remedies that are primarily female, and he in the remedies that are primarily male. In remedies that aren't primarily one or the other, I just randomly picked one. The reader has to be aware that my use of he or she in the text is just a matter of convenience, and that you can have male or female versions of any remedy.

Another matter of convenience was my choice to use remedy names for the characters in the stories, instead of fictitious names. I did this because it makes it easier for the reader to know which constitution the character in the story is, and if the character is a male or female version of a remedy.

One issue that frequently came up anytime I let someone read one of the remedy profiles in Volume 1 were comments about how there isn't a lot of nice traits in the profiles. A comment I often heard was: "Who would want to be with someone like that!" In any book that describes psychological profiles of constitutional remedies, you'll run into the same issue, so I would like to clarify this issue some more.

In every constitution there is a more or less balanced state, where the person feels great on every level and is basically "on his best behavior." We would like to think that we are always balanced beings, and that our behavior is exemplary at all times, but since this is a book about understanding the deeper layers of the psyche and the predictable patterns we see in our relationships, we have to allow ourselves to look into the less than ideal predispositions underneath the surface with an open mind.

It feels great to be in a balanced state, but we all know what happens when daily stresses pile up on us. Sooner or later the niceness disappears and our shadow side takes over. The truth is that we all have a shadow side. The shadow is just as real as the light. The shadow and the light are two complementary aspects that, when put together, make us whole beings, so not only do we have to understand the shadow; we also have to learn to make friends with it to find peace within. You may also argue that I list more negative than positive traits, and that I should have listed an equal amount, but there is a reason for this, too.

If you are sick, you are basically out of balance. If you are stressed and can't cope, you are out of balance. If you have relationship problems which bring out the worst in you, you are out of balance. If you come to see a homeopath, there is an imbalance somewhere that needs to be addressed. So in homeopathy we focus on understanding the imbalance, and that is why the profiles show what happens when we are *not* in a balanced state, and therefore, not necessarily in a state of "niceness."

This is also why I wrote some relationship stories which didn't have good endings. Some of the couples had already split up before I even wrote the story, and some were in the process of splitting up when they came to me. I decided to write the stories anyway, regardless of whether they were still together, or not, because the more we understand what doesn't work, and why, the more we will also understand what works. I was more focused on the understanding that could be gained from the story, rather than what the final outcome of the relationship was. **My perception is that nothing is a mistake if you can learn and gain wisdom from what happened, because anything that happens in your life can help your spiritual growth.** When I previously visited India, I heard a saying that stuck with me: "It isn't what happens that matters, but how you dance with it!" So, I would encourage the reader to keep that in mind. (Just keep dancing!)

Looking at relationships from a homeopathic perspective is an exciting new concept. As homeopaths we have access to very specific information about how different people perceive reality, and why they act, or react, in the ways that they do. Understanding the core issues of the remedies can be an invaluable source of information when it comes to better understanding the dynamics of any relationship, and it can also offer unusual or creative solutions to existing problems.

The purpose for writing this book was to add a new perspective to the information that already exists. I wanted to make the essence of the remedies easier to grasp for anyone who wishes to learn more about the deeper levels of the human psyche, and I also wanted to inspire homeopathic practitioners into looking at homeopathy in a whole new way. I wanted to show that homeopathic remedy profiles are more than just a list of random symptoms; there is actually a relationship between the symptoms, or a "thread" tying them all together, describing a story or a situation that deeply affects everything we do. Once we understand more about how this works, everything starts making sense, and we can begin to see how predictable human behavior actually is. In addition to making it easier to understand human relationships in general, this knowledge will also help homeopaths understand their clients better. If the homeopath can learn to recognize lifelong patterns, or issues, when taking someone's case, it ultimately leads to more appropriate remedy choices and more successful cases.

While writing this book for the purpose of inspiring the readers, I ended up inspiring myself as well. I experienced a continuous deepening of my own understanding of human relationships and also about the spiritual journey of life itself. In Part 4 of the book, I attempted to share some of my newfound insight, so that anyone interested in more than just homeopathic or psychological aspects can follow my journey a few more steps. As a lifelong "seeker of truth," I see everything that happens as a stepping stone to new levels of aware-ness, understanding and wisdom. It doesn't matter if the stepping stone is a relationship, homeopathy, psychology or anything else. All that matters is how we see what is happening, and whether we can allow our perceptions of reality to keep expanding, as well as our understanding of life itself to deepen. There-fore, I have included this part as well, so that anyone, who wishes to delve even deeper into the mystery of life, will have an opportunity to open their hearts and minds still another notch.

PART ONE
Perceptions of Reality

THE MENTAL STATE
What is Real?

What is real? What is truth? The answer depends upon your point of view. Imagine five blind men trying to describe an elephant. One is holding the trunk and describing how soft and round and long it is. Another insists that it is more like a tree trunk. He is describing one of the legs. The one, who is holding the tail, describes how long and narrow it is, with hairs on the end. One of them is holding an ear, which is flat and soft, like a big leaf, and the last one is holding a tusk, pointed and hard with no hair. They are all describing the elephant, but each one can only feel a small part of it.

This story is relevant to all of us because we all do the same thing. We easily jump to conclusions, even though we can't see the whole picture, and we tend to think that our point of view is the only "truth" worth considering. If we were able to see "the bigger picture," there would only be one truth, but since most of us aren't that aware yet, everyone has their own perception of what they *think* the truth is. Unfortunately, what someone thinks the truth is, and what the truth really is, may be two totally different things. So, the first thing we need to understand is how each one of us actually perceives our own personal reality.

The fact is that not only do we see just a small part of the bigger picture, but we also see it through tinted glasses. Our delusions, as well as our underlying cultural beliefs, tint, or distort, our vision in such a way that it is virtually impossible to simply experience reality as it is. This corresponds to the Hindu concept of "Maya." Maya means "that which is not," which refers to the way we perceive the world. Because our perception is clouded by illusion, or delusion, what we perceive, is never the real thing, it is only Maya, illusion, "that which is not." So, how can we get more insight into what is real, if everything we see is just illusion or delusion?

The first thing we have to look at is why we feel the way we do about what happens in our lives. Why do we feel hurt, sad, upset, angry or annoyed when something happens to us? Obviously, our feelings, or reactions, are first of all affected by what is happening in that moment, but the interesting question is, why does the situation we are experiencing trigger *a specific* emotion or reaction? If we try to look deeper into this issue, we may be able to see that our emotions or reactions are always affected by whatever our underlying beliefs are.

As an example of this, we can look at how we perceive the issue of bankruptcy. In America, bankruptcy is not considered a very admirable thing. Someone, who has gone through bankruptcy, has obviously mismanaged his money and spent more than he should have spent; in other words, we are looking at someone with financial problems out of control. Would you want someone like that as a husband for your daughter? I don't think so! However, this is by no means the only way to view the issue of bankruptcy. I have heard that there is a place in India where bankruptcy is actually valued very highly. In this particular community, bankruptcy is considered great business sense. Someone borrows as much money as they can and buys as many things as they need for their business. Then they go bankrupt, they get to keep everything they bought, and they just start over somewhere else. This way, they can build up a lot of wealth very quickly, and not only is it good for business, but it is also an easy way to find a wife. In this place, any parent, who is looking for a man who can provide well for his daughter, would think that someone, who has been through bankruptcy at least once, would be a very desirable mate. The bankruptcy is actually considered proof of how clever he is at accumulating wealth! Here, we can clearly see how our attitude, reaction or feelings about something is totally determined by what our underlying beliefs are.

Our underlying belief system goes a lot deeper than we normally realize. We all know how parents, schools and society actively try to instill a common value system in everyone. These conscious beliefs, which we all share, strongly influence how we perceive our reality and therefore also how we feel and react. The main purpose of instilling these kinds of beliefs, or values, is to make people's reactions and emotions more predictable and acceptable so that it becomes easier for people to live together. This is what we call "cultural values." However, while conscious beliefs, or cultural values, influence us in many ways, our subconscious beliefs, or delusions, influence us even more.

The term subconscious, or unconscious, simply means that the belief, or delusion, is not part of our conscious awareness; in other words, we don't even know that we have these beliefs. This makes it hard to discover what our beliefs, or delusions, really are, but not impossible, because as homeopaths, we have an advantage. We can easily find out more about our delusions by simply studying the mental state that goes with each remedy profile. While doing this, we have to keep in mind that the mental state of a remedy is not just a list of symptoms written in alphabetical order; it is actually a way of perceiving reality. By studying the fears, phobias and delusions associated with each remedy profile, we can get a pretty good idea of what these subconscious beliefs are. Once we know what they are, we can start recognizing them in ourselves, and as our awareness grows, we'll slowly be able to see how deeply we are affected by these beliefs and also what patterns occur as a result.

To shed some more light on this issue, we need to step back for a second and look at how the human mind works. Imagine that you are building your new house and you have designed all the circuits for the electrical system. You have put in a few circuits, but there are still many more to go. When you go to sleep that night, you keep wiring your house in your dreams because the job hasn't been completed in physical reality, so the mind tries to complete it in dreamtime instead. As soon as you complete the whole job, you stop dreaming about electrical work and you can, once again, sleep peacefully.

If this is what happens when a simple job is left incomplete, is it possible that the same phenomenon can happen when any kind of situation is left incomplete or unresolved? Imagine what happens if someone betrays you or treats you unfairly! You go over the situation again and again in your mind until you come to terms with what happened, either by resolving the situation or by letting go. But what if the situation was so severe that you weren't able to resolve it or let it go? Is there a possibility that the unresolved memories and feelings of what happened can change the DNA in such a way that the memory stays, and we can pass down the whole problem to our children, so that they can try to resolve the situation instead? We all know that physical traits are stored in the DNA and passed down to our offspring, so why not mental or emotional issues? The DNA simply holds information, and since there is no separation between body and mind, as I see it, this is a definite possibility. Another possibility is that the information may just be transferred energetically, somehow. I don't know exactly how this works, but the "how" doesn't really matter. The only thing that matters is whether there is *a possibility* that mental or emotional issues, that are incomplete or unresolved, can, indeed, be passed down to our children so that they can complete or resolve the issues instead.

This brings to mind the Buddhist teaching of "the law of Karma," which is basically the law of cause and effect. In this law, it states that every living being is responsible for their actions, as well as the effect of their actions. Here, I would also like to add my own interpretation of the law of Karma. Karma, as I see it, is simply unfinished, unresolved issues which need to be resolved or completed, and the effect of these unresolved issues is pain and suffering for the people involved. It doesn't matter if the completion happens in this lifetime, or if it is passed down to the next generation. The issues will still continue to have an effect until they have been resolved, no matter how long it takes, and only completion or resolution can end our suffering. If this interpretation is accurate, we can easily imagine what the Karmic consequences are. Basically, what this means is that people will be born into this reality with old issues to resolve that may not even have happened to them personally! Something may have happened to your great grandfather, and because he couldn't resolve the issue, you have come in to resolve it instead, even though you have no idea what happened in the original story!

Although this may sound a bit far fetched to some, it does explain why all the people, who need the same remedy, have similar issues in their lives, issues that indicate that they all have the same basic perception of reality, a perception that still reflects the original situation that created the imbalance in the first place. For example: All Arsenicums are worried about being pursued, robbed and attacked, and they often have a strong fear of death, even if they haven't been pursued, attacked or robbed in this life time. Medorrhinums are afraid they are going to be attacked from behind, and Veratrums are afraid they are going to be deceived and betrayed. I was walking in the woods one day with a 3 year old Medorrhinum girl. All of a sudden she got scared and wanted me to carry her. She told me there was a bear in the woods. I asked her: "Where is the bear?" She looked around and said: "Behind me!" Why not "Over there!" or "Under that bush!"? No, she was afraid the bear was going to attack her from behind, which fits the mental symptoms that we find under Medorrhinum.

In addition to explaining why people, who need the same remedy, have similar issues, my theory also explains why we keep repeating the same old patterns in our lives, over and over, and why it is so hard to break these old patterns. We have forgotten what the original situation was; perhaps we never even knew it in the first place. By now the whole situation has become nothing but a set of unconscious beliefs, which basically become our delusions, and these delusions affect the way we feel, act and perceive reality on a daily basis. If someone says or does anything that triggers our subconscious memories of the original situation, all the old feelings reappear, even though we can no longer consciously remember what the original situation was, and we are often left wondering why that particular action or statement affected us so deeply.

One of my cases was a hyperactive Belladonna boy who was creating a big fuss at school. The teacher, who didn't know that Belladonnas are also afraid of being attacked from behind, sneaked up on the boy one day when his behavior was totally out of control. She grabbed him from behind and restrained him until his mom came to pick him up, and by then, the boy was completely traumatized, and the teacher had no idea that she had just triggered his original situation and worst fear by attacking him from behind. Another example of this is what happens if you say to a Natrum Muriaticum woman that she looks really beautiful today. The word "today" might instantly trigger her underlying insecurity, and she might suspiciously wonder if you thought she looked ugly yesterday, instead of enjoying your compliment, because an underlying delusion of ugliness is part of the mental state that goes with Natrum Muriaticum. These are both similar situations because both reactions are simply a reflection of the person's underlying subconscious belief system or delusions.

There is nothing unusual about the reactions I just described in the examples above because this is what we all do. When relating to people, we look at what is happening from our own delusional, or distorted, point of view, and our reactions are always a reflection of this. So, what exactly are delusions? Delusions are simply unconscious beliefs that delude us, deceive us, or fool us; this is why they are called "delusions." This is also why we don't even know what our delusions are, or even that we have delusions in the first place, because delusions only affect us when we don't know that they are there. All we know is that our reactions are not always healthy, and we also know that we may be stuck in old patterns that keep repeating themselves in our lives, even though they no longer serve us. Looking at the mental profiles of the remedies from this point of view makes it easy to predict what is going to trigger somebody's original situation since these reactions are totally predictable. All we have to do is look at the ailments, fears, phobias and delusions under each remedy profile, and we'll have a pretty good idea of how somebody perceives their reality as well as what issues can trigger a state of imbalance in that person.

So far, we have explored how delusions can affect someone's perception of reality, but we can still go deeper into this issue. One of the things that I found, during my studies, was a subconscious mechanism that we use to keep our delusions alive, or "real." The mechanism is very simple; we create or attract what we fear the most in our lives so that we can learn to resolve these issues. This makes sense because most of our fears are still a reflection of the original situation we came in to resolve. If, however, we don't face our fears and resolve these issues, the new situation we have created will simply strengthen our existing delusions, and the result is that we will never even suspect that we have any delusions. If we are unaware of our delusions, we'll naturally believe that our perception of reality is an undistorted version of truth, and we'll never even know that what we think is real, is only Maya, delusion, or "that which is not."

Why do we do this? Why do we try to convince ourselves that our delusions don't exist, and that what we perceive is the real thing? We do this to preserve our "status quo" because we don't like change. Change is uncomfortable, and if we can prove to ourselves that we don't have any delusions, and that what we perceive as real is, in fact, "the truth," we don't have to change! You may argue that your perception of truth is based upon your life experiences, but even your experiences don't necessarily prove that your perception of reality is true. If you end up with a fixed perception of how things are, even if it is based upon your experiences, your perception simply can't be true because life is never a fixed thing. Life is a flux, always changing, moment to moment. Only dead things are fixed.

To illustrate how this works, think of a woman, who believes that men always leave relationships. (The perception that someone *always* does a certain thing is a fixed perception, and therefore a distorted perception of the truth). Why does she believe this? She must have experienced this many times in her life since it has caused her to believe that this is how all men are, but the interesting question is, why does this always happen to her? It happens because she is naturally attracted to men who have problems with commitment, or who are just playing around. When they eventually leave her, it proves to her every time it happens that she is right, and that this is just how all men are. It doesn't even occur to her that, perhaps, she picked a guy who had no intention of staying in a committed relationship in the first place! Or, as another example, think of a man who always feels humiliated and disrespected by others. Why doesn't he get any respect from anyone? He doesn't get any respect because he subconsciously sabotages everything he does in such a way that people will think he is incapable or useless, since that is how he presents himself to the world. And when people respond, by criticizing him for all the mistakes he has made, he feels humiliated and wonders why nobody ever respects him. He doesn't realize that he is actually the one creating the situation in the first place, by acting irresponsibly, or by not doing his job properly, but this is how he keeps his delusions real (in this case, the delusions that he is worthless or incapable). So, the "New Age" concept, that we create our own reality, isn't totally accurate because it is our subconscious beliefs, or delusions, and not our conscious selves, which actually do create that reality. This makes relationships between people much more complicated than we normally realize.

Because patterns arising from our subconscious beliefs are so hard to break, it can be helpful in a relationship between two people if both partners become more aware of the other person's delusions and trigger points, as well as their own, so that they can be avoided to help preserve peace and harmony in the relationship. Or, an even better solution would be to actually realize that our perception of what is happening isn't necessarily a reflection of truth at all, and to simply stop taking everything so personally. Ideally, we can only truly relate to others if we drop our delusional way of perceiving reality, but since that doesn't easily happen, we have to start the process by simply becoming aware of the patterns first, which is what this book is about.

In addition to understanding the perception of reality that goes with each remedy profile, we can also use homeopathic remedies to help shift these perceptions. The homeopathic remedies won't remove our predisposition to seeing reality in a certain way, but they can still help us resolve the original issues that are affecting our lives here and now, so that we can start perceiving reality again more like it really is. You may wonder how a homeopathic remedy can help us resolve issues that we may have inherited from our forefathers, but the process is very simple. If, for example, you find yourself extremely upset about some little thing, you can take a dose of a remedy, and your mental state quickly shifts, even though the situation is still the same. Nothing has changed, except your perception of what is happening, but even a small change in perception is enough to totally change the way you feel about something. The remedy simply takes you from a state of not being able to cope, to a state where you can successfully deal with what is happening.

How is this kind of shift possible? We already know by now that our perception of reality is created by our underlying beliefs, or delusions. Therefore, if a remedy has the ability to change our perception, it must also have the ability to destroy our underlying delusions, even for a short period of time, in order to bring the body back into a state of balance. Therefore, it makes sense to assume that the use of homeopathic remedies, over an extended period of time, can eventually help us let go of our delusions, and in doing so, they can also be helpful in our process of spiritual expansion. Although this may be a somewhat unusual way of looking at the potential benefit of homeopathy, I believe that progress, on any level, is only made if we can look at everything with an open mind and an adventurous spirit, as well as a willingness to explore new possibilities.

WHAT IS HEALTH?

At some point in my writing process, I had a conversation with someone about some of the concepts that I am introducing in this book. This person had a hard time accepting the concept that we come in with an original situation that we are here to resolve. (This, of course, is a common reaction when someone introduces a new concept). Neither could she accept the idea that we pick a mate who can play a part in our story (See the chapter on attraction in Part 4). She wanted to know if these issues still apply if someone is in a very healthy state, and she also wanted to know if I believe that everyone is born in a pathological state. I realized then that this issue also has to be clarified, and first of all, the concept of "health" has to be defined.

Health, as I see it, is a level of inner balance on every level. When you are truly healthy, there will be mental and emotional balance as well as freedom from physical symptoms. In a state of perfect health, there is a sense of well-being that allows you to focus on other things. You don't have to worry about what you do, or what you eat, or how much you sleep. When you are healthy, your body, mind or emotion doesn't require any of your attention because when something is perfect, it doesn't need any more work. However, this level of health is unusual. Most people tend to experience some level of imbalance at all times, either physically, mentally or emotionally. This imbalance may be in the form of physical aches and pains, digestive problems, sleep problems, worry, anxiety, depression and so on. What this means is that on a scale between perfect health and serious pathology, most of us reside somewhere in between. The only difference is that some of us are closer to the healthy end, and others are closer to the pathological end.

In homeopathy, we also see sickness, or pathology, as an imbalance somewhere within the system of body/mind/emotion. The homeopathic remedy has the ability to bring the system back into balance, and when you achieve a new state of balance, the body spontaneously heals itself. What we have to understand, about this "state of balance," is the fact that balance is never a static thing. When studying physiology, this becomes obvious. Physiology describes all the mechanisms that the body uses to keep itself balanced. All the body functions have to be within a very narrow range of acceptable values, or we may become extremely uncomfortable, sick, or even die. For example, if the body temperature isn't within a very specific range, we'll develop hypothermia or fever. If we develop hypothermia, the blood will rush away from the surface and we get goose bumps and start shivering. If we get too hot, the blood will rush to the surface so we can get rid of excess heat by sweating. The PH of the blood also has to be just right, and if for some reason the PH gets too acid or too alkaline, the body will produce chemicals that will quickly bring the PH back within the optimal range. There has to be a balance between sodium and potassium for the nervous system to work properly. The hormonal glands have to produce the exact right amounts of hormones, or some very strange things can happen as a result. Even the sugar level in the blood has to be just right, neither too high nor too low, or the body will have to do many things to compensate for the imbalance. If, for example, the sugar level is too high, sugar will be released through the urine or stored as fat in the body, or the pancreas will produce more insulin in an effort to reduce the levels. If that doesn't help, the person may become very thirsty and start drinking lots of liquids, which can also help dilute the sugar concentration in the blood. If, however, none of these mechanisms bring the body back into a balanced state, the imbalance becomes chronic, and the pathology of diabetes will eventually develop.

What we see, when studying the internal balance mechanisms of the body, is that balance is always a dynamic state. It isn't a solid thing. The system constantly keeps rebalancing itself in an effort to keep the body healthy. If the imbalance becomes chronic because the body has a hard time bringing itself back into equilibrium, pathology, or sickness develops. Pathology is simply a result of a chronic state of imbalance that the immune system isn't able to overcome. In acute pathology, the body eventually overcomes the imbalance and reverts back to a state of health, unless the acute sickness is serious enough to kill the person. In chronic pathology, the normal pattern is that the pathology gradually becomes worse until the person eventually dies. What this means is that no matter what level of health we are experiencing, it is always on a "sliding scale," and therefore, change is always possible.

So, if our level of health is always on a "sliding scale," some of you may wonder at what level of health a baby is born. This, of course, is also different for everyone, since some are born healthier than others. But, again, we need to keep in mind that what we perceive as health, or sickness, can easily change because the level of health we experience is always on "a sliding scale." We slide back and forth on this scale throughout our lives, depending upon our stress levels and the circumstances we are experiencing. When life is easy, we are more likely to be in state of balance where we can experience a sense of health and well-being, and when stressful things happen, the sense of well-being is easily disturbed; it is as simple as that. Some people can handle stress better than others, which means that they are better at keeping themselves in a healthy state of balance, even when outside influences affect them, but their ability to do so is also affected by the kinds of stress they encounter.

There are many different kinds of stress. If you have a manual job, you may experience physical stress. You may have to do the same kinds of movements every day and, eventually, your joints can start wearing down, and your tendons may become inflamed. Or, your health may be affected by mental or emotional stress. We often find that different kinds of stress tend to affect different people in different ways.

A friend of mine is very good at handling large amounts of stress. She is absolutely brilliant at making money. She knows how to invest her money in things that have a potential for great returns, and she doesn't mind taking risks and juggling payments and loans without blinking an eyelid. Someone else in her situation could easily develop acute anxiety and sleeplessness, but these kinds of issues don't bother her at all because they are not even close to her core issues. If, however, a new man comes into her life, and she ends up falling in love, she'll call me and tell me the "horrible" news: "I am in love! What shall I do???" Since I love being in love, I tell her "Go with it, enjoy it, celebrate it! Being in love is so awesome!" She will sigh deeply and say: "Easy for you to say! It scares me to the core!"

Why does it scare her to the core? Why do relationships have this affect on her when she can handle other types of stress with absolute ease? The answer is easy. The underlying core issue that goes with her remedy profile is like a pre-disposition for pathology or imbalance. The core issue is her "sore spot," or trigger button, or her inherent weakness. If nothing triggers her core issue, she may never even know that the issue is there, but the predisposition is still there, even though it can be hidden at times, and it is this predisposition I am describing in the remedy profiles.

The original situation that goes with each remedy profile is simply a predisposition to become affected by specific types of stress. Any time an issue is close to the core issue that goes with your constitutional remedy profile, it will affect you more strongly than any other kinds of stress, and it will naturally be harder to deal with as well. For Natrum Muriaticum the core issue has to do with disappointing relationships, for Arsenicum Album it has to do with someone taking their money or conspiring against them, for Medorrhinum it has to do with someone dying or leaving, for Carcinosinum it has to do with losing control in a chaotic situation and having to sacrifice themselves in an effort to restore order, and so on.

When something triggers our core issues, it hits us very hard. When stressed, we slide into a pattern of action and re-action that fits the original situation that goes with our constitutional picture, and when that happens, everything becomes predictable. This is why we can look back on our lives and see the same patterns going through our relationships or job situations, time and time again. Every time something triggers our core issues, we feel the familiarity and tend to think to ourselves: "Here we go again! This is how life is! Why does this always happen to me?" And, whenever we say this to ourselves, it shows that we are stuck in some kind of fixed perception of life, or delusional point of view, which is a sure indication that we are dealing with an old core issue or a pattern that needs to be resolved. And, if we aren't able to learn from what is happening and resolve these issues, we'll get even more stuck in our own distorted perception of reality. Eventually, the mental stuckness may become too much, and we end up becoming physically sick as a result.

Arthritis is a good example of how someone's stuckness and fixed perception of reality can create a reflection of stuckness in the body, as well, in the form of inflexible, painful joints. Allergies are another example of how a distorted perception of reality can make us sick. Allergies have to do with a sense of being attacked or criticized, and not being able to fully express this feeling. (The theme, or delusion, of being attacked, or criticized, or simply having to be perfect, is often reflected in the remedies that work for allergies, like Arsenicum, Nux, Lachesis, Nat Mur, and so on). What happens is the person becomes so oversensitive to the idea of being attacked that he or she eventually develops an over-defensive attitude as a result. They can, in fact, become so defensive that they may even feel attacked by the smallest speck of dust, pollen or cat hair, or even the smoke of a cigarette or the smell of a flower. The allergy is simply an over-reaction in the body's defense mechanism which stems from an underlying fear of criticism, or of not being able to fulfill someone's expectations. The person basically feels that he or she isn't good enough, or worthy enough, or perfect enough, in other words, something is lacking within them, and their defensive attitude eventually turns into some kind of allergic response. This allergic response is simply a result of the person's effort to compensate, or over-compensate, for their internal sense of lack (which also reflects the Psoric miasm). Here we can easily see that the key, to bringing the body back into a healthy state, is to understand how the physical symptoms are linked with the existing mental or emotional symptoms that are actually causing the imbalance, and for the homeopath, this is also the key to finding the right remedy.

Although we know, by now, that health can easily change into sickness; there are still many people who live most of their lives on the healthy end of the scale. Knowing this, it is natural to ask what happens when people, who are so healthy that they don't even know what their core issues are, relate to others. Do they still have underlying core issues that they are here to resolve, and do they still pick a mate that will play a part in their core story? Again, the answer is yes. Whether they are consciously aware of their core issues, or not, doesn't really make a whole lot of difference, since nobody is consciously aware of why they feel attracted to someone anyway. There is a part of us that intuitively knows what our core issues are, and this same part also knows what partner to pick so that we can get an opportunity to deal with these issues. Even though we would prefer to pick a mate we can live with happily ever after, this, unfortunately, only happens in the fairytales. In real life we get to experience both happiness and unhappiness in our relationships, and that is how it should be because that is what gives us the opportunity to learn. Therefore, it doesn't matter so much if we end up in a rotten relationship or an awesome relationship, as long as it helps us grow to new levels of awareness and as long as it deepens our understanding of life. We are here to resolve the core issues we came in with, regardless of whether we are aware of these issues, or not. The relationships in our lives help us along so that we can achieve this because if we don't, these issues do eventually end up making us sick. However, nature is very generous. If we don't learn a lesson at the first opportunity, many more opportunities to deal with our core issues follow, since resolving old issues and breaking core patterns are what we are here to do.

So, if we pick partners who can help us deal with old issues, do we tend to pick a more dysfunctional partner if we are in a state of greater imbalance? Yes, we do. In an unbalanced state we may pick a partner who triggers our core issues on a daily basis, or in a more balanced state, we may pick a partner who only triggers our core issues once in a while. If core issues are being triggered daily, the relationship has very little chance of surviving, simply because it becomes too intense and too emotionally disturbing. So when we look at compatibility in relationships, we are actually looking at how often two people trigger core issues in each other. Two people can be considered compatible if their core issues are only triggered once in a while. Not only is the relationship itself going to be healthier if core issues aren't triggered too often, but the relationship dynamics isn't going to make anyone in the relationship sick, either, as a result of emotional stress.

So far, we have looked at how the body is affected by both outside influences, like stress, as well as inside influences, like disturbed emotions and fixed, or distorted, perceptions of reality. We have also looked at the fact that what we perceive as health is simply a reflection of a dynamic state of balance that can easily change. Therefore, the next thing to look at is what we can do to maintain this balance. Besides eating well and taking good care of our physical bodies with herbs, vitamins and lots of sleep, we also need to be aware of the effect of daily stress and actively do what we can to bring ourselves back into balance when the stress becomes too much. This can be as simple as taking a deep breath, relaxing for a moment with a hot cup of tea, going for a walk, or taking a nice, warm bath before going to bed. Or, if we are dealing with core issues and old patterns, we may have to make a conscious effort to break these patterns because if we don't, chances are that sickness will eventually occur as a result.

WHAT IS HEALTH?

One of the things we have to understand, about staying healthy, is the importance of not wasting our energy unnecessarily, which is what we tend to do when our daily stress becomes too much. Most of the stress we are dealing with has to do with what is going to happen if we can't cope efficiently with the task at hand, in other words, we worry about something that might happen, as a result, in the future. Or, if we are dealing with old issues or patterns, our energy is often wasted on things that have already happened in the past. Both are a waste of precious life energy that could be used for healing. So, if we want to get well, or simply maintain a comfortable level of health, it is very important to let go of old issues that we are holding on to and to stop worrying so much about the future. By living more in the NOW, we can stop wasting our energy on things that are not essential, and this frees up energy that can be used to maintain our health instead. Therefore, the most important thing we can do to keep ourselves healthy, is to live in the NOW, to leave the past behind, and to stop worrying about the future. This, of course, is easier said than done, but nobody has ever said that life is supposed to be easy...

PART TWO
THE REMEDY PROFILES
The Deeper Levels of the Psyche

DO I EXIST?
Alumina

REMEDY DESCRIPTION

Alumina is a timid, mild mannered, quiet person, with a tendency to be serious, absent minded and somewhat spaced out. Because she has a weak sense of self, she needs a lot of recognition, support and respect from others. She likes being in control in relationships and has a natural tendency to be both critical and judgmental in her views. She is fastidious and usually does things as perfectly as she can, hoping she might impress someone. She often compensates for her weak sense of self by being ambitious, obstinate, headstrong and quarrelsome. Because Alumina needs recognition, support and respect from the people around her to make her sense of self more solid, relationships are very important to her, but unfortunately, her relationships are often as undefined as her personal sense of self.

When her relationships don't work out, Alumina tends to fall apart. She often suffers from grief and disappointment and she may end up feeling both humiliated and hurt. Her moods can be like a roller coaster, changing frequently. One moment she can feel weepy, gloomy and depressed, with a feeling of total hopelessness and a sense that she will never recover, and the next moment she may feel alright. Her confidence suffers, and she may have no energy to do anything. Because Alumina is mentally unstable, she can also become very confused about her own reactions and impulses. Her identity becomes so weak that she often doesn't even know if she exists. She may develop a sense of duality, or a sense that everything is unreal, as if in a dream. She may even feel as if her head belongs to someone else, or that she is about to totally lose her mind. At times, her mind can become so dull and sluggish that it makes any kind of thinking and comprehension almost impossible, and she may not even remember what words to use, or what she was about to say.

When Alumina finds herself in this kind of unbalanced state, even the simplest tasks can become so overwhelming that she becomes anxious and fearful about everything. At this point, it is very hard for her to make any decisions on her own, and she may start feeling numb, both emotionally and physically. If her condition deteriorates even further, she can eventually become completely paralyzed, both mentally as well as physically.

When Alumina starts falling apart like this, her sense of time also becomes distorted. Time either passes too quickly or too slowly, and she feels like she always has to hurry. The problem is, the more she hurries, the less she accomplishes, so her sense of hurry is more of a feeling rather than a physical reality. If she doesn't accomplish what she is trying to do, no matter how much she hurries, she is likely to react with frustration, irritability and anger.

When Alumina is angry, everything offends. Lack of support or recognition is one of the things that tend to bring out Alumina's mental instability as well as her weak sense of identity. Grief, disappointment and anxiety can also aggravate her, and when she becomes angry, her body often starts trembling. She may complain, or behave in childish or foolish ways, and she may even feel a strong impulse to strike or kill someone, especially with a knife. She often fears her own impulses because she is afraid she could totally lose control over herself and do something horrible. Because she has a tendency toward hysteria and mania, she may also start howling, shrieking, screaming and shouting.

One Alumina woman often had the impulse to kill her newborn baby, especially when she was tired and felt unsupported. Every time she saw a sharp knife, she could feel "the pull." Even though she was disturbed by her unusual feelings, she thought that perhaps everyone else had similar feelings that nobody ever spoke about. Another Alumina woman felt an almost irresistible urge to kill her husband with a kitchen knife when he casually introduced her to one of his girlfriends. Her feelings are definitely understandable, but the interesting thing here is how her husband treated her - as if her feelings didn't exist. He was even puzzled when she got hysterical and threw both of them out of the house. His total disregard for her feelings shows that he didn't treat her like a real person, and it was this lack of consideration and care that disturbed her the most.

At a later time, when she was able to confront her husband about the incident, he defended himself by explaining to her that he didn't really consider their marriage a real marriage because he felt that she wasn't his soul mate. Even though they were legally married, Alumina's marriage seemed to be as shaky and non-existent as her weak sense of self.

Alumina often feels guilty and blames herself for her situation. Her moods can alternate between courage and fear, and she is often anxious about her future as well as her health. Alumina is so full of cares and worries about everything that she may even fear that some day she won't be able to take care of herself. She fears that something very bad will happen, or that she will be attacked from behind, and she can even develop a fear of people in general.

Because she can't cope, she also feels strong anticipation anxiety. Alumina is aware that something is very wrong with her mind, and she is afraid she is going to lose her sanity. She may even feel an impulse to commit suicide if her life seems to become too meaningless and hopeless. In this state, Alumina really needs someone who can help her define her sense of self, but finding someone who will be there for her is very difficult because she is not really there for herself.

When Alumina's relationships turn out to be as non-existent as her own sense of self, her feeling of grief and disappointment is so deep that she often has a hard time recovering. If she can't find someone who can take care of her or give her the support that she needs, she can become totally indifferent and sink into apathy. At this point, she becomes discontented with everything and just wants to be alone in bed, brooding. She feels how weak her will is, and she may turn to spirituality for courage and inspiration.

When Alumina feels really forsaken and friendless, her biggest worry is the fact that her mind doesn't function well. She would love for someone to take care of her, because she is so unable to cope that she sometimes loses her desire to live. But, even in her relationships, she tends to lose her identity and play the role of "the invisible one."

One Alumina woman had dreams in which she was standing in a room full of people, and nobody even knew she was there. She would seriously question whether she actually existed or not, and she couldn't really find an answer. She could see herself in the mirror, but she didn't feel as if she were real inside. Her confusion about the whole issue would sometimes lead to suicidal thoughts, especially when seeing a knife or a razor. This sense of total hopelessness and despair, as well as her lack of identity, can often be helped with the use of homeopathic Alumina in a high potency.

ALUMINA IN RELATIONSHIPS

Alumina has experienced so many disappointing relationships in her life that she doesn't feel comfortable around people at all. She is afraid of feeling anything, afraid of being hurt and afraid of disappointment. In relationships with people, Alumina always has the feeling that nothing is real. She doesn't even know if she is real, so how can any of her relationships be real? And if her relationships aren't real, how can anyone expect them to last? These are the kinds of questions she will ask herself when she is about to get involved in another relationship, and she often starts feeling indifferent towards the whole concept because there doesn't seem to be any point in even trying.

One Alumina man told me a very odd statement in his initial consultation with me. He said: "I don't happen to life – life happens to me." In other words "nothing is in my hands!" or, "I'm totally powerless!" These kinds of odd statements are always clues as to what kind of remedy or miasm we are dealing with. In this case, the sense of hopelessness shows a strong syphilitic influence, which fits the Alumina profile. When Alumina finds herself in this kind of a hopeless state, the familiar numbness returns so she doesn't have to feel any pain. In fact, she won't have to feel anything at all, and this makes her secure and safe, but it doesn't help her create intimacy with anyone.

The idea of becoming real is very scary for Alumina. If she were to become real, she would open herself up to conflicts and disappointments, as well as to grief and pain. One of my Alumina clients was adopted as a baby by a family where her step mom was an alcoholic, and her step dad was never around much. It was a matter of survival for her to be as invisible as possible to avoid being caught in the middle of some conflict. The problem was, she didn't know who she was, and she had no role models to guide her. Therefore, her sense of self was almost non-existent.

In her relationships with men, she always had a tendency to lose herself. Sometimes she would end up with someone who was dominating and wanted to be in charge, which she didn't really mind, but the person would often be emotionally unavailable as well. If he didn't pay any attention to her, it would make her feel almost non-existent. Or she would end up with someone who simply wasn't around very much. If her mate kept coming or going, and she never even knew if he would come back, she couldn't really tell if the relationship actually existed or not. She always kept playing the role of "the invisible one" because she simply didn't know how to become more real.

She came to me for help, and after taking the remedy for a while, she had a dream in which her husband complained that she was becoming too real because she wanted him to be around more, and he was not happy about it. This dream proved to be prophetic. Having a wife who was aware of her own needs was too much trouble for the husband to deal with, and he simply stopped coming home after a while. She waited for him, month after month, making excuses for his behavior and hoping he would come back to her some day, until she finally realized that she actually deserved a man in her life who would appreciate her more. She filed for divorce and tried to nurture herself the best she could.

Eventually, she was able to attract a new man who paid more attention to her. He wanted to see her and loved spending time with her, and she started feeling like a real person. Her numbness disappeared, and she was able to feel again, both physically and emotionally. The intensity of her emotions scared her and she was amazed at how vulnerable she was becoming, but she was courageous enough to stay open to her new experience of love. Her healing was happening: she was finally becoming visible and gaining a sense of identity again, but unfortunately; this relationship also became very short lived. After a few months together, she found out that he had changed his mind about divorcing his wife, and she also found out that he had another girlfriend on the side. It took her a very long time to get over the disappointment of another broken relationship, but she is still hoping that, some day, she will be able to find someone who truly loves her. This brings to mind the story of the velveteen rabbit where the rabbit asks the skin horse how to become real, and the horse answers that the secret to becoming real is to find someone who truly loves you. Alumina's quest to become real seems to have a lot in common with the little velveteen rabbit's quest for the same.

Alumina needs a lot of encouragement and support from the people around her, even if she doesn't usually ask for it. The worst thing people can do is to ignore her because, when they do, she starts feeling invisible again. Alumina is happy in relationships as long as her mate or friends pay attention to her. It is also important that nobody criticizes her, or puts her down, because that will also trigger her confusion and further weaken her sense of self. The situation that goes with the Alumina picture is one of being totally ignored, and she can only reverse that sensation if people really pay attention to her and give her lots of love, support and encouragement.

I'M RIGHT AND YOU'RE NOT!
Arsenicum Album

REMEDY DESCRIPTION

Arsenicum Album can often be cheerful, affectionate and passionate in his relationships with others. When something interests him, he can easily become excited, vivacious and talkative, which is not really surprising since he loves a good discussion. But Arsenicum also has another side to his personality, a more quiet, reserved and somewhat timid side. He is generally mild mannered, and because he also tends to be both serious and cautious, he loves to live in tranquility and peace. In addition, he is often very sentimental and likes to celebrate anniversaries, birthdays and other types of memorable days.

Because Arsenicum has very high standards, which he applies to everything and everybody in his life, he is also extremely fastidious and conscientious about little things, and he has to have order and control, as if his survival depends on it. If there is any chaos in his life, it often makes him anxious, so he is very picky about how he wants things done. For an Arsenicum, there are only two ways of doing things, the wrong way and his way, and there is usually nothing in between. On the positive side, Arsenicum has a great eye for detail. He often picks a line of work which requires accuracy, and he is very reliable, hard working and always does the job perfectly.

Arsenicum's senses are extremely acute. He is oversensitive to sensual and mental impressions, and also to horrible things and sad stories. In female Arsenicums, symptoms are worse during menses and during the climacteric period. Because Arsenicum is so hypersensitive, he is easily offended and often takes everything in bad part. One Arsenicum friend of mine couldn't stand it if his girlfriend looked at him for more than a few seconds at a time. The same Arsenicum also had an aversion to being touched, so when he was going for a walk with his girlfriend, he would never hold hands, and he would get very upset if she accidentally bumped into him while walking next to him. Arsenicum's touchiness can sometimes become so extreme that he may even develop a fear of pins and sharp, pointed things.

Arsenicum is also very sensitive to odors and noise; in fact his sensitivity to both can be so extreme that it almost becomes delusional. One male Arsenicum described how enraged he would feel if he could hear someone crinkling paper in another room, which was the most annoying sound he could possibly think of. He couldn't possibly fall asleep if there was one single dog barking in the distance, and he would open the window and yell at the birds if they woke him up in the morning. Needless to say, he also had to have his bedroom totally dark when he wanted to sleep, and his partner had to sleep on the edge of the bed as far away from him as possible, so her body wouldn't accidentally touch his while he was sleeping.

Another Arsenicum, who happened to have the idea that women shouldn't wear makeup, conveniently became allergic to his girlfriend's mascara just by sitting next to her on the couch. (Even though his physical reaction was real – eyes burning and tearing – I must admit my suspicion that it also might have had something to do with his attitude towards her wearing makeup. Could he have managed to bring on an allergic reaction just to control her? We'll probably never know...) The same Arsenicum also frequently demanded that his bedding be rinsed in the washing machine in the middle of the night because he was certain that there was still laundry soap left in the fabric that was making his eyes burn. This kind of sensitivity, however unimaginable to most of us, can actually be very real for an Arsenicum, and if nobody believes him, he feels very disturbed and misunderstood.

As you may have guessed by now, Arsenicum is basically a very nervous type. He is easily frightened, even about little things. He often wakes up from frightful dreams after midnight and can't go back to sleep again easily, so it comes as no surprise that his worst time is between 12 and 3 am in the morning. Sometimes he feels so restless at that time that he has to get out of bed and sip a cup of hot tea before trying to go back to sleep again, since hot drinks usually has a calming effect on him.

Because Arsenicum always expects so much from himself, he often fears undertaking anything new, and as a result, he tends to suffer from anticipation anxiety, mainly because he is afraid that someone will judge him if what he has done isn't perfect enough. The whole idea, that everything has to be perfect, makes him put a lot of pressure on both himself and the people in his life. In addition, he is also full of cares and worries about what bad things could possibly happen to him in the future. He is basically pessimistic by nature and often paces around the room in restless anxiety. His fear of misfortune is so strong that it is almost impossible for anyone to cheer him up. This is because his mindset tends to be extremely fixed.

However, when looking at an Arsencium, he doesn't easily give you the impression that he is as anxious, sensitive and vulnerable as he really is. This is because these characteristics are usually carefully hidden behind a proud and critical façade. He is often brilliantly intelligent, and he knows it well. He doesn't mind boasting and bragging about his abilities, and, of course, with such brilliant intelligence, he is always right. He is intolerant of contradiction and doesn't mind criticizing or reproaching others. He can be both intolerant and contemptuous of other people's point of view, and when he has made a decision, he obstinately sticks to it. Whether he adopts a prejudiced, conservative, or a more eccentric point of view, his ideas are always fixed and hard for anyone to change once he has made up his mind.

One of Arsenicum's more positive traits is his great ability for business and finance. He loves working and can often be a bit of a workaholic. Work makes him feel less anxious, especially if he is making good money. Arsenicum is impulsive, impatient and always in a hurry. He loves accomplishing things and seeing tangible results from his efforts. One problem is that Arsenicum isn't always happy with what he has. Because he has a strong fear of poverty and often feels that what he has isn't enough, he can sometimes be greedy, ungrateful and envious of what others have, and he may even turn to dishonesty or kleptomania to get what he wants. This shadow side of Arsenicum reflects his inner sense of weakness and vulnerability that he won't normally admit to anyone. But, the truth is that he simply doesn't feel safe. He feels weak and vulnerable in a scary world where people are out to get him and his money, and he tries to compensate for this feeling by creating more physical security in his life any way he can. Because of Arsenicum's tendency to think about scary things, once he starts thinking, he simply can't stop, and one thought easily leads to another.

To better understand Arsenicum's sense of weakness and vulnerability, we have to remember how sensitive he is to all kinds of influences and also take a look at the delusions that go with the Arsenicum remedy picture. Even though he does everything he can to be absolutely perfect, he often has the feeling that he has done something wrong, or that what he has done isn't good enough. His expectations of himself are so high that he may feel angry with himself if he thinks he has made a mistake, or he may feel guilty and blame himself if something isn't 100% right. In Arsenicum's mind, he simply can't afford to make even the smallest mistake. This also reflects Arsenicum's core belief about himself, that unless he is absolutely perfect, nobody will love him!

Because Arsenicum is basically insecure and often feels unloved and forsaken by his friends and family, he is also very affected by discord between family members or friends. He doesn't feel good about being alone, and he is afraid that the people in his life will somehow turn on him and leave him. He is afraid to offend people, and he even fears that he may already have offended a friend without even knowing it. He may feel anxious for his friend, and he may even fear that his friend, whom he thinks he has offended, is going to have an accident. And if his friend does have an accident, Arsenicum will blame himself and forever think it was his fault. Or, he could start imagining that something even worse could happen. Not only could his friend end up having an accident, but he might even die from it!

Should something like that actually happen in real life, Arsenicum would feel as if he had murdered his friend, and fear that he would soon be pursued by the police and get arrested. He suspiciously feels that there is always a possibility for conspiracies against him, and he never knows who to trust in his life. He is always afraid that he is going to be persecuted or pursued by enemies, and if they find him, he fears that he is going to be punished, injured, or maybe even killed. He believes that others are conspiring to murder him, and he is sure that he will die very soon. (It wouldn't surprise me if this feeling reflects back to a time when arsenic was commonly used to get rid of unwanted people. Perhaps someone in his household, someone that he trusted, put poison in his food and he almost lost his life as a result! No wonder he can't trust anyone...)

All of these delusions reflect something of the original situation which Arsenicum is still responding to. In the original situation, Arsenicum was obviously blamed for something he didn't do, or that he can't remember doing, and he was pursued and injured (or possibly poisoned) by his enemies. He was too weak to defend himself and almost lost his life during the attack. This is why his sense of weakness and vulnerability in a scary world is still such a strong part of Arsenicum's perception of reality, and it also explains why he is always defensive, and always on guard.

Because Arsenicum doesn't know who is conspiring against him, and he doesn't know who to trust in his life, he may not even feel safe in his own house. He feels weak and sick, and he is afraid that he could be attacked again. He feels that there could be criminals anywhere, even inside his own house. They could be watching him right now! He can see their faces when he closes his eyes, and he is sure they are hiding under his bed, waiting for a chance to steal his things or attack him. He keeps looking under his bed, and searching for thieves in the night, and he simply can't relax. Once his trust has been betrayed by anyone, Arsenicum is on guard! If he has been betrayed in some way by a person he knows, it can become almost impossible for him to ever trust that person again, and if his trust has been betrayed by some kind of organization, Arsenicum will definitely sue!

As a result, Arsenicum's moods are often repulsive, spiteful or even malicious, but we have to understand that his maliciousness is simply a defense against his perceived or imagined enemies. As long as Arsenicum feels that he is right in his assessment of a situation, he doesn't really mind being cruel, hard-hearted or unfeeling to get his point across, simply because, to him, it is a matter of survival! (This, of course, also reflects the original situation where it actually *was* a matter of survival; therefore Arsenicum still acts *as if* this is still the case).

Arsenicum also has a tendency to gossip and slander, and he can sometimes be very sarcastic and hurtful in his expressions. If someone gets their feelings hurt, it doesn't concern him very much, because he is fighting for what he thinks is right, as if his survival depends on it. In the situation that goes with Arsenicum, he was unjustly accused of something he didn't do, and the consequences almost cost him his life, so now he has to prove to everyone that he is right, at any cost, to compensate for what happened then and to make sure it can never happen again. Here, we can see another one of Arsenicum's core beliefs; that not only does he have to be perfect to be loved; he also has to be right for anyone to love him. So, now you can understand why he loves to argue so much, and also why he doesn't care if you happen to get your feelings hurt in the process. If that is what it takes for him to get his point across to convince you that he is right, then so be it!

As you may have guessed, Arsenicum has never really gotten over what happened in the original situation. Even though he can no longer remember what the original situation was, the feelings of what happened are still there and the whole situation still makes him angry! Every little thing irritates, especially in the morning after waking up. He gets angry from contradiction, and he gets angry when he has to answer questions. He even gets angry if someone is expecting him to eat, since he doesn't totally trust the people who are preparing his food either. His digestive system is so sensitive that he would rather not eat at all, than eat anything that he doesn't think his body can handle. He can be cheerful one moment and furiously angry the next and this makes him both unpredictable and very difficult to live with. His fury can easily turn into a violent rage, with Arsenicum cursing, swearing, screaming, shouting, throwing things, biting or pulling his own hair, and when Arsenicum expresses this level of rage, he can be quite intimidating to the people he lives with. They'll most likely withdraw, rather than arguing back, since they are bound to lose in an argument with Arsenicum anyway. With his quick, brilliant mind, he is usually able to talk circles around anyone who wants to challenge him, but for the people he lives with, it simply isn't worth going there.

We can easily sense how this rage is an act of desperation. He feels like he is doomed or lost, and that his family will starve if he doesn't succeed. His fear may become so overpowering that he feels claustrophobic and may fear suffocation as well. He worries about the people in his life and what they may do to him, and he often feels that he can't really trust anyone.

So, what can he possibly do to protect himself from his enemies? If some-one is in his house, his first impulse may be to hide, or, he may have to kill the person with a knife, which scares him more than anything. But this time, he will do whatever he can to defend himself because he is determined not to let anyone hurt or attack him again, like they did in the original story!

An Arsenicum woman experienced all these feelings after a woman in her neighborhood was raped, and the rapist got away. She was convinced that he was hiding in her house, under her bed, and when her husband had to leave the house, she would lock her front door and grab the biggest kitchen knife she could find, preparing herself for possible battle while hoping her husband would return home as soon as possible.

The sense of weakness and vulnerability, and the fear of being attacked again, makes it almost unbearable for Arsenicum to be alone. His anguish is so intense that his whole body feels constricted. He is afraid that he will get hurt or die if he is left alone, and his fear of death is so strong that he will do almost anything to find someone who can keep him company.

Arsenicum can be quite clingy and emotionally dependent when his anxi-ety is out of control like this. He needs someone who can talk to him and reas-sure him that he is not in danger, and that nothing bad is going to happen to him. Physical contact also helps him feel better, since it makes him feel safer and more protected against possible attacks. This is why Arsenicum needs physical security in his life more than anything else.

Arsenicum's biggest problem, besides feeling weak and unloved, is that his imagination is too vivid. The more he thinks about all the bad things that can possibly happen to him or the people he loves, the worse it gets. His thoughts intrude and crowd around each other, persistently tormenting him. At some point he doesn't even know what is real, and he gets very confused about the whole situation. His confusion often affects his behavior. He doesn't know what to do, and sometimes he feels better after washing his face, his hands or even his whole body.

One Arsenicum woman felt so anxious about everything in her life that she couldn't get through the day unless she had at least 4 long showers every day. If she could, she would have probably preferred to stay in the shower all day since the running water made her feel so much better.

Obviously, Arsenicum has a hard time relaxing since his anxiety tends to be quite overwhelming. He fears the future, since the future represents the unknown, and his anguish makes him so restless that he can't even sit still. He has to constantly move around and is often pacing the floor, tossing about in his bed or driving from place to place. He can't rest if anything isn't in its proper place, because any kind of chaos makes him feel even more anxious, and also more compelled to clean and create order in his surroundings. This need for order and structure is typical for all of the metal remedies, but in Arsenicum, this need can be rather extreme, or even obsessive.

One Arsenicum woman told me that after doing a dose of 10M of Arsenicum, she was finally able to relax enough to sit through a whole movie for the first time in years. She was less anxious in bed at night, and her ability to sleep also improved.

Because Arsenicum has extremely high standards about everything, he is not an easy person to please. He needs company and physical contact to feel safe, but because he feels worse thinking about bad things, he may also feel worse talking about bad things. So, even though he feels better in good company, he will only enjoy the conversation if it is going in a direction where he wants it to go. If it takes a turn that he doesn't like, he often feels better if nobody talks to him at all. He still wants people around, but he may become irritable when spoken to, especially in the morning, and he may even develop an aversion to answering questions. If he does have to answer a question, he often answers abruptly and shortly, or he may not even bother to finish his sentences. If Arsenicum desires to be silent and the people in his life don't honor his request, he often answers in abusive or insulting ways. Again, he is not too concerned about hurting anyone's feelings because taking care of his own needs is usually his main priority.

Arsenicum basically doesn't like it if any of the people in his life require too much of his attention. If they do, he may start to develop an aversion to his family or his wife, since he is not really interested in what other people's needs are. At that point, he may want to sleep in a different bed or a different room. Even though he is afraid to be alone, he may feel fine sleeping alone as long as he knows that someone else is still in the house; he just doesn't want to have to interact with any of them.

The ideal situation for Arsenicum is to find a relationship where there is a person in the house, so he doesn't have to be alone, but she doesn't talk to him or ask anything from him unless he wants to have a conversation with her (This is similar to Lycopodium, but Lycopodium is usually less extreme in his views). Everything has to be on his terms since he feels that his needs are more important than those of anyone else that he lives with. This clearly reflects the defensive posture that goes with Arsenicum's perception of reality, that: "Either you take care of my needs, or you are also my enemy!"

Arsenicum experiences the same internal conflict when it comes to health and sickness. He is very fearful of anything to do with his health. He has a tendency toward hysteria and hypochondriasis, especially when he is alone. If he thinks he is seriously ill, he needs someone there to talk to him and make him feel better by calming his fears, but at the same time, he knows that he often feels worse if he pays too much attention to his ailments, and he may try to pretend that he is not really that sick. He may refuse treatment, even when he is very sick, and he doesn't want anyone to talk to him about it. Again, he wants someone to be there for him, but it has to be totally on his terms, and he may, or may not want to talk to that person.

This also applies to other people's sickness. One Arsenicum man never went with his wife to the hospital. He didn't go when she was having babies, and he didn't go when, later, she went in for cancer treatment. In both cases, he simply couldn't deal with the intensity and the seriousness of the situation. He was so afraid she was going to die that he preferred to wait and see what would happen, rather than having to be in the middle of it while it was actually happening. His wife's needs were obviously less important to him than getting a handle on his own fears.

Another Arsenicum man refused to go to a local restaurant and bring food back for his wife who was sick in bed with pneumonia. When I told him that his wife needed him to take care of her because she couldn't take care of herself, his answer was: "Then who is going to take care of me???" At the time, I didn't understand where he was coming from. I just thought he was being mean, selfish and uncaring. But, now that I know the Arsenicum core issue, I can see that the man must have been an Arsenicum constitutionally, and that his wife's sickness had basically triggered his own fear of death. That is why his main concern was "Who is going to take care of me?" rather than "What can I do for you?" By going to the restaurant and feeding himself, while being in denial about his wife's condition and needs, he wasn't really trying to be heartless; he was simply trying to get a handle on his own fears about what was going to happen next.

As you can easily imagine, deep down Arsenicum knows very well that he isn't an easy person to live with, even though he would never admit it. Therefore, one of his greatest fears is that his partner will eventually get tired of the whole situation and leave him. If that happens, Arsenicum is inconsolable. He is beside himself with grief, and he can become deeply depressed for a very long time, especially if he also lost his house or his money, or both. He will complain, moan and whine to his friends, or just to sit and sulk.

The truth is, Arsenicum is actually quite fragile and doesn't handle any kind of stress well. He can often become really exhausted from too much mental or emotional stress, or from too much thinking. When that happens, his mind can become dull, sluggish and slow, and he may find it very difficult to concentrate. He may even find it impossible to do any kind of mental work, or he may develop a complete loss of ambition as well as an aversion to business in general. Because his will isn't very strong, Arsenicum can easily feel both discouraged and discontented with everything in his life, including himself. He can even get so disgusted with his life that he develops complete indifference to absolutely everything, including loved ones, pleasure, his own recovery, the welfare of others, or even to life itself because life, as he knows it, can be so totally meaningless that he sees no point in going on. His depression is so deep that he may feel like his life is never going to get any better, and this can put him into a state of total despair. In this state, Arsenicum may reach for alcohol or drugs to try to drown his sorrow, anxiety and despair, or he may turn to religion for courage and support. Arsenicum fears evil, and sometimes ends up with religious delusions. He may see frightful images of ghosts, spirits or devils when he closes his eyes, and he may even end up on the floor, kneeling and praying for help.

Sometimes he even fears going insane, and in many cases, Arsenicum actually does go insane. His grief and paranoia can get so out of hand that he may seriously consider suicide; although his fear of death would probably stop him from actually going through with it. When Arsenicum's outlook on life becomes this gloomy, a dose of homeopathic Arsenicum is probably the only thing that will make a difference, if only you can convince him to take the remedy...

ARSENICUM ALBUM IN RELATIONSHIPS

Arsenicums often come from a wealthy family background where physical security in the form of money or property is very important, and they always feel more comfortable when they are able to achieve a high standard of living for themselves and their families. They usually have excellent understanding of money and business in general, and they normally have very expensive taste.

Arsenicum's need for order, as well as his keen eye for detail, makes him a dream come true for any employer. He is reliable, punctual and hard working. He doesn't mind responsibility, and he is often good management material. Arsenicum always does his job to the best of his ability, and if he is in a position where he is in charge, he expects the same from the people who work for him. If you hire an Arsenicum, you can be sure the job is done, and done right, the first time. Arsenicum feels good when working hard and can often be a bit of a workaholic.

There are two reasons for this. The first one is obvious; he is making money, which helps him create the physical security he needs for himself. The other reason he likes to work is the fact that business and distraction also takes the focus away from his anxiety, so it doesn't trigger his more negative traits. However, that only applies as long as the stress isn't too much. Arsenicum doesn't handle stress too well, and he can easily start feeling overloaded and anxious, even at work, especially if he feels that too much is expected of him.

In personal relationships Arsenicum feels good as long as none of his fears are triggered, and he can be playful, affectionate, caring and warm towards others. One of my Arsenicum friends often comes over on the weekends just to play with my kids, and they love it. He is funny and playful, and he told me he is able to relate to most kids in the same way. I have seen the same playfulness in several other Arsenicums as well, both male and female. Arsenicums often like children because children are so innocent that they don't trigger any trust issues. Arsenicum's more challenging sides only show up in his relationships if he is sick, stressed out, feeling overloaded, or if he feels threatened in some way.

I saw an example of this once when I went to a birthday party for a small Arsenicum girl. Birthday parties are often stressful for the birthday child, and she was obviously not having a good time with so many children messing with all her toys. She is usually a sweet girl, but this particular day she showed a very different side of herself. At some point, one of the other little girls happened to step onto her favorite scarf, which was lying on the floor at the time. As soon as the Arsenicum girl saw this, she quickly yanked the scarf away, and the little girl went flying, landed on her butt and got really hurt. The little girl's mother became very upset and told the Arsenicum girl that what she had done wasn't nice. She explained to her that she could have just asked the little girl to step off the scarf instead of yanking it away. The Arsenicum girl answered that the scarf was hers, and that she wanted the little girl and her mother to go home. She showed no remorse or concern that the little girl was hurt because the scarf was hers, and she wanted it back!

From a homeopathic point of view, the little girl's behavior totally fits the Arsenicum remedy picture. Arsenicum is afraid of thieves taking their possessions. They need physical security, which they create by collecting things, money and property, and by keeping their things in order. In this case, the children had made a big mess out of her toys, and the Arsenicum girl probably thought the girl, who stepped on her scarf, was going to take it from her. This triggered her fears and made her feel vulnerable. She defended herself, in this case by yanking the scarf away in order to take it back. The Arsenicum girl felt that she was right. It was her scarf, and she wasn't concerned if someone got hurt in the process. Because she was in "defense mode," her survival and physical security was the only thing that mattered to her. She wanted her scarf back and simply didn't care what happened to the other little girl.

This pattern is often seen in couples as well. A friend of mine shared with me how her Arsenicum boyfriend behaved after he felt betrayed by something she had said to his mom. Her Arsenicum boyfriend had been in a grumpy and critical mood for several weeks, and the girl was feeling very sad about the situation. In the middle of this, they went to visit Arsenicum's parents. Arsenicum's mom quickly realized that the girl was feeling sad about something and wanted to know what was wrong. The girl told her how grumpy and critical Arsenicum had been over the last few weeks, and the mother, who only wanted to help the situation, gave Arsenicum a hug when they were about to leave, and very casually said to him that he should be nice to his girlfriend.

Arsenicum wasn't stupid. He immediately put together two and two and realized that she had been talking to his mother about him. He felt betrayed, stabbed in the back, and he yelled at her the whole way home. The poor girl was intimidated by Arsenicum's rage and didn't argue back, but Arsenicum still kept going, non-stop, for several hours. He didn't care that she was crying because he was justifying his anger and malicious behavior by the fact that she shouldn't have involved his mother in his private affairs. In other words, he was right and she was not, and that made it right for him to be as cruel as he felt he needed to be to really get the point across. He did get the point across, loud and clear, but not in the way he intended. The girlfriend saw very clearly where he was coming from and closed her heart to him, and she eventually ended up leaving the relationship, which he wasn't very happy about at the time.

When hearing stories about Arsenicum's uncaring attitude in relationships, it is important to understand the original story that goes with the Arsenicum perception of reality. Arsenicum still responds *as if* he were unjustly accused of something he didn't do. He was attacked, lost his money and possessions, and almost lost his life. He didn't know who conspired against him so he didn't know who to trust, and this created a high degree of suspiciousness towards almost everyone, even the people within his own home.

From this point of view, he has to convince the people in his life that he is right at any cost because to him, it is still a matter of survival. This is why Arsenicums are intolerant of contradiction as well as other people's opinions because it all comes down to who is right and who is not. Any time Arsenicum finds himself in a defensive mode, all the feelings that go with this situation are triggered, and at that point, the only thing that matters to him is proving that he is right, and you are wrong, no matter what it takes. He behaves *as if* you are his worst enemy (that is why he doesn't care if your feelings are hurt in the process) because, in his perception you are, until you agree with him so he can feel safe again.

In the example above, the girlfriend could have easily avoided Arsenicum's non-stop rage if only she had agreed, right away, that he was absolutely right. Her choice of being silent during the argument was worse, to Arsenicum, than if she had been arguing against him. If she had at least argued back, he could have easily destroyed her arguments and won the battle, but how do you argue against silence? How can you have a debate with someone who doesn't respond to your arguments? It must have been frustrating for Arsenicum because her silence didn't put his mind at ease at all. He had no way to determine whether or not she had been convinced yet because she wasn't giving him any reassurance that his point had been understood. So he kept screaming at her for several hours, just to make sure that she really got the message.

Arsenicum's girlfriend was so intimidated by his anger that she chose to be silent during the argument, hoping he would "run out of steam" if she didn't ad any more fuel to the fire. However, she found that the effect of her silence was exactly the opposite. If only she had known this, she could have possibly avoided what she experienced as psychological abuse on a regular basis for the whole time they were together. This is why it is so important to understand the underlying patterns that determine people's behavior. Who would have ever thought that silence could be a trigger for abusive behavior? But, by looking at the delusions that create Arsenicum's perception of reality, this actually does make sense! He doesn't feel at ease unless he can convince the other that he is right, and because he didn't feel convinced by her silence, he became emotionally abusive in an effort to force his point of view across.

The issue of money and property is another difficult area for Arsenicum. If he has enough physical security in his life, he feels less vulnerable, but as the next example shows, the feeling of security can easily change if there is a chance that someone can take it away from him.

One Arsenicum man and his wife decided to buy a house together. They agreed to pay the loan off as quickly as possible, and both put as much money into the house as they could afford to each month. As long as Arsenicum put in more money than his wife did, he felt fine, but the day his wife put in a lump sum so she actually had more money invested in the house than he had, he felt quite disturbed. He immediately felt his physical security threatened by the possibility that she could claim a bigger part of the house should she ever decide to divorce him. By putting more money into the house than her husband, the wife had unknowingly triggered Arsenicum's fear of being alone and vulnerable, as well as his fear of losing the house, which represented his only physical security.

The pessimistic outlook based in the fear of losing his security is also a typical part of the Arsenicum perception of reality. Deep down Arsenicum feels forsaken and unloved. He tries to control relationships through logic and intimidation because he doesn't know any other way. This is why Arsenicum knows, from experience, that emotional security isn't something he can count on, so he chooses physical security instead, since it is easier to create, hold on to and control. Again, we can see how the need for security and control reflects Arsenicum's inner sense of weakness and vulnerability. It is interesting to note that unless we know what Arsenicum's perception of reality is, none of his reactions make any sense, but as soon as we relate his behavior to the Arsenicum core issues, we can see that everything actually does make sense! This is why it is so important to study the core issues associated with each remedy type.

Here is another example which reflects the same kind of issue: This story is about an Arsenicum man who was engaged to be married for 12 years. He kept postponing the marriage because he wanted to accumulate enough money first to ensure that he could properly take care of a wife and a family. This reminds me of the story of Ebenezer Scrooge in Charles Dicken's Christmas Carol, who also let the years go by because he never thought he had enough money to get married, and his girlfriend finally realized that he loved his money more than he loved her. But unlike Scrooge, our Arsenicum man finally did get married and went on to raise a family of his own. Years later, when his own daughter brought home her first boyfriend, Arsenicum's behavior towards him was extremely critical and judgmental. Although the young man had borrowed a suit and a pipe in an effort to impress Arsenicum, it made no difference to Arsenicum because he was determined not to let anything impress him. All he could see was that his daughter's new friend was just too young. He wasn't from a wealthy family, he didn't have any money saved up, he didn't have a proper education and he simply wasn't good enough for his daughter. When they decided to get married anyway, Arsenicum didn't even give them a proper wedding gift, since he didn't want to waste his money unless her new husband could first prove to him that he was good enough for his daughter.

Five years later, after his son in-law graduated from college, Arsenicum finally decided to buy proper silverware for his daughter and her family as some kind of delayed wedding gift. The boy had finally proven himself to be both ambitious and responsible, and Arsenicum finally found him worthy enough to approve of their marriage. He never even considered the hurt feelings and physical hardship he put his daughter through by not supporting her choice of husband because he just wanted what was best for her, and that intention justified his insensitive behavior.

This shows how important physical security is for Arsenicum. The father didn't even consider the fact that his daughter loved the man she wanted to marry, in fact, love was the least of his concerns. All he could focus on was the fact that the boy wasn't wealthy enough, and that he couldn't provide the amount of security that he wanted for his daughter since physical security was the only thing that mattered to him.

From the example above, we can see how easy it is for many Arsenicums to end up feeling unappreciated by the people they love, since people tend to resent their seemingly callous behavior rather than appreciating their good intentions. (The expression: "It is the thought that counts!" must have been invented by an Arsenicum!)

Arsenicum's behavior can easily be understood if we look at what his underlying feelings are. If Arsenicum wants to establish his superiority, he will self-righteously defend himself and his point of view, and he will justify, to himself, the use of any harshness needed to get this point across. If, however, his underlying feeling is fear, rather than self-righteousness, his behavior can be totally different. Coming from a place of fear, or insecurity, he will surround himself with people who can help him feel better, even though he is still afraid that the people he is relying on are going to take advantage of him in some way. He doesn't like being taken advantage of, but if he feels that he needs them in his life for some reason, he will still be very nice to them to make sure that they don't leave him.

One Arsenicum therapist kept bending over backwards in an effort to be nice to her clients, even though many of them were calling her any time of the day or night. When I asked her why she kept putting up with it, and why she didn't draw the line somewhere, she admitted that she was afraid they would quit coming to see her if she drew the line, and if they quit coming, she wouldn't be making any money (fear of poverty again). So because she relied on her clients to give her money, she was willing to allow them to take as much advantage of her as they wanted to. If this was the price she had to pay to have wealthy clients come to her for therapy, then so be it!

Another Arsenicum client had hired a project manager to help him build his new house. The project manager charged top dollar, took very long lunch breaks, made lots of mistakes on the project, came late, left early, and obviously, to everyone who could see clearly, took advantage of Arsenicum any way he knew how. When asked why he didn't fire the guy, it became obvious that Arsenicum thought he needed him on the project. He didn't trust that his house would be built without his help, so he was just putting up with all his nonsense because he thought it was a necessary part of the project. Fortunately, he did eventually fire him. Later, I heard what happened after he was fired. The guy became so upset about being fired that he took some of Arsenicum's tools as he was packing up to leave, and not only that, he even charged Arsenicum for the time it took to pack up the tools he had taken! Only an Arsenicum would be nice to someone like that!

If Arsenicum isn't coming from a place of fear, or insecurity, he isn't nearly as nice to the people in his life. He is always ready to defend himself, or justify his position, opinion or action, thinking that if he can prove, beyond any doubt, that he is right, others will eventually come to their senses and even love him for making things so clear to them. (Arsenicum has this peculiar underlying feeling, or delusion, that if he can just prove that he is right, he will be loved!) This can make Arsenicum controlling in relationships because he can only see his own point of view most of the time, and, in his opinion, there is no other way of looking at a situation.

An amusing example of how Arsenicum tends to control others happened to me one day when an Arsenicum friend came over for tea. As soon as I poured the boiling water over the tea bags, he jumped up and found two small plates that he put on top of each cup. I told him that I didn't want my tea bag steeping too long since I don't like my tea very strong, and I also told him I didn't want my tea too hot, so I didn't want the plate on top of my cup. I reached out to take off the plate when my friend said "Don't touch!" He explained to me that this is the only proper way to make tea, and that I had to wait until my tea bag had finished brewing before I was allowed to remove the plate. When he finally handed the cup to me, he got a look of horror on his face when I went to the sink and added cold water so I could drink it without burning my tongue. The adding of cold water definitely wasn't part of his recipe! This Arsenicum man, who was a guest in my house, behaved in a controlling way without any concern for the fact that I didn't want my tea the way he made it. He felt that he was right, and that justified his behavior, regardless of how I felt about it, since he knew the right way to make tea, and I obviously didn't.

To complete the picture of Arsenicum's behavior in relationships, I want to show that Arsenicums also have a very caring side. They usually have good intentions, even though it doesn't always look like it, and they always try to do for others what they think is the best for them. One Arsenicum woman was so dedicated to her two children that even "super mom" couldn't have done any better. It was a full time job for her just to drive her children from one class to another. Anything they wanted to learn, she wanted them to experience, and she didn't care how many hours of driving or waiting she had to do each day. She bought the best shoes, clothes and food for them because only the best was good enough for her children. By the end of each day, she was so tired she went to bed by 7 or 8 every night. She admitted that she didn't feel like she had much time for herself, which bothered her at times, but she felt that because she had chosen to have children, she should be prepared to be totally committed and follow through all the way. She was trying to be the most perfect mom anyone could ever be. In return, she was very controlling and had high expectations of her kids, and I can only guess that, some day, her kids will rebel against her need to control, and she will end up feeling totally unappreciated after all she has done for them. Unfortunately, this is a problem for many Arsenicums; they mean so well, but they eventually discover that good intentions aren't always enough.

Another example of how Arsenicums can be caring in relationships is the story of a woman who was living with her alcoholic mother. She was terrified when her mother went out every night. She knew her mother would drink, and she also knew she would be driving back drunk some time during the night. She was so afraid that her mother was going to have an accident on the way home, which she frequently had, that she couldn't sleep until her mom came back late at night. This eventually turned into a chronic sleep problem for the girl, even after she moved out and got her own place. Years later, she is still terrified that her mother is going to die some day, and she'll be on her own. She loves and cares about her mother very much, and she wishes she could help her get over her addiction.

Arsenicums often feel a lot of anxiety for others. They really do care about the people in their lives, but underneath their caring attitude, there is almost always an underlying fear that they will be on their own if something bad happens to the people that they love. This shows that most of Arsenicum's behavior is fear based; even the caring and worrying about others comes from their underlying fear of aloneness, or even the fear of death.

Sometimes, I think, Arsenicum's need to control a situation is such a part of their nature that they aren't even aware that they are doing it. But even when Arsenicum can totally justify his behavior, he is often afraid that the people he loves are going to leave him some day because, deep down, he knows that he isn't treating them very nicely. He just can't stop behaving that way because he feels less anxious when he is in control. Since Arsenicum's perception of reality is so fear based, the use of homeopathic Arsenicum is the best way to make him less controlling. Over time, it will reduce his fears and defensive attitude and help bring out his more playful, caring and loving side instead.

I JUST WANT TO FEEL SAFE
Calcarea Carbonica

REMEDY DESCRIPTION

Calcarea Carbonica is generally a good natured, happy, easygoing individual. She is slow by nature and often tends to be late for things, but being on time doesn't really matter to her. She is cheerful, optimistic, somewhat timid and absentminded, and some Calcareas may even have clairvoyant qualities. Calcareas are usually earthy, grounded, practical people who can be quite stable emotionally as long as they feel safe.

Calcarea loves stability. Like the oyster, she doesn't like things to change very much. Therefore, Calcarea Carbonica has a tendency to be extremely stubborn. If she doesn't agree with what she is told to do, she won't necessarily confront or create conflict, she will just quietly and stubbornly keep doing what she is doing, in her own way, and she doesn't easily budge when her mind is made up. Therefore, it is no surprise to find that Calcarea also tends to be very picky about things. She likes things to be a certain way and can sometimes be critical, prejudiced, pompous and selfish in her views. She applies her "pickiness" not just to things, but to people as well. She may prefer to only be around certain people that she likes and feels safe with, and if you aren't part of her group, it may be hard to get "a foot in the door." Again, we see a strong lack of flexibility, lack of movement and resistance to change.

Interestingly, even though Calcarea resists change, she is often a very passionate type since her sex drive is quite high. She loves being at home, relaxing, eating good food (especially potatoes and eggs) and making love. If her mate can't match her sex drive, she can become very unhappy and start looking for sex from other sources. Calcareas usually feel good about the way they look, even when they are quite overweight, and it is very important for Calcarea to have a mate she can make love with whenever she wants to.

There are two types of Calcareas. One type is slow and mentally sluggish, and the other type is brilliant. The slow type has difficulty learning, concentrating or remembering anything, and she gets tired just thinking about the effort it will take. The other type is able to remember very well, once the material has been understood properly, but in both types comprehension is usually slow, and learning happens step by step and often takes a lot of effort.

Calcarea feels easily overloaded from too much mental work. Her brain simply can't take in, or process, a lot of information at one time because it processes slowly and can only do it bit by bit. It takes a lot of effort for Calcarea to remember things, and she often has problems remembering what was heard or said, like facts, places and words.

Basically, everything Calcarea wants to achieve takes a lot of effort on her part. When seeing how seemingly easy things come to other people, Calcarea often feels envious. She stops appreciating what she has and becomes ungrateful and sulky. Even though she may feel restless and want to do something about her situation, she may not have a clue what to do since doing isn't really her thing. She much prefers to hope, or trust, that somebody will come along and save her and take care of her.

Calcarea feels safe inside her home. The worst thing that can happen to Calcarea (the oyster) is that she loses her home. Like an oyster without a shell, she feels totally unprotected in an unfamiliar environment. According to the Calcarea delusions, when she is in unfamiliar territory, everything in her life feels like a dream and she may fear that she is going insane! She feels vulnerable, as if she is being watched, or she feels that somebody could come and get her. Horrible things could happen! Her body could be dashed to pieces, she could disappear, she could die, or even worse, be murdered by some hideous monster. And if she somehow survives, she would probably end up getting some incurable disease, or at least heart disease, anyway. So, if you have ever wondered why Calcareas are so happy being at home, and why they have so little desire for adventure, this is why! They simply don't feel safe leaving their nice, cozy "shells," going out in a big, scary world where horrible things can happen to them.

When Calcarea feels unsafe, unprotected or stressed, she often becomes oversensitive to the rudeness of others and worried about what others may think about her. She has a strong sense of responsibility and often feels guilty if there is a possibility that she is to blame for something. Calcarea also feels strongly affected by bad news and by hearing about cruel and horrible things. This affects her so much because it reminds her of how terrifying the world outside her cozy little house is. Calcarea would probably be better off not listening to the news at all since there are no good news, anyway.

When Calcarea feels anxious, frightened or doesn't feel safe, she easily becomes angry or picky about little things. She can become critical if the people she encounters don't measure up to her standards, or she can be very controlling in her relationships with others. If she doesn't get what she wants, she sometimes becomes furiously angry, even to the point of violence. Therefore, Calcarea is often a very good remedy for temper tantrums in children. If they stubbornly want something they can't have, and you can't easily distract them or make them change their minds. They may dig their heels in and start raging, and your best option may be to quickly give them a dose of Calcarea Carbonica to make them a little bit easier to deal with.

Calcarea adults can also become furiously angry at times. In an angry Calcarea adult, you will be surprised to find that she can sometimes be abrupt, malicious, spiteful, vindictive or even cursing. If that doesn't change things, she doesn't mind becoming mischievous, deceitful, sly or dishonest to get what she wants. Because she isn't very brave, she much prefers sneaking around rather than confronting someone directly.

Calcarea isn't very strong physically, either. She gets exhausted and over heated easily, and because she feels weak and vulnerable, she often develops many anxieties. She is full of cares and worries about pretty much everything, especially in the evening and in bed while going to sleep. She is afraid to be alone and often wakes up full of anxiety from frightful dreams.

One of the things Calcareas often feel anxious about is business and money issues. She is often anxious about the future and feels worse the more she thinks about it. Having to make money and pay bills is a constant source of aggravation for Calcarea, it just isn't her thing! She would much prefer to win the lottery or find a mate who can take care of all her needs so she doesn't have to. She often dreams about ascending this dimension to a better dimension where all she has to do is think a thought, and it will manifest instantly and effortlessly. This, for a Calcarea, is her version of heaven – a place where no effort is needed!

Calcarea is also anxious about health issues. She suffers from anticipation anxiety since she always expects bad things to happen, and she worries about going to the doctor or the dentist since she can easily imagine that she might have some kind of incurable disease that she didn't know about. She has a tendency towards hypochondriasis and is often anguished if she feels any signs of heart palpitation.

When Calcarea finds herself in an anxious or non-coping mode, she can sometimes sink into a deep, dark state of depression. She will sit brooding, dwelling on past disagreeable occurrences, like grief and various other disappointments. She can go into an extremely discontented, displeased and discouraged state. If her confidence is low, she avoids any kind of company, including family members, and she may not want to talk to anyone since talking often makes her feel worse. If she doesn't know what to do, she'll feel both confused and gloomy. She feels slow, heavy and lazy, and she easily develops aversion to any kind of work. She simply isn't the kind of person who will do something to make a change in her own life.

Here, I do need to add that there are some Calcareas who will go out, work hard and do what it takes to create the kind of life that they want for themselves, but they are normally few and far between, because they basically have to force themselves to do so, as it isn't really part of their nature. Normally, help has to come from the outside, and until that happens, Calcarea feels very hopeless and unfortunate about her situation.

Some Calcareas have such an aversion to solitude that they do want to be around people. It gives them someone to complain to. In a weeping, tearful mood, she pities herself and has a very pessimistic outlook on her situation. She torments those around her by talking about her symptoms for hours, even though it doesn't really make her feel any better. She desires to have someone to tell her what to do, or even better, to take care of her, and if that doesn't happen, she can become totally apathetic and indifferent to everything.

If she can't find anyone who is willing to take care of her, Calcarea often turns to religion for comfort instead, since trust and faith are qualities that really appeal to her, in fact it gives her great hope and helps lift her spirits. If, however, her earthly concerns still keep dragging her down, she can still go into deep despair and become quite suicidal. She probably doesn't have the courage or the energy to actually kill herself, even though she may wish to be dead at times, so her suffering in this dimension can be over with for good.

CALCAREA CARBONICA IN RELATIONSHIPS

The main thing for Calcarea is to feel safe and secure, with nothing to worry about. She is sweet, affectionate, loving and easygoing as long as she feels safe, and as long as her partner takes care of her needs. Because her standards are high, she may criticize and try to change him if he doesn't live up to her standards, or if he doesn't do things the way she likes them done because she likes things done her own way. If her mate criticizes her in return, it affects her emotionally, but it doesn't affect the way she does things. Calcarea is one of the most stubborn of all the remedies. She controls the people in her life in a gentle, quiet, stubborn kind of way, by doing what she is doing without even arguing about it, even when someone tells her not to. That way she always gets her way in the end.

If Calcarea ends up with a mate who doesn't take care of her needs, or who doesn't make her feel safe, or that she can't change or control, Calcarea becomes angry: very, very angry. At this point she is no longer her happy, easygoing self. She will fight for what she wants, she becomes oversensitive to insults, and she will complain to her friends about her impossible mate. The same can also happen to Calcareas who don't have a mate. If they don't have a mate that they can control, they can always try to tell God what they want instead!

One Calcarea client had been told by "spirit" that she didn't have to work for a living. She was helping people expand their consciousness, and as a new age "light worker" she believed that she deserved being taken care of and should not have to worry about any earthly concerns. She expected everything in her life to mysteriously be taken care of, simply by trusting that it would. One of her friends, who had a house she wanted to sell, offered it to Calcarea on very good terms. The owner would finance the house, Calcarea didn't have to give her anything as a down payment, and she could pay it off like a regular loan, but with no interest. Calcarea joyfully accepted the offer and immediately moved all her things in. She opened up her house to anyone who wanted her services, but most of the people who wanted her help had no money and gave her no donations to speak of. By the time her first monthly payment was due, Calcarea knew she didn't have enough money for the payment. She spent the last week of the month doing a lot of praying to God and trusting that he would provide what she needed at exactly the right time, but unfortunately nothing happened. When, by the end of the month, she still didn't have the money for her monthly payment, she promised to pay her friend as soon as the money came in. She explained that she only needed a little more time to get it together, and the friend agreed to wait.

Every month the same story happened. She clearly told God what she needed, and when it didn't magically manifest, she figured that it was simply a test of her level of trust. In addition to her house payment she also had car payments due. She stopped paying her car insurance since she was short on money, rationalizing this decision by saying that her trust was strong enough that no accidents could possibly happen to her, so she no longer felt that she needed any car insurance.

The friend, who had offered to sell her the house, was unbelievably patient about receiving payments. However, even her patience eventually came to an end after about 6 months of not receiving any payments from Calcarea, who were still living in the house. She finally decided to take her house back and sell it in a traditional manner, and Calcarea had to move into a rental. She borrowed money from her friends to pay the first month's rent and the security deposit, and then the same story repeated itself. Month after month she would pray, trust and not pay her rent, and she kept having to move from place to place. At some point she borrowed several thousand dollars from a bank and got a friend to cosign for the loan. Unfortunately, she didn't make any payments on this loan either, and her friend ended up having to pay it back.

The bank eventually foreclosed on her car, and she had to sell most of her possessions in order to get some cash. The last time I had contact with her, she was traveling from place to place, living wherever people would give her free room and board out of compassion, and basically heading for a life on the streets.

The interesting thing about this story is the fact that she wasn't willing to take any kind of action to change her situation, no matter how bad things were. At some point, I tried to tell her that trust alone wasn't enough. She would also need to take action if she wanted things to change, but she stubbornly stuck to her own point of view, and no one could convince her otherwise. Once, I asked for her help with a project I was in the middle of, and I offered to pay her $200.00 just to lend me a hand. And even though she had no money to pay her upcoming bills, she told me, in true Calcarea style, that it was going to take more than $200.00 to get her out of her house!

All she wanted was to be in her house, to feel safe and to be taken care of. She was truly an "oyster" waiting for some kind of miracle to happen, like winning the lottery, or marrying someone who was independently rich, or being beamed up on a space ship, or simply ascending to the fifth dimension where no more effort was needed.

I admit that the story above is a somewhat extreme example of how a Calcarea may choose to live her life, but it still clearly describes the essence of the Calcarea personality where making an effort simply isn't part of their reality. However, we have to also keep in mind that this doesn't apply to all Calcareas. There are Calcareas who sincerely work for a living, and put in a lot of effort, even when they are tired or exhausted. This kind of Calcarea may be slow in what she does, although she is often very reliable, capable and conscientious, and she may put a lot of effort in to get the job completed. Calcarea's main problem is that she doesn't have a lot of energy, or endurance, and this is why she has a tendency to be on the lazy side and live her life accordingly.

ALWAYS FIGHTING FOR A CAUSE
Causticum Hahnemanni

REMEDY DESCRIPTION

Causticum Hahnemanni is a timid, gentle, mild mannered type. He has a tendency to be both serious and cautious, and he usually has a calm, quiet disposition. In addition, he can also be reserved and introspective. His mind is sharp and analytical, and he loves to bury himself in deep thoughts.

In some ways Causticum is like an absent minded professor. He can sometimes be so absorbed in his own thoughts that he can easily forget his groceries and walk out of the store without them. Not surprisingly, he often has a feeling that he has forgotten something, but he doesn't know what it is. One of my Causticum clients lost his homeopathic remedy bottle the day after he received it, even though he was excited about using the remedy. He always lives in a state of slight chaos, and things just seem to naturally disappear on their own. However, Causticum doesn't really care if there is chaos in his life because his dreams, visions and ideals are much more important to him than ordinary, mundane physical details, such as whether he can find two matching socks in his drawer, or not.

Causticum has a big heart and a sympathetic nature. He is usually cheerful and affectionate and has a good sense of humor. He likes to tease, and he often loves to go out dancing. Causticum is a very passionate type who loves being around people, and he may even become obsessed by the idea of marriage, since family means a lot to him. Although he loves being around people, his passion and excitement can sometimes make it difficult for him to relate to others because he has a tendency to become either too emotionally intense, or too controlling in his relationships. However, it is a fact that Causticum is a type who truly cares about people. Not only does he care about his own family and friends, but he is also deeply concerned about humanity in general. In fact, he is so sympathetic that he often worries about others a lot of the time, and he is also very affected by horrible things and sad stories.

Because Causticum is so full of cares and worries, there is often an underlying feeling that something bad is going to happen, like some kind of danger or misfortune, and he tends to have a somewhat pessimistic attitude that can easily bring him into a state of anguish. He reacts to this inner sense of impending danger by becoming anxious, suspicious, mistrustful and secretive, since he often doesn't know what the danger is, or even where it is going to come from.

When looking at the delusions that go with the Causticum picture, we see the same kinds of fears reflected there. His imagination is so vivid that he can easily create some pretty scary visions of phantoms, ghosts or evil. Sometimes he sees hideous faces, dead people, or even people that are larger than normal. There are also delusions about criminals and about being robbed, as well as the delusion that he is unfortunate.

Causticum's fears and delusions about something bad happening reflects the original situation that goes with the Causticum profile. In this situation, he found himself in grave danger. Someone, bigger and stronger than himself, robbed him and took away his fortune. Therefore, he still perceives his reality *as if* a similar thing could happen again at any time.

This explains why Causticum can develop anxiety when he finds himself in a crowd, or he can develop fear of strangers, especially if someone he doesn't know is approaching him. He also has a tendency to fear animals, especially dogs, since dogs can be dangerous, too, and he doesn't know if they are going to bite or attack him.

However, Causticum isn't just concerned with the possibility of his own misfortune. He also knows that the same can happen to other people. This fills him with anxiety for others, especially about the future, because he feels that something bad can definitely happen to the people in his life as well. The more he thinks about it, the more anxious he feels. Every little thing makes him feel worse. The fear is often overpowering, his body starts trembling, and he may find himself making involuntary gestures with his hands.

Although Causticum knows that it isn't his fault that bad things can happen to people, he somehow feels responsible, and if something bad does happen to anyone he knows, he feels very guilty that he didn't do something to prevent it. This makes Causticum extremely sensitive, and because he feels guilty, and he also tends to take everything personally. It is almost as if Causticum takes on the part of tribal leader, where he feels that the he alone is responsible for the welfare of the other members in the "tribe." He can sense that danger is coming, and he feels that he is the only one who can prevent it from happening. We can easily imagine how much pressure Causticum feels on his shoulders, being in this kind of position, especially since he often doesn't know what the danger is, or even where it is going to come from. However, Causticum takes his "assignment" very seriously, so seriously, in fact, that he is in a state of anxiety a lot of the time. He is often anxious first thing in the morning, but it is even worse in twilight, in the dark or in the evening in bed. Causticum dreads the evenings, especially if he is alone, and sometimes he feels so anxious that he fears going to bed. He can even develop a fear or aversion to the bed itself, because his anxiety often increases when he is trying to go to sleep.

One of Causticum's main problems is his inability to stop thinking about frightful things. There may be a rush or flow of thoughts, tormenting and haunting him about persistent and unpleasant subjects. His thoughts are often frightful and rapid, and one thought usually leads to the next. The more he thinks, the worse he feels, and if he finally does fall asleep, his sleep is far from peaceful.

Causticum has a tendency to startle on falling asleep. Either he is sleepless from too many thoughts, or he falls into a very restless sleep that makes him tired the next day. He is often so full of restlessness that he keeps tossing and turning throughout the night, and it may even drive him out of bed because he just has to keep moving. And even when he does fall asleep, his mind is not necessarily at peace. He may laugh, weep, talk, moan, groan or whine during his sleep, which shows how hard it is for him to truly rest.

However, Causticum knows how to put this restlessness to good use. Because he feels responsible for the welfare of others, he is not just going to sit and do nothing. Causticum is basically a practical idealist, which means that he is a man of action and practical solutions. (He may not be practical in his day to day life, but that is a different issue). He feels compelled to find creative solutions to the problems he can see, and he often becomes deeply involved in political or religious issues, and sometimes even both. His views can be eccentric, and he is usually not a great supporter of the status quo. He may be somewhat of an anarchist, dreaming about utopian solutions to the impending disaster that is sure to come at some point in the future. He may be involved with environmental issues, protesting against gold mining and tree cutting, trying to keep the government from stealing our ground water or reducing medical care for the poor, or saving baby seals and whales. He may hand out flyers or write books or articles for newspapers or magazines, and he may even be ready to die for his cause if it seems necessary. His mind is clear, his ideas are abundant, and he often feels extremely excited talking about "his vision."

Sometimes his idealism can even seem a bit too fanatical to others. He can easily become manic, obsessive and obstinate about his political or religious passions, or he may become critical, dictatorial or intolerant of other points of view. He has a disposition to contradict, and often refuses to follow any kind of rules that don't make sense to him. Causticum is basically a natural born campaigner. He is a natural revolutionary who simply isn't happy unless he is fighting for some kind of cause that he can put all his passion into.

However, if he gets too obsessive about his cause, it can eventually throw him off balance. He may start feeling sorry for himself and become ungrateful and unappreciative about what he has, and may also start slandering others, especially if they don't agree with him. Being heard and understood is so essential to Causticum that he can become extremely depressed if the world isn't ready for "his vision," and he doesn't get the support or recognition he needs and wants. Not only does he tend to feel depressed if the world isn't ready to hear what he has to say, but his excitement can easily turn into a complete loss of self-control where he becomes quarrelsome and abusive, with harsh screaming, shouting and swearing. He may also start feeling a sense of urgency, as if he has to get the point across to people quickly, before time runs out.

When Causticum feels stressed, he often reacts with anger and irritability, especially in the morning. Little things often aggravate, and his moods can become so repulsive that he can't even take a joke. At times, his irritability can alternate with cheerfulness, or it can just as easily turn into violent anger. After all, he only wants what is best for the people he is concerned about, and he feels very upset if they don't know what is in their best interest, or they don't appreciate or understand his efforts. (This explains why Causticum is so controlling in relationships. It is because he can see what needs to happen, but he can only help people if they cooperate with him and do what he tells them to do. So, although he has "the vision," he still needs the support from the group he is trying to help, and this usually becomes his biggest dilemma: How can he convince them to listen to what he has to say, when they don't know what is in their best interest? Prophets, dooms-day preachers and fanatic revolutionaries come to mind...)

Sometimes Causticum gets so absorbed in his desire to do something to make the world a better place that it will start affecting his home life as well. The people in his life will most likely start to complain, but their complaints will only increase his sense of anxiety, pressure and urgency which, in turn, will make him even more irritable and harder to live with. Even though Causticum loves his family and often feels devastated if they leave him, his cause will always be his first priority in life, whether his family likes it, or not, because Causticum doesn't feel happy if anyone stops him from pursuing his vision. At the same time, he doesn't want to lose his family either. So basically, he has to try to find a balance between pursuing his vision and keeping his loved ones happy, although this is not an easy thing for him to do since he absolutely hates compromising. The problem is that if he can't find this balance, there is every chance that he will, eventually, lose his family and end up feeling totally beside himself with grief and disappointment. His behavior can then become hysterical and childish, and he may even start thinking he is sick and refuse to go to work, since there is no point in doing anything if even his closest friends and family don't understand him! He is brooding, complaining and whining, and if he has to move out of his own house, he will miss his family terribly and suffer from homesickness. He doesn't like being alone because he always feels better if he has someone he can talk to. If his sadness and gloom gets deep enough, he can even start feeling suicidal. He has dedicated his life to making the world a better place to be, but if nobody else seems to care, he can feel totally discouraged and misunderstood and can sink into a deep depression about the state of things.

At this point he might not believe that anything in his life is ever going to get any better, and he keeps dwelling on disagreeable occurrences, especially at night. He is discontented, displeased and dissatisfied with himself, and he feels remorse for having failed his mission. He may be so disgusted with everything that he doesn't even feel like eating and he may even turn to alcohol for comfort, since things can't really get much worse anyway.

When Causticum feels really inconsolable, he can become both indifferent and apathetic. He neglects everything and just wants to escape. Because he isn't very brave, and he may want to travel as far away as he can from whatever is dragging him down. He may be in a tearful mood, easily weeping at little things. He weeps in his drunkenness, and sometimes he can't even stop. The weeping can even become spasmodic, which points towards the remedy's ability to deal with different kinds of muscle spasms as well.

When Causticum is depressed, his ideas, which used to be so abundantly available, are now pretty much gone. He feels confused and can't think clearly. Concentration is difficult, and he feels exhausted if he tries too hard. His memory becomes weak, and he can't even remember familiar names. Everything seems to slow down, and his mind becomes dull and sluggish. Sometimes he can't even understand a question unless he repeats it to himself first. He may feel better if he takes a walk in open air. It is almost as if his brain needs more oxygen to function properly.

If his condition keeps deteriorating, Causticum can gradually become slower and more sluggish in everything he does. The worst thing that can happen to him is that he goes completely unconscious, like a state of mental paralysis. He may be sitting on his chair with eyes fixed and unmoving, and if the condition deteriorates even further, he could eventually end up in a coma. There is also a possibility that he could develop paralysis or epilepsy at some point, especially if his brain or nervous system becomes too overloaded. Therefore, Causticum can be a good remedy for both paralysis and epilepsy, especially if the epilepsy is preceded by dullness, forgetfulness, idiotic actions or foolish behavior. He may even be laughing before, during or after the fits.

When Causticum's brain starts to become sluggish, he may no longer enjoy being around people. In this state he may lose interest in talking to anyone or answering their questions, or he could even develop an aversion to people in general, especially if they previously hurt his feelings or worked against his cause in some way. Causticum may also become afraid that he has some kind of sickness, even when there is no reason to think so. But even if he does become really sick, he may still refuse treatment. He may also go completely insane, especially if he develops persecution mania.

At some point Causticum could come to a place in his life where he no longer has a strong will to live. He may become suicidal from disappointment and sadness, or he may become so weary of life that he starts thinking of death, especially if it seems like his life work has been in vain and his mission has failed.

The best way to get Causticum back on his feet again, after too much hardship and disappointment, is to see if you can get him interested in another cause he can put his energy into. If he can find something else that makes him excited and sparks his passion for life again, preferably something that only he can do, and he feels that his work is needed because people depend on his skills and creativity, his depression will lift and he'll start moving forward again. This is because, for Causticum, helping others is what gives his life meaning and purpose.

CAUSTICUM HAHNEMANNI IN RELATIONSHIPS

Causticum is a gentle soul with a big vision and a strong sense of justice. As a result of his caring attitude, he often works towards some kind of political or religious vision that will make the world a better place to be, for at least some of the people in it. And, although he isn't always an easy person to live with, it is very rare to find someone with more passion and dedication than Causticum when it comes to really making a difference in the world.

One Causticum man wanted to do whatever he could to protect the individual's rights according to the constitution. He knew that many of the political decisions made are unconstitutional, so he made it his mission in life to go to as many local political meetings as possible to make sure that all decisions made were in accordance with the constitution. If he discovered any signs of individuals losing their natural rights, he would step in and quote the law and become as much of a nuisance as he possibly could. Whenever people came to visit him in his home, the conversation would always take a political turn because there were so many injustices out there, and he felt personally responsible for doing whatsoever he could to make things better. Several times he was asked to leave the political meetings because he was viewed as a major trouble maker, and when this happened it affected him deeply. He often felt discouraged and hopeless, and would eventually look for another town to move to, hoping that people there would be more sensible.

Another Causticum man told me how he had visions of creating a utopian world even when he was quite young. He was interested in space colonization and self sufficient floating cities, and he kept reading everything he could find to learn more about the possibilities of doing so. He also wanted to find the link between religion and science to show that they have things in common, even though they may seem different at first, because he felt that if people could see this clearly, they could all work together for a common cause.

Causticum is very intelligent and has a sharp, analytical mind, so it is easy for him to find patterns and connections between seemingly unrelated issues while trying to show people a bigger picture of how things really are. This particular Causticum urgently felt that we all have to work towards a common goal for the purpose of saving humanity, and that we need to understand how important this issue is before it becomes too late to change the way things are going. In true Causticum style, he felt personally responsible for saving humanity because he felt that his own vision was the most practical solution he had encountered so far.

Another Causticum client was concerned about how people could get their needs met after a possible apocalypse. He designed numerous original solutions for creating quick and easy shelter, extremely practical clothing that has many uses and is simple to make, as well as alternative energy sources and healthy food production. His visions are often fuelled by vivid dreams of apocalypse, where he is playing his part and helping save people in trouble.

Causticum is so passionately convinced about what he has to do to bring about change that he tends to neglect everything else in his life. Two of my Causticum clients were both facing bankruptcy at some point in their lives. One actually went through it, and the other is still on the edge of possible bankruptcy.

The Causticum who went through bankruptcy has a good business where he makes lots of money each year, but he doesn't know how to manage the money well because money doesn't really matter to him that much. He looked at the bankruptcy as a great relief, and felt good getting the pressure off, so he could stop worrying about having to pay all his bills.

The other Causticum is working a part time job, so he can have more time for his utopian research work, and he often uses his credit cards too much when he needs something he can't really afford. Again, he feels that his cause is more important than covering his daily living requirements because his work is so valuable that he simply can't stop until he has achieved his goal.

It is easy to imagine how Causticum's passion and dedication to some kind of future vision can affect his personal relationships here and now. Although he is affectionate and romantic by nature, and his family means a lot to him, his cause or vision is where he puts most of his energy because that is where his main priority lies. He can become obsessive and work on his vision day and night, neglecting his family members and their needs, even though he means well and he does care, or he may constantly talk about his cause and forget to ask how his wife is doing because he has such a strong sense of urgency that nothing else really matters. There may be a feeling that he is the only person who can achieve the goal he has set for himself, and he feels a lot of pressure on his shoulders as well as anxiety and fear of failure. The cause tends to consume him, both physically and mentally, and this can be hard for the people in his life, since he is always so pre-occupied with the bigger picture that he forgets to pay attention to what is happening here and now. He can easily come across as boring, fanatical, emotionally intense or controlling, and sometimes he ends up as a loner because people can't put up with his level of intensity and dedication for more than short periods of time. It means a lot to Causticum that his family understands how important his cause is to him. If they don't understand, Causticum feels sad, misunderstood and discouraged.

The perfect relationship for a Causticum would be to find a mate who shares his passion for the same issues that he is working towards. Such a mate would work with him and help him achieve his goal, and this would take a lot of pressure and anxiety off his shoulders. However, it is often hard, or even impossible, to find a mate who is that dedicated to the same goals that he is working towards, so he often ends up finding mates who are much too practical or sensible for this taste.

One Causticum expressed to me how all his previous partners tried to "get him out of the clouds" and "back to earth," so he could learn how to function in a more practical way in this dimension. He told me that if someone should ever succeed in getting him "back to earth," they would kill his passion and inspiration, and he would no longer be who he loves being. They would destroy the very thing that gives him joy, and if that happened, his life wouldn't be worth living. He is still dreaming about finding his "dream woman" or "soul mate," which would be someone who would embrace his vision and be as excited about it as he is. Someone who would inspire him to think even more utopian thoughts, rather than pulling him back to earth again. Perhaps another Causticum could be a good match, if only he can find one who has the same goals as he does?

Another interesting thing about this same man was how he treated his ex-girlfriends. He may have decided to move on in his life because he realized that his girlfriend wasn't supportive enough, or she may have been too practical or too demanding, but even after they split up, he would never turn his back on any of them. He was always there to help or support them if they ever needed anything, which shows how sympathetic and caring a Causticum can be.

Another example of a similar situation is a Causticum friend of mine who let a single mom and her two children move in with him and stay for free in his house for as long as they needed to, since she didn't have anywhere else to go. He would even baby-sit her children when she needed to do things on her own, and he didn't ask for anything from her in return. This also shows how much Causticums truly care about people, and how they are always ready to help anyone in need.

Causticum lives in a state of passion or compassion at all times, and it is this inner fire of intensity that drives him to do what he does in his life. Because idealistic campaigning for something is part of Causticum's nature, he won't change his passionate pursuits no matter how his mate feels about it. His cause is the most important priority in his life, and his family comes second, whether they like it or not. This leaves two options for his mate, either to join him in his efforts, or surrender to the fact that this is just how he is. If his mate tries to "talk sense" into him instead, the relationship will surely break up. He simply can't be happy unless he has some kind of cause that he feels passionate about and wants to pursue, and this is something his mate has to understand if she wants to be with him. She needs to do what she can to nurture her own needs, and stop trying to change Causticum into something that he can't be. Causticum also has to understand that his partner may not be as excited about his vision as he is, and let her be who she is without any pressure from him. He probably won't like this idea very much, since he has a tendency to want to control the people in his life and make them do what he wants them to do. However, I still believe that relationships work better if each partner focuses on their own happiness instead of trying to change the other.

The money issues, that are bound to come up in a relationship with a passionate Causticum, can also cause a lot of problems, but I don't think there is an easy solution to this issue. Maybe the best thing Causticum can do is to surrender all his money to his mate and let her manage the money and pay his bills. That way he doesn't have to worry or spend more than he can afford. Another solution would be to live in two different households, where Causticum is responsible for paying his own bills, and his mate has a separate household so she doesn't have to worry about his money issues.

Causticum may be a very difficult mate to live with, mainly because he has an inner fire that can't, and shouldn't be, quenched, and also because the relationship to his mate is never his main priority. However, our society is in great need of idealistic people with a vision like his because these are the people who can really make a difference and bring about much needed change that will benefit all of us in the long run.

FAMILY AND FRIENDS
ARE IMPORTANT
Kali Carbonicum

REMEDY DESCRIPTION

We often think of Kali Carbonicum as a responsible, serious, conventional and rigid type. She is often timid and reserved, and usually prefers to dress in earth tones, like grays and browns, which don't attract much attention.

Kali Carbonicum can sometimes be critical and stubborn in her views, but there is also a cheerful and passionate side to Kali that we don't always find in the Materia Medicas. One Kali client described herself as timid, shy, reserved and serious, but quickly added that she could also be spontaneous, cheerful and fun-loving, especially around her family or friends.

Kali Carbonica has a great love for logic and prefers to live her life through her intellect. She feels comfortable being rational most of the time, simply because it makes more sense to her. Although Kali's rational way of perceiving reality makes her quite emotionally stable, it also gives her a somewhat rigid quality. By sticking with what she knows, she feels safe because if she does what she is expected to do, she is less likely to get herself into trouble. This is why Kalis like to follow rules.

The remedy also covers a sense of weakness, both physically and mentally, which causes Kali to not always get excited about going to work. She may develop dread or aversion to work, either from laziness or weariness. She is easily exhausted from too much mental effort, and she sometimes feels like sitting and doing nothing at all. Her will is weak, and she would love for someone to take care of her. This is something she has in common with her sister, Calcarea Carbonica.

Ambitious Kalis do exist. They sometimes become very successful businessmen since they often have the same need for physical security as Arsenicum Album. They can be workaholics in high positions, who have been working their way to the top in a cautious, methodical, way. What they don't have in social skills, they make up for in politeness, reliability and trustworthiness. Kali absolutely loves being part of a team, where decisions are made together.

To understand why Kali prefers to be rigid, even though there is a cheerful and passionate side to her as well, we need to take a deeper look at her fears and delusions, so we can see more clearly what the situation is that creates this perception of reality.

Because Kali is a predominantly mental type, she tends to think a lot, especially in the evening. Her mind is often clear with abundant ideas. Thoughts continue to rush through her mind even after she has gone to bed. Her thoughts are often hard to turn away, and she may be haunted by persistent thoughts about unpleasant subjects, especially if she is alone. Her imagination is often so vivid that she may not be able to sleep easily. She is full of cares and worries, and she may become so anxious that she can even develop a fear of the bed, since her anxiety is usually worse after she goes to bed. Kali is extremely sensitive, especially at night. She feels frightened by unfamiliar noises, and startles easily, both when she is about to fall asleep, and also while sleeping. She startles if somebody touches her unexpectedly, and she may even develop aversion to touch because she is very ticklish.

In addition to being sensitive, Kali can also be very excitable, especially after hearing bad news. Because Kali has a sense of internal weakness, any kind of bad news will make her feel vulnerable since she knows that whatever it is, it can easily happen to her, too. This is another issue that she has in common with Calcarea Carbonica.

When Kali is excited or anxious, her speech can be hasty, and she may feel impatient and hurried in her work, even to the point of mania. Kali's anxiety is usually worse before midnight or around 3 am in the morning, especially if she is alone. There is fear, apprehension and dread of aloneness, and she often worries about what can happen. Her main worries are about future and health, or about something bad happening to herself, her family or her friends. She may have fear of impending diseases, or feel that she is already sick for no particular reason. There is fear of solitude and fear of death, and it is often worse in the morning, just after waking up.

Even little things can scare her, and she often feels the fear in the pit of her stomach. She is so afraid of getting hurt that she can sometimes become anxious around people, especially if she is in a crowd. Some Kalis may even develop a fear touch in general, which also reflects how "touchy" she can be, both mentally and emotionally.

In addition to this, Kali also fears poverty, which can indicate that some-one took her money in the original situation that goes with the remedy picture. She compensates for this fear by accumulating wealth, so she can create physi-cal security for herself, similar to what Arsenicum does. The question is why she feels so anxious, fearful and vulnerable. What is the situation that Kali is still responding to? The answer to this question is often found in the delusions that go with each remedy profile.

Kali's delusions are frightening. She may have imaginations, hallucina-tions or illusions both day and night. At night there is the delusion that the bed is sinking, or there is an abyss behind her that she could fall into. There is a sense of emptiness, or a delusion that the body is hollow. This describes a situa-tion where Kali is not in control of what could happen to her because she is not standing on solid ground. She compensates for this feeling by being rigid and logical, so it will make her feel less vulnerable, and more in control. There are also delusions about ghosts, spirits and devils. She may see frightful phantoms or hideous faces. Maybe they are wearing masks, or maybe they are thieves, who are going to take her money. She can see people in her visions, and some of them are dead, probably murdered. She is certain that this will happen to her, too. And there are worms creeping ...

The delusions are so real that she is obliged to scream, or strike out at imaginary objects. No wonder she feels anxious and fearful when she is alone! Kali was obviously attacked and robbed, and many people died during the event. Kali's sleep is often disturbed by what she sees. She may feel like scream-ing from her disturbing visions, or she may have nightmares and wake up screaming. She may be walking or talking in her sleep, and she may scream if anyone touches her while she is asleep. Kali still seems to perceive reality *as if* she expects a similar situation to happen to her again. She compensates for this feeling by being around other people as much as possible, because it makes her feel safer to be part of a group.

Kali loves being around people. She has such a strong aversion to solitude that she will do anything to find company. Aloneness can make her feel quite beside herself, and she may beg for someone to stay with her. She feels better if someone holds her, carries her or rocks her, since aloneness brings up all her old fears. This is why Kali has such a strong bond with her family because in the family unit, she feels less vulnerable (together we stand ...) She only feels safe when she belongs to a group, or gets the support of a group. She may have many friends, or she may be part of a sports team, or she may join a religious or political group, so that she always has a sense of belonging and security. It is interesting to note that Kali feels dependent on the people who give her support, and she may voice her opinion strongly if they don't provide the support she needs or wants. This is different from Calcarea Carbonica. Calcarea feels safe if she has a nice house that she can hide in, and Kali feels safe when she has support from family, friends or a group of some kind.

Because Kali fears that something bad is going to happen to her, naturally, we can expect to find ailments from anticipation anxiety and bad news. There are also ailments from fright, emotional excitement and from disappointed love relationships. Because family relationships are so important to Kali, she may feel jealous if someone threatens the security she needs from her close relationships.

The other day I heard a car sales commercial on the radio. The person was talking in a slow, monotonous voice (definitely a Kali of some kind) about how great it was to work for Ford. And the very best thing about his workplace was the fact that: "Here, we work as a team!" The feeling that clearly came across from the commercial was a sense that if you went to see this man for your next car purchase, you'd be in very good hands, safe and secure, with no worries whatsoever. At that moment I finally understood why car dealers tend to pick Kalis to read their commercials, rather than a more dynamic type. It's all about gaining the customer's trust and confidence, and Kalis always come across as solid, reliable, no nonsense people who would never even think of ripping anyone off! In other words, nothing bad could possibly happen to you if you buy your car from this man! Very clever advertising!

Because Kali is so dependent on her relationships to others, she tends to become very sad and weepy if her relationships don't work out. The same applies if a close friend or family member should fall ill, get injured or leave the group. This is because the strength of the group, or family as a unit, is weakened when one of its members are missing, or aren't well. But, things could get even worse! The very worst thing that can possibly happen to Kali is being disowned from her family, or told to leave the group that she belongs to. If something like that were to happen, she would feel so forsaken and heart broken that her sadness would be almost unbearable. Being on her own would bring out her vulnerability and sense of weakness so much that it would significantly increase her anxiety level. In this kind of situation, the logical, rational Kali can all of a sudden act chaotic, confused or even foolish. She may feel confused and not know what to do, since she isn't very confident, or she may feel unfortunate and sulky. However, although her despair is deep, she may still have moments of hopefulness and optimism (a Tubercular trait).

Irresolution is also a common trait of all the mild mannered types. Lack of fiery energy causes lack of confidence, which in turn causes confusion of mind. Kali tends to feel confused in the morning and after waking, and she always feels better if someone can help her make the right decision.

I saw an example of this when I watched the movie Fahrenheit 911, which is a movie made about the bombing of the World Trade Center. President Bush, who is most certainly a Kali, was being filmed just after the first tower had been hit. He was visiting a preschool that day, and when the message was delivered to him, he was in the middle of reading a story to the children. His total lack of reaction or emotion was remarkable. He just sat on his chair and stared into the air. After a minute or two, he kept reading the story to the children, as if nothing had happened. A few minutes later the message came that the second tower had also been hit. Again, he said nothing, just sat on his chair, staring in front of himself. He didn't get up or make any comments. He just looked absolutely stunned. He obviously didn't know what to say, and he must have felt very lost and confused without his team of advisors there. As a Kali, he needed input from his advisors before he could respond appropriately to the situation, and since they weren't there at the time, he became literally speechless.

This reaction is typical for any Kali who would have to make serious decisions without the advice of others. Kalis often find it very difficult, or even impossible, to make decisions on their own. If they are required to do so anyway, especially if the situation is serious, it makes them feel extremely uncomfortable, almost to the point of mental paralysis.

Looking at the rubrics associated with the Kali picture, this issue is reflected on many levels, as weakness for business, weakness for expressing oneself, and weakness for finding the rights words. (This weakness is also reflected as physical weakness, which is one of the key symptoms of the Kali Carbonicum picture). Kali may also experience difficulty with concentration, especially if she has a headache. Her problem is worse from mental exertion or stress, especially if she is studying or reading something. She tends to make mistakes in speaking, by misplacing words or by using the wrong words, and also in writing, by spelling the words wrongly. She may also have difficulty with mathematics and numbers.

Kali Carbonicum can therefore be a good remedy for mental dullness and lack of comprehension. It covers stupefaction, as if intoxicated, imbecility and dull or vanishing senses. It can also cover unconsciousness during vertigo, and moments of sudden or transient unconsciousness or coma.

One of the main key symptoms of Kali Carbonicum is her tendency to be discontent, displeased and dissatisfied. Her emotions are predominated by her intellect, which often gives her fixed ideas of how things should be. Things should be a certain way because that is the logical way and also because it is the only thing that makes sense to her. If something doesn't make sense, Kali will protest.

FAMILY AND FRIENDS ARE IMPORTANT Kali Carbonicum

One Kali woman told me that her parents had very idealistic family values and her family members had to live by them. They should have peace and harmony in the family, everyone should be easy going and get along with each other, and everyone should basically be cheerful. If she finds herself in a relationship with someone who isn't necessarily cheerful or easy going, she becomes critical, and if that doesn't work, she can easily fall into a terrible mood. When this happens, she doesn't let go easily and often dwells on disagreeable occurrences at night. This makes her irritable, especially towards her family members, or even the members of the group she is associated with. Because she is so sensitive, many things may bother her. She may be irritable on waking or eating, after intercourse or even from consolation. She is very sensitive to noise and can easily feel aggravated from music, especially if it is played on the piano or the violin.

Because of this irritability, it is no surprise that the remedy Kali Carb is one of the main remedies for PMS, since Kali can also be horribly irritable before and during menses. Her oncoming periods can trigger restlessness, anxiety and issues of dependency, so even though Kali is normally quite stable emotionally, this often changes before and during her periods, and also around the time of menopause. At these times she has a tendency to treat the people in her life outrageously; her moods can become repulsive, she may change her opinions frequently and she may totally lose her sense of humor. I can just imagine other family members carefully tip-toeing on eggshells...

Kali's normally mild disposition can also suddenly alternate with anger if something doesn't make sense to her, especially in the morning or in the evening. She can become furiously angry, even while she is still in bed in the morning, or she can become malicious, spiteful or vindictive any time she finds it necessary. She may become violently angry, even with persons who are absent, or she may become quarrelsome and scolding towards her family members, especially if they aren't providing her with the kind of emotional support she feels that she needs and deserves. She may have many fixed ideas of how she wants things to be, and she has no problems expressing how she feels when things aren't that way. Sometimes she treats her family members worse than she treats her friends, in spite of the fact that she is dependent on the people she is angry with! (Or, perhaps it is *because* she is dependent on them?) If she can't resolve her discontent, she may eventually withdraw from people all together. In that case, she either develops aversion to company in general, or to specific family members, including her husband. Eventually, she just wants to be alone, in peace, so she doesn't have to talk to anyone, and it may bother her to even hear others talking to each other in the next room.

Kali may feel so much despair about her family or work situation that she chooses to turn to alcohol for comfort. She may sink into a state of indifference and apathy about company, about money, and even about pleasure. She may have a feeling that she is going to die soon, or she may even wish she were dead. However, there is not much of a chance that she would actually kill herself, since she doesn't really have what it takes to physically go through with it. (She would probably talk herself out of it anyway...)

The best thing Kali can do, to get out of her depression, is to either make friends with the people she doesn't get along with, or make new friends. As soon as she feels a sense of belonging again, it usually lifts her mood and makes her feel safe, loved and included as part of a group again, which is all she really wants.

KALI CARBONICUM IN RELATIONSHIPS

Kali Carbonicum's three main issues in life are: fear of aloneness, irritability, and a tendency to be outrageously unkind to the people in her life, and these issues can affect Kali's relationships in many different ways.

When interviewing Kalis about their childhood experiences, I am struck by how many fond memories they often have. One Kali Carbonica woman told me that she felt closest to her mom, who encouraged everyone to truly be themselves. Her father was rather strict and stern and wasn't around very much, but they were still very close to each other as a family. She described how they were always doing things together, like playing together and going on outings, picnics and family re-unions. She told me that once you are part of the family, you can't do anything to get out of it. Even if you do something the family disapproves of, they may pretend it never happened, but they would never even consider disowning anyone. She also explained how, when she became a teenager and needed more space to do her own things, the connection to her family was almost too much because there was always something they were supposed to be doing together.

When she was a child, she used to play with her brother and sister, and the neighbor's children. One of the hardest thing she experienced as a child was when she went inside to get a drink, or to use the bathroom, and the other children were gone when she came back out. If they had run away, or if they were hiding from her somewhere, she felt totally left out, sad and forsaken. She felt that you should always be able to depend on your family and friends, and that nobody should ever have to be left out of the group.

I have seen the same tendency in other Kali clients as well. One Kali woman was a sports enthusiast, and most of her friends were team mates. Her father had taught her how to be good in sports, and that became the way she chose to relate to people and make friends. Another Kali joined a local religious group and spent much of her spare time pursuing her religious interests with likeminded people. Kali feels anxious and vulnerable when she has to be alone, and she is much happier if she can be part of a group of some kind.

A Kali is probably one of the best team mates you can find, whether it is in sports or in business. They love company, and they like making decisions together with others. In addition to being good team players, Kalis are reliable and responsible by nature. If Kali says she is going to do something, you can count on it. One Kali woman told me that she considers herself "over-responsible." She always tries to keep her word, even if she sometimes wishes that she hadn't committed herself in the first place. Another Kali woman was working in a government building. She was so conscientious that she would go to work an hour early every day, just to organize her desk and make sure she was properly prepared for the work she was expected to do that day. That kind of conscientiousness and dedication is very rare, so she is probably much appreciated by the company she works for.

Kalis are often so reliable that people find it easy to trust them. They usually stick to the rules and do what is expected, and they have a good eye for detail. They work systematically and often do well in areas of science and research.

Kali's whole life revolves around relationships, family relationships, work relationships or groups of friends doing things together. Kali may have a hard time dealing with casual contacts. They often don't feel socially at ease unless they know they have common areas of interest, so they do better when joining some kind of group first, and then getting to know the people in the group. Light and superficial "chit-chat" usually doesn't appeal to Kali at all.

There are certain issues that often show up more in Kali's personal relationships than in business relationships. In personal relationships Kali is, first of all, looking for friendship, and secondly, intellectual connection. Kali loves stimulating conversation, and because she is primarily a mental type, the mental connection is very important to her. She often looks at everything from a very rational point of view, and she can easily develop fixed ideas of how things should be. Kali Carbonicum is a metal remedy, and metal remedies are often stubborn when it comes to what they like or don't like. Kali likes being in control; and things need to make sense to her in a very logical way. If someone acts irrationally in any way, Kali will step in and give advice or criticism, regardless of whether someone has asked her for advice, or not. She has good intentions and means well when she expresses her opinions. She only expresses what makes sense to her, and she is convinced that her advice is in the other person's best interest. If, however, the other person doesn't take her advice, she often feels offended and irritable. This can lead to discontent and general irritability and quarrelsomeness. We can often see this kind of irritability and desire to scold or criticize, especially towards her mate or children, if they don't listen to her advice. In this situation, Kali may not treat any of them very nicely, hence the rubric "Company, desire for, treats them outrageously, yet".

Kali's stubbornness can also make her less spontaneous than other types, and this can also become an issue in her relationships. She likes to stick with a daily routine, and she likes planning things ahead of time in a logical manner. She is not too happy when someone spontaneously wants her to change her plans. A Kali would probably never go on a vacation without having a proper travel itinerary. She would like to know, ahead of time, where she is going to stay, what she is going to see, and how long she is going to be in each place. She simply doesn't like surprises because surprises aren't always pleasant, and she always feels better when she is more in control.

However, the lack of spontaneity is often well balanced with what Kali has to offer in a relationship. She is loyal, dedicated to her family, responsible, trustworthy and consistent in her views. She has a great ability to create a safe, secure environment for herself, her mate and her children. She shares her sense of integrity and values with the people in her life, and in return she needs other people's support so she can also feel secure. Kali feels the happiest in relationships where everyone involved value mutual dependence and togetherness, and everybody supports everybody else. In this kind of relationship, she will always feel a great sense of belonging that quickly puts her mind at ease.

I NEED TO ACHIEVE MY GOALS
Lycopodium Clavatum

REMEDY DESCRIPTIONS

Lycopodium Clavatum is a mild mannered, reserved and timid type who is both serious and quiet by nature. Interestingly, there are two opposite tendencies in Lycopodium; either he is yielding and submissive, or he is dictatorial and controlling. This is an unusual combination of traits in the same type of person, and the reason is probably this; he loves being in a position of power, but because he isn't very brave, he will be submissive if someone else challenges his position, even though he much prefers to be in charge.

Lycopodium is not a "heavy" remedy emotionally. He is often optimistic and cheerful, and he may have a somewhat refined sense of humor. He laughs easily and can be both affectionate and passionate in his relationships. He often becomes excited about little things, and his sexual desire can be quite high.

Lycopodium is a very sensitive being. He is sensitive to sensual impressions and can be profoundly affected by horrible things and sad stories. He startles easily from fright, or a slight noise, and he may become so "touchy" that he can even develop an aversion to touch. He is sympathetic and compassionate, and also has a tendency towards being sentimental.

In all the mild mannered remedies we often see confusion about identity, or a weak sense of self. In Lycopodium there can also be a sense of duality, or a sense of being double, or even a sense of being in two different places at the same time. In addition to a weak sense of self and a general lack of confidence, there is also vivid imagination. Sometimes his imagination creates frightening images, and at other times it can cause sleeplessness. There is often anxiety and worry on his face, and because he tends to make frowns on his forehead, he often looks older than he is. Even Lycopodium babies sometimes look like ancient little beings.

To understand the situation that goes with Lycopodium, we first have to study the delusions associated with the remedy profile. The Lycopodium delusions show that he may have horrible visions. He may hear voices, or have a sense that someone else is there. Someone may be in another room, or somewhere else in the house. He feels anxious because the house is full of people that he doesn't know. He can see them. They have horrible, hideous faces. He thinks that, perhaps, he has neglected his duty and is now being pursued by enemies for having failed. He feels doomed and unfortunate, and he knows they are going to hurt him. Maybe he will even die from the injuries, or maybe someone actually intends to murder him.

If Lycopodium was pursued or attacked by enemies in the original story, it is no wonder that he has now developed a fear of people. He may feel apprehension or dread when approached by strangers, he may feel fearful when meeting new people, or he may intensely dislike being in a crowd. From the delusions above we also see that Lycopodium's enemies were already inside his house, so naturally, Lycopodium has a tendency to feel anxious if the doorbell rings, or if he has to open the door, especially if he doesn't know who is there. Who knows? An enemy could be standing outside, ready to enter his house as soon as he opens the door! His imagination plays tricks on him and he dreads being alone. He doesn't feel safe, especially in the dark, and it really helps if someone else is there to keep him company, even though he may not want to speak to them. He may also develop claustrophobia in narrow places, or fear of suffocation at night, and he could even develop fear of ghosts.

Because something bad happened to Lycopodium in the original story, he often has a feeling that something bad could easily happen to him again. This leads to anticipation anxiety and worry about the future. There are ailments and complaints from anticipation, especially before an engagement, and there is fear of undertaking anything new, fear of failure, and also fear of being unable to reach his destination.

This is an interesting combination of symptoms. On one hand, there is fear of failure, and fear of undertaking new things, and on the other hand, there is fear of being unable to reach his destination. But how can he reach his destination if he avoids undertaking new things? There is only one way; he has to find enough courage to overcome his fear of failure and punishment! So, this has become the core issue associated with Lycopodium: He feels small, weak and defenseless, but he wants to be big and strong. He feels like "nobody" and he wants to become "somebody important." He may be nowhere right now, but he is working hard to reach his destination, even though he has to overcome his fear of new undertakings to do so. Lycopodium has even come to believe that he will only be loved if he performs well, or if he reaches his goal. And if he fails, he will, according to his delusions, be pursued by enemies and punished severely. So he has to keep moving towards his goals, even though his confidence is low and his anxiety level high. However, his fear of not amounting to anything in life makes him ambitious enough to keep going anyway. Feeling both anxious and cautious, he carefully proceeds in a conscientious and methodical way, and eventually he is most likely to end up very successful. These qualities are perfect for doing any kind of scientific work, so we can expect to find many Lycopodiums among scientists and intellectuals.

Lycopodium is also timid about talking in public, but if he actually gets up and talks, he is perfectly capable. It is his confidence that is lacking, not his ability. His low confidence makes him feel somewhat helpless. His will is not strong, and he may yield to other people's wishes and end up doing things against his intentions, very similar to Sepia.

One Lycopodium teacher didn't know how to say no to his boss, so when he was asked to take on more work than he could handle, he kept working overtime, constantly trying to catch up, rather than telling his superior that the workload was too much for him. Perhaps he was afraid of losing the position he had achieved through a lifetime of hard work, so he chose not to say anything. Instead, he was willing to keep working, harder than he wanted to, just to keep his position secure. (Every achievement has a price, I suppose...) This clearly shows the issue I mentioned earlier, about Lycopodium being either dictatorial or submissive. At work, he is usually dictatorial towards subordinates and submissive towards people of higher rank than himself, but at home he definitely prefers to be in a dictatorial position.

Lycopodium often develops anxiety about his health, and can sometimes become a bit of a hypochondriac. He may feel anxiety arising from his heart or his stomach, and he often feels better when he is around people who support his confidence. He may develop fear of possible disease, or even a delusion that he is already sick. His anxiety is often worse between 4 and 8 pm, and open air usually makes him feel better.

There are many different types of Lycopodium. Some stay weak and fearful throughout their lives, and others find ways to cover up or compensate for their inner weakness, either intellectually or physically. Some Lycopodiums feel a constant need to prove to themselves, and the rest of the world, that they are immensely competent and indispensable. They don't like being questioned or told what to do, and they may become defiant if anyone tries to control them.

There is often a certain amount of selfishness or egotism in Lycopodium, and he may seem overly confident to the rest of the world. This is how he covers up his inner sense of inner weakness, and it may be hard for others to imagine that his display of great confidence is not quite as solid as it seems. Once Lycopodium discovers "the love of power," he tends to demand it any way he can. He may stubbornly stick to his views and expect others to obey. His answers may become dictatorial with little room for differing views, and he loves to be in a position of authority, preferably all the time if possible.

I NEED TO ACHIEVE MY GOALS Lycopodium Clavatum

The most important thing for a Lycopodium is to reach whatever goal or destination he has set for himself. Reaching his goal is basically what gives his life purpose. Therefore, if he experiences any kind of obstacles and becomes worried about the possibility of reaching his destination, he will naturally tend to become envious of anyone who is ahead of him. He might envy their qualities or competence level, or he may feel greedy about the amount of money they are making. It is easy for Lycopodium to feel ungrateful or unfortunate about his own situation and he may try to achieve his goals faster by gambling, or even stealing.

Obviously, Lycopodium is very ambitious and will employ every possible means to achieve his goals. He may be industrious and put in long hours at work, regardless of how his family feels about it, and he often feels impatient and has a sense that time passes too slowly. Being engaged in an occupation, or some other diversion, usually makes him feel good since he enjoys being productive and making money. He tends to undertake many things but doesn't always complete what he starts, often from a lack of discipline. He may wish he were rich, and he has a tendency to show off or boast about all his new possessions or accomplishments. A shiny, new car or a brand new house is always a good way to boost the image he wants to present to the world. He tends to flatter others, and he loves it when others flatter him in return. If Lycopodium somehow manages to accomplish his goals, it becomes important for him to secure his position, and in the process of doing so, he may become deceitful, sly, corrupt, secretive or suspicious as a result. He may even want to slander others to make himself look better. We often see this when politicians "battle" each other in public by doing whatever they can to degrade their opponent. Lycopodium's message to the world is: "I'm bigger than you, I'm better than you, I'm smarter than you, and I should be in charge!"

Most Lycopodiums have very strong minds. They are mentally active with abundant ideas and clear thinking. They often talk quickly and can easily change from one subject to another. Sometimes Lycopodiums can be unbearably longwinded since they normally love to hear themselves talk. (That is, of course, why a lot of teachers are Lycopodiums). They have strong intellectual capacity and can easily understand things, even when it comes to abstract ideas. Therefore, we often find that intellectuals and scholars are likely to be Lycopodiums, and it comes as no surprise that many Lycopodiums have huge libraries and love reading books. Even Lycopodium children often spend long hours reading, rather than playing with other kids. The most intellectual Lycopodiums often end up writing books on scientific subjects, but you can also come across more poetic types at times. Both types express themselves quite easily with words, although they tend to get exhausted from too much mental effort.

Lycopodium has such a fear of failure that if it actually happens to him, it affects him very deeply, especially literary or scientific failure. Any kind of failure will most certainly affect his self confidence, and he may become both depressed and discouraged as a result. He also has a tendency to develop digestive problems when the stress becomes too much. Intestinal fermentation, rumbling and flatus in the lower part of the abdomen are common problems for Lycopodiums.

Lycopodium is also affected by things like disappointment, grief, humiliation, deception and scorn. Because his level of confidence is not very high, even though he does whatever he can to hide his insecurity, he will often react to these issues with anxiety, worry, irritability or anger, since anger with indignation, suppressed anger, and anger with silent grief are all part of the Lycopodium picture.

Lycopodium is known for his tendency to be irritable, especially when sick or before menses. Little things aggravate, so even the smallest noise, like the crackling of a newspaper, can trigger his irritability or anger. (This is similar to Arsenicum's over-sensitivity to noise). He also tends to feel angry or irritable when he wakes up in the morning, especially if he didn't sleep well the night before. In addition, there is also a tendency for his symptoms to become aggravated in the afternoon, or evening, especially between 4 and 8 pm.

Lycopodium is extremely sensitive to criticism. Therefore he feels offended easily and often takes things the wrong way. Sometimes he holds on to past offenses too long. He may feel angry while thinking about the people who have offended him, or he becomes angry if he meets any kind of opposition. He either blames himself, or he blames others. It is common for Lycopodium to be hard on inferiors and kind to superiors, and he has a tendency to become quarrelsome and difficult to be around at times.

Lycopodium's moods are generally very changeable. He can be both ill-humored and sulky when he isn't happy about something, so the word "cranky" seems to fit him very well. When Lycopodium is angry, he can sometimes be abusive or insulting to the people in his life. It is not unusual for Lycopodium to feel both furious and hateful. When that happens, he can also become malicious, spiteful and vindictive. He may start shrieking, screaming, shouting, cursing and swearing. He often trembles when he is angry, and his anger can even be violent, especially in the morning. He may feel like striking someone, or he may even feel a desire to kill at times.

When Lycopodium's isn't feeling well emotionally, consolation or sympathy isn't likely to make him feel any better, either. He usually prefers to be alone when he doesn't feel good and doesn't want anyone to speak to him. He just wants to be quiet, and sometimes he can't even bear to be looked at. His speech can also be affected with a tendency to wander from subject to subject, or even muttering quietly to himself. When Lycopodium is unhappy, he can easily feel discontented, dissatisfied or discouraged, too. He may completely lose his motivation and prefers to just sit around, doing nothing. He can even develop an aversion to work or to business, and he often feels better if someone holds him.

Lycopodium doesn't handle disappointments well. When he feels disappointed, he may become so upset that he is quite beside himself, brooding, complaining and dwelling on past disagreeable occurrences or memories. Sometimes he blames himself and thinks he may have done something wrong, or if the disappointment has anything to do with relationships, he may suffer from jealousy. Eventually, he can become very depressed and melancholic. It is common for Lycopodium to complain about his grief and sadness, and he may feel both unfortunate and worried about the future. He also has a tendency to sigh deeply when he is feeling low spirited, and he can easily become weepy, especially between 4 and 8 pm. He may weep aloud about past misfortunes, or about the insecurity he feels about the future, or he may weep when someone thanks him. Sometimes his weeping alternates with laughter, but even when he is in a weepy mood, consolation usually annoys him.

If he feels inconsolable, he simply doesn't want to be cheered up by anyone. He tends to go into a state of indifference about everything, including his children and family. He may feel forsaken and unloved by his parents, wife or friends because he is such a mental type that he often has a hard time connecting with anyone emotionally. When the stress becomes too much for him, he may be tempted to escape from his family and children just to get away from the stress he is feeling. This is because Lycopodium takes everything very seriously, and sometimes the responsibility of having a family and children becomes too much for him. If we remember Lycopodium's fear of failure, and the fear of not reaching his destination, we can easily see how family obligations, in addition to his natural fears, can make it tempting to run away from it all. If his family puts too many demands on him, he will most likely develop an aversion to his whole family and start longing for solitude, or he may even consider the possibility of divorce just to get his freedom back.

Under too much stress or mental exhaustion, Lycopodium sometimes experiences brain-fag, where his thoughts tend to vanish and concentration is difficult. He may find it hard to concentrate while studying or reading, or he may have difficulties expressing his ideas through writing. He misplaces words, uses the wrong words, or spells the words wrongly by omitting letters or syllables. If this is happening, Lycopodium can also develop an aversion to any kind of mental work, including reading, writing and math. Again, we see in Lycopodium the desire to escape from whatever is uncomfortable, difficult or too much of a challenge. When feeling challenged or stressed, homeopathic Lycopodium in a medium to high potency can be very helpful, and it can also be helpful for children with learning disabilities.

In addition to brain-fag and difficulties with concentration, Lycopodium also experiences confusion at times. He may be confused, mostly in the morning or in the evening, especially from 4 to 8 pm. His confusion can be about daily affairs, or he can be confused from mental exertion or too much reading. All his mental symptoms are usually better when opening the windows, or walking in open air.

It is also common for Lycopodium to be forgetful. He may have a hard time remembering words or names, or he may forget what he just did. He may have difficulties expressing himself, or he may have a tendency to forget what he just read, as well as facts from the past. (The absentminded professor...) The fact is, that not all Lycopodiums are intellectually sharp or brilliant, although most of them are. Occasionally, you may see a certain degree of dullness in Lycopodium, which causes difficult thinking or comprehension. This dullness is often seen in children or in old people, where it tends to manifest as a tendency for idiocy or senility with deficiency of ideas. In extreme cases, Lycopodium can even enter a coma if the room is too crowded or stuffy. And as usual, open air, always makes him feel better.

Lycopodium may also at times suffer from restlessness, especially between 4 and 8 pm. The restlessness is often combined with anxiety, which can make it difficult for him to go to sleep. He may do a lot of tossing and turning after going to bed, and sometimes the restlessness may even drive him out of bed. This is usually caused by an overactive mind that makes it hard for him to relax. Sometimes he can't even sleep at all because of tormenting thoughts, and at other times he may simply feel too anxious or worried to sleep. He may startle easily from any little sound, and if his worry or anxiety becomes too intense, he may even develop an aversion to the bed itself. However, if he does eventually fall asleep, his sleep isn't necessarily restful. He may talk in his sleep, or scream, shout, laugh, bark or growl. Sometimes he walks in his sleep and he may even climb a roof, or the railing of a bridge or balcony while still asleep! He may wake up fearful from a scary dream, and because his sleep is seldom peaceful or refreshing, he is usually irritable or grumpy when he wakes up in the morning.

Lycopodium usually copes with his excessive anxiety and worry by rationalizing solutions in his mind. If he becomes too anxious about the welfare of his soul, he may turn to religion for comfort, or he may adopt a totally atheistic point of view instead, since religiousness just as often defies his sense of logic. It all depends on how convinced he is, intellectually, one way or the other. Whatever makes the most sense to him is what he will choose.

It is, however, important to understand that whenever someone's perceptions are based solely on belief, intellect or simple rationalization, there is always going to be an element of underlying doubt behind the façade; no matter how confident the person seems to be on the surface. Lycopodium makes up for this doubt by either performing his religious practices without fail, or by arguing his atheistic views in a very self righteous way. The problem is that intellectualizing or theorizing can never really dissolve any underlying doubt. Doubt can only disappear if your perceptions are based on personal experience. But because Lycopodium usually prefers to explore everything through his mind, rather than through first hand experience, he will always have to struggle to cover up or ignore his feelings of underlying doubt. Unfortunately, the doubt will remain, regardless of how convincing his arguments are, and of course, he would never admit to anyone that the doubt he is feeling even exists!

If Lycopodium doesn't find any comfort in his choice of religion, he may turn to alcohol instead. Dipsomania, alcoholism and delirium tremens are also part of the Lycopodium remedy profile. The next story is a good example of what can happen when Lycopodium comes to a point in his life where he realizes that he can't possibly reach his goal. This story is about a Lycopodium man who worked his whole life as a clerk in a store. He was secretly hoping that if he did his best, he would eventually be asked to take over the owner's position in the company when the owner decided to retire. I suspect that Lycopodium never expressed his secret desire to the owner of the company because, when the time came for the owner to retire, he gave his position to one of his relatives instead, even though this relative had never even worked in the company previously. When Lycopodium found out what had happened, he relieved his feelings of grief, disappointment and failure by turning to alcohol. His core fear, of not being able to reach his destination, had been triggered. He felt like a failure and could see no other solutions to his problems than to drown them in alcohol.

If Lycopodium feels that his life has been nothing but a failure, he may eventually become so weary of life that he becomes suicidal, seriously wishing he were dead since his life no longer seems to have any purpose or meaning. He may have thoughts of death, or presentiment of death, but since he is not very brave, it is doubtful that he will have the courage to actually kill himself. It is more likely that his weariness and desire for death will just turn into a state of deep depression, which homeopathic Lycopodium can help lift.

LYCOPODIUM CLAVATUM IN RELATIONSHIPS

One of the most obvious things about Lycopodium is his intellectual strength. He often loves reading for hours at a time, and he tends to theorize and intellectualize about everything. It is common to find that young children, and even teenagers, often have more interest in books or computers, than in playing with other children, or even pursuing girls. One Lycopodium teenager spent so much time reading in his room, that his mom was absolutely certain he would never find a girlfriend or get married. He was very intellectual and felt rather shy around girls, but eventually he did find a girl that he liked, who, luckily, liked him, too. She was also rather shy, and they decided to get married shortly after they met. His mom silently breathed a sigh of relief, secretly anticipating the grand children she was hoping for.

In both personal and work relationships, Lycopodium likes to put himself in a leader position. Whether his confidence is high or low, he has a tendency to constantly want to prove himself to everyone. He wants to establish quickly how capable he is, or how intelligent he is. If someone threatens his authority, he will argue logically, or if that doesn't work, he will try to belittle the other arrogantly. He usually comes across as someone who is extremely self-confident, and because he is so seemingly confident, others listen to his expertise and tend to take his word for it.

At a drumming workshop I went to recently, I saw a good example of how Lycopodium always has to prove himself. The teacher was showing us some very unusual and complicated rhythms, and the Lycopodium man kept making mistakes. He tried to intellectualize about what kind of rhythms they were, but still kept making mistakes, almost constantly. All of a sudden he got up and started banging some different drums in a rhythm that he had learned somewhere else. He kept banging away and asking the teacher if he had ever heard that kind of rhythm before. Then he turned around to the others and started telling them how difficult it was to do what he was doing. When the teacher didn't really respond, he started doing it even faster (more impressive!), and held up the whole class while showing off what he could do (to cover up what he couldn't do). And for a short time, he actually took over the teacher's position, demanding everyone's attention!

I believe that this kind of behavior is a totally unconscious part of the remedy picture, and that Lycopodium isn't even slightly aware of what he is doing. I saw a similar example when I invited a Lycopodium friend for dinner one day. There were two chairs evenly spaced along the longest side of the table, and Lycopodium was supposed to sit on one of those chairs, next to another guest. He unconsciously moved his chair to the middle of the table so the other person had to sit almost on the corner. This way Lycopodium was sure to have everyone's attention and didn't have a clue that he had actually pushed the other person out of the way (and out of the conversation). In both these examples we can see in Lycopodium the fear of being small and insignificant, the desire to be considered important, and an almost instinctive knowledge of how to do so.

In personal relationships, Lycopodium can sometimes have difficulties with commitments. He is shy, timid and somewhat awkward in his relationships with women since women in general make no sense to him. This, combined with fear of undertaking new things, could easily hold him back from commitments. If, however, he does decide to commit, his commitment is usually quite solid, since he doesn't want the relationship to fail (fear of failure). So if he does decide to have a family, he is quite willing to do whatever it takes to make that possible (to make sure he will reach his goals). He is often ambitious and will work hard and long to provide for his family and achieve his dreams, but he may not always be sensitive to the needs of others while doing so. It is almost as if he expects his efforts to provide, to make up for his lack of emotional availability in the relationship. This, of course, comes back to his core belief, that he will be loved if only he achieves his goal, so all he has to do in relationships is to keep achieving. Nobody ever said anything about having to be emotionally available, too...

Lycopodium likes to be in a position of authority, both at home and at work, and he has a tendency to become quite dictatorial in his views. He likes having people in his life who don't question his authority. You often see Lycopodium fathers ruling the family with a dictatorial hand. Although he means well and is usually ambitious about his children's future, (making sure they will also reach their destinations), he isn't too happy if he has to face any contradictions from anyone. This is why he usually doesn't ask anyone else what they wish to do. This is because he wants to avoid arguments, and he already thinks he knows what is best for everyone, anyway. And, since he hates having his authority questioned, he usually picks a mate who is willing to let *him* be the person who knows all the answers. He needs a wife who won't be too demanding in the relationship, and who won't question his position of authority in the family. It would be best if she looks up to him, encourages him and takes care of his home and children without becoming too much of a nuisance in his life (Nat Mur and Pulsatilla are often good choices). Together they can make a good husband and wife team, although she won't always get her needs met since Lycopodium prefers to be clueless as to what her needs really are.

A friend of mine, who was married to a Lycopodium man, told me how he would often make family decisions without asking what anyone else wanted. This is very similar to what a Nux, or an Arsenicum, would do, although there is a slight difference. Nux doesn't even think of asking what others want because he doesn't need anyone else's input to make the right decision. Arsenicum will ask what his mate thinks, but if the answer isn't what he wants to hear, he will destroy her arguments and convince her that he is right. So, although he asks for advice, he isn't really interested in anyone else's opinion. He only asks so he can prove himself right. Lycopodium, however, makes decisions without consulting with anyone else for a very different reason. He doesn't want t*o know* what anyone else thinks, simply because he doesn't want anyone to question his authority, and he doesn't want to have to explain anything to anyone. If someone asks him why he wants them to do something, he is often tempted to answer "Because I said so," self righteously thinking that this is a good enough explanation.

Nux acts in a similar way, but for a totally different reason. He doesn't care if anyone questions his authority because authority is in his nature, and being questioned is more of a hassle than a threat to his self-confidence. Arsenicum likes to be questioned because arguing, and convincing someone that he is right, is such an enjoyable challenge to him. Lycopodium, however, doesn't have the same level of confidence that Nux or Arsenicum have, so he prefers not to be questioned at all. That way, his lack of confidence or knowledge won't be exposed, or even questioned. He tries to establish his position of leadership by surrounding himself with an "air of authority" that very few have the courage to question. Because his "air of authority" often has an intimidating effect on most people, he normally doesn't have to explain himself, or justify his point of view to anyone, which is exactly how he wants things to be.

This is why Lycopodium often ends up in a position of leadership at school, at work and also in his family relationships. He requires everyone in his life to honor his position of authority and to obey his decisions without argument. This often works until his children become teenagers, but when they start rebelling against their father's authority, you can expect big problems, power struggles and rage. Since Lycopodium hates being opposed, and teenagers hate being controlled, conflict is unavoidable. And if his wife also gets corrupted by some kind of local self-empowerment group for women, he might even be heading for a divorce, since he is not likely to change his authoritarian ways and become more open to accepting other people's point of view, when his own view makes so much more sense to him!

At work Lycopodium is often both capable and ambitious. He is cautious, methodical and often well suited to intellectual or scientific endeavors. Many Lycopodiums become teachers because they love having an attentive audience, and also because they enjoy being in a position of natural authority that nobody can question.

Becoming a car salesman or a computer salesman are other popular lines of work for Lycopodium. He comes across with an amount of authority and self confidence that can be very convincing to someone who knows less about cars or computers than he does. The "pushy car salesman" is often a Lycopodium, doing his very best to prove to you what a great car he is trying to sell you. His approach is very different from how a Nux salesman would sell cars (see example in the Nux profile). Nux isn't trying to convince anyone by being pushy. He will simply try to help you find the car that is best suited for you, your situation and your wallet, and because he isn't trying to prove anything to anyone, his approach is not as pushy as Lycopodium's.

I NEED TO ACHIEVE MY GOALS Lycopodium Clavatum

By comparing Lycopodium to Nux, we can see how Nux already *is* where Lycopodium is striving to be. We can imagine two brothers, Nux - first born, clever, confident, natural leader, and Lycopodium - second born, less confident, but just as clever, with a strong desire to be exactly like his older brother. This makes Lycopodium both ambitious and competitive in an effort to overcome his general lack of confidence and achieve his goals. He wants to prove that he is at least as good as his brother, or preferably even better than him! This example describes Lycopodium's situation. He has to overcome his fears and strive to get where he wants to be. It also shows why Lycopodium's main fear in life is that of not amounting to anything, or of not reaching his goals. He just can't bear living a life of failure...

If Lycopodium should ever want to break free of all these old patterns, he would simply have to let go, practice self acceptance and learn to be happy no matter what his position or achievements in life are. It is such a simple solution, but very hard for a Lycopodium to do. The key is to understand that all of these issues are simply old patterns we came in with to resolve in this lifetime, and that none of it really matters as much as we think it does...

EXPLORING EVERYTHING TO THE MAX
Medorrhinum

REMEDY DESCRIPTION

Medorrhinum is an interesting and complex personality type. There is often a tendency in Medorrhinum for being extreme on every level; from the level of emotional intensity to the fact that there are usually very opposite qualities present in the same person. Medorrhinum can be rude, harsh, cruel and selfish one moment, and sweet, compassionate, affectionate and full of care and sympathy the next. One moment he is concerned about trifles; the next moment he doesn't care. He doesn't try to suppress his negative side, like Anacardium tends to do. He can easily switch from one state of mind to another, and back again, depending on what is happening in his life each moment.

Medorrhinum is a passionate, impulsive spirit who is always ready for new adventures. Fortunately for him, he tends to recover remarkably well from all the troubles he gets himself into, and he doesn't dwell much on issues that he leaves behind.

Medorrhinum doesn't have a very strong sense of self. He isn't sure of his identity, and he sometimes feels confused and can't tell what is real. Strange things may seem familiar, and sometimes he may feel like he is in a dream. He fears that someone is behind him, or that someone is touching his head, and he doesn't always feel emotionally stable. In addition, Medorrhinums often have strong clairvoyant abilities. Having a weak sense of identity with a general lack of boundaries is a common trait for anyone who has psychic ability. This is because psychics receive their information from other dimensions, and this can only happen if their personal boundaries aren't too strongly defined.

Medorrhinum's psychic ability is interesting; it mainly has to do with the ability to accurately predict disagreeable events, like someone's impending death. Now, why would he have the ability to predict someone's impending death? It must have something to do with what originally happened to Medorrhinum, and now it has become part of the core story associated with Medorrhinum's remedy profile. In this story, Medorrhinum is predicting the death of someone he is close to, and he is worried about what the consequences of this person's death is going to be in his own life. He is basically predicting, or anticipating, that something very bad is going to happen, and while he is waiting for it to happen, the waiting and uncertainty becomes almost unbearable. This is why Medorrhinums absolutely hate waiting for anything, because even while waiting for something good, anxiety is still going to be there until the outcome becomes certain.

However, it isn't just someone's impending death that will trigger Medorrhinum's core fears. The same thing also happens if anyone, whom he is close to, comes down with some kind of serious or possibly fatal disease. He immediately suffers from anticipation anxiety about the future, both for the person who is sick, and for himself. This issue is also easily triggered if one of his family members is away from home and doesn't come back at a pre-determined time. The anxiety is always worse if an actual time has been set because if the person doesn't show up on time, Medorrhinum is convinced that something horrible must have happened to him, and he can't relax until the person actually shows up.

The main reason why someone's impending illness or death affects Medorrhinum so much is that he has major issues about responsibility. He is basically an independent type who doesn't like anyone telling him what to do, so he has an aversion to responsibility and tries to avoid it at any cost. Because of this aversion, his greatest challenge in life is to overcome this issue and basically "grow up." Since spiritual growth and maturity always happen as a result of overcoming various fears, challenges and weaknesses, it is likely that Medorrhinum will have to take on a position of responsibility at some point in his life, whether he likes it or not. Therefore, it is very possible that the person, who is seriously sick or dying, is Medorrhinum's parent, caretaker, or boss. Most likely, he is someone in a position of power, or authority, which Medorrhinum is expected to take over after his death. Therefore, Medorrhinum's main lesson in life has to do with finding a healthy balance between freedom and responsibility since you can't really have one without the other.

The possibility of having to become more responsible fills Medorrhinum with anticipation anxiety and dread about how it is going to affect his life. His biggest fear is how the added responsibility will impact his desire for freedom, independence and spontaneity. At the same time, he doesn't want anyone to know how insecure he feels, since he won't admit to anyone that he has a problem with responsibility. He compensates, either by being egotistical, selfish, cruel and harsh, or by pretending to be very confident, in an effort to hide his inner weakness and postpone the need for immediate action.

Medorrhinum can also become jealous of anyone, who is better than he, or who threatens his future position, even though he doesn't really want the position in the first place. Or, perhaps he does want the position, but he may not feel quite ready for the level of commitment which is required. However, that doesn't mean that he wants someone else to be in charge instead. This dilemma creates both confusion and anticipation anxiety in Medorrhinum, and the more he thinks about it, the worse he feels. He bites his fingers nervously, or he keeps washing his hands repeatedly because he feels dirty. Time passes so slowly that the waiting seems to last forever, and he simply can't stand living in this kind of uncertainty.

When Medorrhinum has to wait for anything, especially something bad or uncomfortable, time stops and his mind seems to be doing the same. In this state, he can't remember anything, even his own name. He can't remember certain words while speaking, or what he was going to do, or what he just did. He feels so restless that he has a hard time focusing his attention on anything. Because his mind seems to go blank, he just can't concentrate or think clearly. He may feel so confused that he makes mistakes while speaking, and he often has a hard time even finishing his sentences. When someone asks him a question, he can hardly remember the question, and often has to repeat it again before he can answer.

Because Medorrhinum lacks inner strength and confidence, he may also develop all kinds of fears. He is afraid he is going to be pursued or attacked from behind, and he is afraid of aloneness and misfortune. Because he doesn't know what to do, or what is going to happen, the anticipation anxiety can become so intolerable that he fears going insane. At this point, he may be tempted to turn to religion and prayer out of despair.

If his king, boss, father or other family member does end up dying, it affects Medorrhinum very deeply. He cries, which makes him feel better, and he feels very sad, gloomy, melancholic, and maybe even suicidal. He doesn't have any idea how to cope with the new situation, and he may feel doomed and full of cares and worries. He tends to blame himself and feels guilty for what has happened. If he becomes angry, he may start pulling his own hair, and there is sometimes a wild feeling in his head. He hates being in a state of uncertainty, and the big question is: "Now what?" He won't feel any better until he has been able to find an answer which can relieve his unbearable anxiety about the unknown. (Interestingly, Medorrhinum's mental or emotional symptoms always feel worse in the daytime and improve at night).

Medorrhinum's clairvoyant quality tends to make him both superstitious and suspicious. He doesn't know who he can trust, and he often develops oversensitivity to noise, as well as an aversion to being touched (he feels "touchy"). On the mental/emotional level Medorrhinum's touchiness manifests as oversensitivity to any kind of critique or reproach. Even a mild scolding affects him deeply. He almost falls apart if someone is too harsh towards him, which is quite interesting, considering the fact that he himself often acts pretty harshly towards others. He just can't bear it if he is the one who is being criticized. Here, it is important to remember that Medorrhinum compensates for his inner sense of weakness with outer harshness. If, however, he is the one being reproached, he tends to fall apart because he isn't good at covering up or pretending that things are all right. He doesn't have the kind of self control that we see in Natrum Muriaticum, although he can be just as withdrawn and moody when it suits him.

If Medorrhinum can get over his depression without going insane or committing suicide, he'll eventually try to figure out what he can do for himself, since doing something is better than just sitting there in limbo. He has plenty of ideas, but he doesn't always carry them out well or follow through all the way. He enjoys his ideas so much that he may even prefer to postpone everything and spend his time daydreaming instead, or he will go to the opposite extreme where he becomes so focused and industrious that he can turn into a workaholic.

At work, Medorrhinum is usually conscientious about trifles and does the job well, but he tends to become irritable and impatient about little things, which makes it easy to mistake him for a Nux. He is always in a hurry and wants things to happen RIGHT NOW, since he absolutely hates waiting for anything. He likes working on his own, and he doesn't like interruptions because of his tendency to become distracted. Sometimes he can even be in so much of a hurry that he walks around in circles and accomplishes nothing. Medorrhinums can also be extremely absent minded at times. Because he has no sense of time when he is deeply focused on the task at hand, he may completely forget everything else, like upcoming appointments or even meal times.

However, at work Medorrhinum can be as fastidious, efficient or bossy as any Nux, but he is less reliable than a Nux because he doesn't have the same stamina, persistence or tolerance for boring tasks. He tends to become easily distracted if something more interesting catches his attention, and when this happens, he often doesn't complete the task he is in the middle of. If he loses interest in what he is doing, he could even decide to drop the whole project or simply quit the job because he always feels tempted to go with the new rather than sticking with the old. This makes it a bit of a challenge to hire a Medorrhinum. Although he can be super efficient and reliable one moment, he can be just as independent and unpredictable the next. He very much lives in the moment and doesn't like being tied down in any way. Medorrhinum is probably better off being self employed, since he needs to have enough freedom in his life that it doesn't destroy his independence and spontaneity, and of course, he doesn't want his aversion to responsibility to be challenged!

It is also interesting that Medorrhinum is perfectly capable of being responsible if he really wants to. He just drags his feet and dreads *the idea* of responsibility, either because he doubts himself or because he doesn't like being tied down. He likes to be able to "go with the flow," whenever he wants to, without having to feel tied down. If, however, a situation should arise where someone is required to be in charge, he can easily rise to the challenge and take on the responsibility without too much trouble. His lack of confidence and general aversion to responsibility is the only thing that truly stands in his way...

MEDORRHINUM IN RELATIONSHIPS

Medorrhinums often have fixed ideas about how they want things to be, although they can also be flexible when needed. They like to know where everything is, and they may like their laundry folded in a certain way, or the dishes done just right. They like their little rituals and can be quite obsessive about how things have to be. One Medorrhinum girl refused to take a bath if she could see one hair floating in the bathtub, and when she went to the local park, she was cleaning up all the cigarette butts and bottle caps instead of enjoying the swings and slides. The same little girl didn't mind spreading her things all over the house and making horrible messes. She was stubbornly picky about certain things and totally flexible and easy going in other areas.

Medorrhinums are so impulsive by nature that they spontaneously change their minds anytime it suits them (Forget about asking a Medorrhinum to make you a promise!) If you invite a Medorrhinum to go to the movies or to a party, he will simply pick up his jacket and car keys and be out the door in a matter of minutes. Being fastidious and conscientious about trifles one moment and spontaneous and impulsive the next moment is an unusual combination of traits that is rarely found in other remedy types. This makes Medorrhinums unpredictable, which can be a bit of a challenge both in relationships and in a work situation.

Medorrhinums are often very outspoken and direct in their relationships. They don't avoid confrontations, even though they don't like being criticized or reproached by others, and they often speak up clearly when they have a problem or an opinion about something regardless of the consequences. This can be both embarrassing and annoying for Medorrhinum's mate or friends. You can see this quality even in very young Medorrhinum children. The strangest things can come out of their mouths, things that you didn't expect from someone of such a young age.

A 3 year old Medorrhinum girl walked off at a local music festival with a woman she knows who is a friend of the family. They walked around looking at things, and the woman she was walking with said to her, "We are two gorgeous goddesses, you and I!" The little girl thought about this statement for a few seconds, and then said, "No, we are two sexy bitches!" Nobody knew she had picked up this sentence from an Austin Power's movie that her big brother was watching, but she remembered it and saved it for the perfect situation.

Another Medorrhinum girl was invited to a dinner party with her parents. The hostess had invited too many people to the party, and she was very stressed about the whole thing. Five or six children were also there, and the woman had only bought one big bottle of soda pop. She poured it into the glasses, and handed it to each of the children, one at a time. By the time she poured the last glass, the bottle was empty and the glass was only half full when she handed it to the Medorrhinum girl. The little girl looked at the half full glass and told the woman in a loud scolding voice: "You should have bought more soda pop! If you invite this many children, you should have bought two bottles! Look, I didn't even get a full glass!" The little girl didn't mean to be horrible; she just wanted to make sure the hostess wouldn't make the same mistake next time she decided to have a party. Because the little girl didn't have any sense of hierarchy or respect for authority or elders, she couldn't see anything wrong with a small girl telling a grown woman what to do since the woman had obviously made a mistake which needed to be pointed out. You could hear a pin drop, and the little girl and her family didn't get invited to any more dinner parties for a while.

Medorrhinums often have a sharp mind which they apply in both creative and mischievous ways in their interactions with others. One Medorrhinum boy asked his father for a glass of milk, and because he forgot to ask with a "please," the father turned around and said, "What is the magic word?" The little boy thought for a second and then he uttered with a big smile, "Bibbedy, bobbedy, boo!" It wasn't the answer his father had in mind, but it was definitely a magic word (and a very creative answer), so he had to give him his milk.

Because Medorrhinums generally have no respect for authority, especially when it is based upon position or age rather than skill, the issue of who is in charge often comes up in relationships, both at work and at home. Medorrhinum's don't mind being in a relationship where someone else is in charge, as long as the person in charge is responsible and does his job well, and as long as the person in charge doesn't interfere with Medorrhinum's need for independence. If the person in charge fulfills Medorrhinum's strict requirements or expectations, there is no problem, but if, or when, they don't, Medorrhinum has a tendency to take over the situation. We can easily see how this can create problems in his relationships. At work, Medorrhinum will follow orders from the boss, as long as the orders are reasonable and make sense, but if they are unreasonable in any way, Medorrhinum can be very tempted to make his own decisions, regardless of the consequences, and often ends up getting fired for not doing what he was told to do. You can even see the same tendency in small Medorrhinum children, who tend to carry on with whatever they are doing in spite of the possibility of a time out, or worse.

These are the kinds of contradictions that show what a complex type Medorrhinum is. On one hand, he has aversion to responsibility and doesn't want to be in charge, and on the other hand he could change his mind at any time and simply take over in a dictatorial way. The main reason for this kind of behavior has to do with Medorrhinum's high expectations about how things should be. He may be so particular or picky about all kinds of details that if someone doesn't fulfill his rather high expectations, he may choose to put his aversion to responsibility aside and become dictatorial, pushy and arrogant instead.

In personal relationships, you can often see similar patterns of behavior. If the person in charge doesn't do things the right way, or make the right decisions, Medorrhinum can easily decide to step in and take over. This kind of behavior usually has a disastrous effect on the relationship and often signifies the beginning of the end. Nobody likes to be in charge at first, and then lose his position because somebody thinks they aren't doing things right. Even when Medorrhinum agrees to let another make most of the decisions in the relationship, the other can still feel somewhat threatened by Medorrhinum, sensing, on a subconscious level, that the positions could easily change.

Looking at the original situation that goes with Medorrhinum, this issue makes very much sense. Medorrhinum is still responding to life as if he were someone who is waiting to take over a position of responsibility and dictatorial power, even though he doesn't really want to, and Medorrhinum's mate can sense this underlying possibility very strongly.

In addition to pickiness, bossiness and arrogant behavior, Medorrhinum's need for independence can be another source of conflict in relationships. Medorrhinums are naturally independent beings who like doing "their own thing," regardless of who is in charge. They often make decisions quickly and impulsively, and they don't ask for advice unless they really want it (similar to Nux Vomica). If someone tries to stop Medorrhinum from being independent, he may defend his independence in a harsh, cruel, hardhearted manner, regardless of consequences, because his independence is so important to him. After being harsh, Medorrhinum often hates himself for having been so horrible to the people in his life, but he simply can't stop himself from doing so when somebody tries to tie him down. Sometimes he feels like there are two different people inside him, a sweet and caring self, and a cruel and harsh self. This sense of duality, which comes from being so full of extremes, is unfortunately not listed in the repertories. If the sense of duality is very strong in an individual, it may cause the homeopath, in some cases, to confuse Medorrhinum with Anacardium, which is listed in the repertories under "sense of duality." However, there are still subtle differences between the two. Medorrhinum doesn't suppress his shadow side, like Anacardium would, so there isn't really the same kind of split between good and evil. He allows his "good self" and his "shadow self" to express themselves freely and spontaneously, and this "shadow self" comes out mostly whenever he feels that his freedom or independence is trapped or restricted.

A young Medorrhinum teenager described herself as having two distinct personalities, one sweet and loving and one heartless and cruel, which made me think of Anacardium at first. However, when I inquired more about what triggered her meanness, she told me how she felt about having to take care of her alcoholic mother, who wasn't taking care of herself, after her father left the family. Taking care of her mother, whom she loved more than anything, was interfering with the independence she needed as a teenager. When her mother continuously avoided eating well, and still kept drinking too much alcohol, the Medorrhinum girl became furious and treated her horribly. She felt very badly about the way she treated her mother, because she really loved her very much, but she expected her mother to be responsible enough to get her life in order and stop being such a burden. When she didn't do that, the Medorrhinum girl felt trapped and became very angry towards her. She also harbored resentment towards her father for leaving the family, since she had to take over his position of responsibility and take care of her alcoholic mother, which she wasn't really ready for. This corresponds exactly with the situation that goes with Medorrhinum: somebody, in a position of responsibility or power, is going to die (or leave, like her father did), and Medorrhinum is expected to take over the position even though he doesn't feel ready to do so. This situation caused both physical and mental problems for the young girl, and she did very well on occasional doses of Medorrhinum 1M.

Medorrhinum teenagers are usually extremely rebellious and won't tolerate any restrictions from anyone of their freedom or independence. They often do whatsoever they want, regardless of any consequences, and the parents are actually better off if they can just allow their Medorrhinum teenager total freedom, or Medorrhinum could end up running away from home or simply decide never speak to them again. When those are the options, the parents are better off trying to stay on friendly terms with Medorrhinum, no matter what trouble he gets himself into. That way, there is at least an opportunity for the parents to be able to help when things don't work out.

Another example of Medorrhinum's need for independence is the story of a woman who had two children whom she loved very much. She was a devoted and loving mother as long as she had enough time for herself, but as a mother, that is not an easy thing to ask for. She liked working on her computer 3-4 hours a day, and she wanted her children to leave her alone, and play by themselves or with each other, while she was busy doing her own thing. She wasn't willing to wait (too impatient) until the children were grown before she could take care of her own needs. She felt that it was important for her as a mom to have a little break from her children every day, but her children didn't necessarily agree. She took care of her children's needs as much as possible, even while working on the computer, but if they were interrupting her too much, she would start becoming irritable and aggressive and close the door to her room. If they still didn't honor her need to have space, she would eventually scream at them and feel horrible later. She, too, did well on occasional doses of Medorrhinum 1M or 10M.

A third example was the case of a Medorrhinum woman who lived in a remote rural area with a husband who saw no reason for her to have her own car. She wasn't allowed to drive his car and ended up living in total isolation from her friends. She could call them on the phone, but that isn't the same as seeing someone in person. Or, she could ask her husband to take her somewhere, but as every woman knows, you can't really talk to your girlfriend when your husband is sitting at the same table. This Medorrhinum woman ended up buying herself a car with her mom's help, and against her husband's wishes, and it wasn't long after she got her new car that she packed up her things and left her husband.

If Medorrhinum loses her independence in a relationship, I can guarantee that the relationship won't survive, since Medorrhinum values freedom and independence more than any job or personal relationship. In relationships with Medorrhinum, a partner may or may not appreciate this independent quality. I have noticed that partners often try to control their mate's behavior if their mate is doing something they don't like, but this simply doesn't work if their mate is a Medorrhinum. If the partner doesn't appreciate Medorrhinum's independence and tries to interfere or restrict him in any way, Medorrhinum won't be happy about it and will express himself as harshly as the situation requires. When he reaches the limit of how much restriction he is willing to take, he will eventually get up and leave the job, or the relationship, behind without looking back.

Medorrhinum is an animal remedy, and all animal remedies have an issue of fighting for survival, which explains why Medorrhinums can be quite extreme sometimes. I saw this clearly when observing a small Medorrhinum girl, who easily switched from being her big brother's worst nightmare, bossing him around and acting very mean if she didn't get her way, to being her brother's main protector if somebody else was trying to bully him. One day she saw some bullies in the park pushing her big brother around. She immediately ran over to them and kicked one of them as hard as she could, while screaming, "Don't you dare hurt my brother, or you'll be sorry!" The big bully looked at the little girl, and laughed, saying, "You are so little, you can't hurt me!" The little girl answered fearlessly with a stern expression on her face, and her arms crossed: "Yes I can! I am a fighter, that is what I do!"

In addition to being outspoken, bossy, independent or harsh, there is one more issue that is very characteristic in relationships with Medorrhinums. This issue has to do with waiting. Waiting for something is probably the worst thing that can happen to Medorrhinum. The combination of anticipation anxiety, a sense of foreboding, impatience, restlessness and a feeling that time has stopped, can drive Medorrhinum insane very quickly. Medorrhinum feels the anticipation anxiety in his stomach and will pace around the room. He won't be able to relax, eat, or sleep and will keep looking out the window. It is even worse if a specific time has been set, and something doesn't happen when it is supposed to. He can't help worrying, even though a part of him knows that everything is probably going to be fine. By the time the person finally shows up, Medorrhinum's worry will either turn into great relief or violent anger, depending on the reason why he was kept waiting.

Medorrhinum's tend to live life as if it were a great adventure, and they trust that whatever happens in their relationships, they will be able to roll with the punches and recover from their pains. In spite of Medorrhinum's more questionable qualities, they can be both affectionate and loving, since they tend to let go of old pains and hurts from past relationships fairly easily, and they don't carry too many trust issues around. If their parents, mate, or boss can allow them enough freedom and independence, Medorrhinums can actually be easy going, happy and fun to be around.

A NEW PERSPECTIVE ON ADD
Medorrhinum

These days we often hear in the news that more and more people are diagnosed with a condition called ADD, or attention deficit disorder. This condition describes a state which is characterized by distractibility and difficulty concentrating. It wasn't until I studied the case of one of my ADD clients, a Medorrhinum case, that I first started to understand what ADD really is. There are actually two different manifestations of ADD, one type works like a floodlight, and the other is more like a laser beam. To clarify what I am talking about, imagine a large, dark room with only one light in it. If the light is a floodlight, it will light up the whole room, and you'll be able to see everything in the room. If, however, you look at everything at once, chances are that you'll feel overwhelmed, and you won't be able to pay any attention to the individual details. This is one version of ADD, lack of ability to focus on details because they are too sensitive to everything in their environment. They don't know how to filter out what is not important, and they end up with too much sensory input all at once, which creates confusion and overload. In this case they often become hyperactive in an effort to release some of the input since they don't know any other way to deal with it.

To clarify what the second type of ADD is like, one can imagine the same dark room containing only one light, but this time the light emitted is more like a highly concentrated laser beam. This time, the whole room remains dark, except for a small area the size of a quarter. This small area is very bright, and you can easily see every detail, but you can't see any part of the bigger picture around the lit area since it is still in the dark. If someone with the laser beam type ADD wants to shift his attention to another area, which is what happens when he gets distracted, he will have to move the laser beam to a different place. This puts the other place back into the darkness of the rest of the room, and he forgets all about it. He can only focus on what is right in front of him because that is the only thing that is lit up by the laser beam (his area of attention, or focus). Everything else has disappeared.

In a so called "normal" way of perceiving sensory input, we actually have the ability to narrow or widen the focus of our attention voluntarily depending on what is needed in each situation. The normal way of perceiving input is more like a camera, where you can turn the lens until the object comes into focus. The person with ADD has actually lost their ability to change their focus like the rest of us do. They operate with one fixed way of seeing everything in their lives, and this can become a big problem because the ability to change the focus is necessary for efficiency. We need to be able to adapt the way we look at something to the situation that we are experiencing, and this is something a person with ADD can't easily do. Imagine what would happen if you had to take pictures with a camera with a fixed focus. Once in a while you would probably take a really great picture, where everything was in focus, but most of your pictures would surely be out of focus, no matter how hard you tried. Imagine how frustrating it would be if you were hoping, or expecting, the pictures to be as good as pictures taken by anyone else, and yours always ended up being out of focus in spite of your efforts! You may eventually start suspecting that something is wrong with your camera, without knowing what it could be. It is the same for someone with ADD. They know something is wrong, but have no idea what it is...

The Medorrhinum type ADD is like the laser beam. There is nothing wrong with Medorrhinum's ability to focus, but his focus is so concentrated that everything else in his environment disappears, or ceases to exist. His focus is so total, that he brings all his energy to the present moment. Most people are living in the past, holding on to old stuff, or living in the future, constantly trying to prepare for what is going to happen next, but very few people ever experience living in the present, which is another name for the HERENOW. In the present there is no time, because in the NOW time simply doesn't exist. This explains why Medorrhinum has no sense of time. He has no sense of time because his focus takes him to a place where time doesn't exist. However, when occasionally he is not focused in the HERENOW, if for example he has to wait for something that is going to happen in the future, the waiting is like torture. Because he doesn't have any normal sense of time, he can't tell if 10 minutes has passed, or an hour; and it feels like time is moving too slowly and the waiting goes on forever. This is one reason why Medorrhinums have no patience. They want things NOW, because that is where they are, and in the NOW the future never happens. Therefore, waiting for anything just seems like a huge waste of time, and they can't stand it.

The opposite is also true. Medorrhinum can be so focused on what he is doing, that when he finally looks at the watch, many hours have passed, and he may have missed important appointments that were scheduled previously. In this case he doesn't have any idea where the time went; it just feels like it passed too quickly. The whole time distortion is a result of his tendency to be in the present most of the time, and this, unfortunately, creates nothing but problems when trying to function in "the real world" where everything has to be planned and scheduled ahead of time. This is an interesting problem. What exactly is the value of functioning the way "the real world" expects you to? Besides the fact that you'll fit in, are there any spiritual benefits to "fitting in?" If we look at the teachings of any enlightened being, they all have one thing in common; they teach you to bring your total energy to the present moment! They don't tell you to schedule your day properly, or plan for the future, their whole focus is on living in the NOW. Seen from this point of view, maybe Medorrhinum lives in a way that should actually be honored, rather than criticized? (Just a thought...)

In my Medorrhinum client's case, he told me that tests had been done where it was determined that his blood flow to the frontal lobes were only at 40%. My personal opinion is that this is just a physical manifestation of what is happening on the mental plane, and that the condition, most likely, can be reversed. If you had to concentrate 100% of your attention on one task, you would most likely start feeling very tense after a while. What happens when you are tense? Everything contracts, not just muscles, but also blood vessels. And, when blood vessels contract, it will obviously result in less blood flow to certain parts of the body. Therefore, the blood flow to the frontal lobes can most likely be restored, if he can only learn to focus on things in a more relaxed way.

My Medorrhinum client also expressed to me how frustrated he feels about people's tendency to judge him and think he is lazy, irresponsible and uncaring, when the truth is, he is putting enormous effort into what he is doing. It is easy for people to only pay attention to the fact that he has a hard time working efficiently and getting things done on time, but it is important to understand that this, in no way, reflects the amount of effort he is actually putting into his work. He is probably more focused on what he is doing each moment than any of us can ever understand because his focus is so total that nothing else exists.

You may wonder, then, why it is that someone, who is so intensely focused, and puts so much of his energy into what he is doing, can't accomplish what he sets out to do. Here we have to go back to the example about the laser beam in the dark room. His focus is total, but it can only focus on one thing at a time. If someone calls my client on the phone and asks him to do something else, he'll start working on it right away, while it is still fresh in his memory, and he immediately forgets what he was working on before the phone call. This is why he rarely completes the task he is working on because as soon as he becomes distracted, his attention moves on to the new, and he completely forgets about the old.

My Medorrhinum client's inability to focus on more than one thing at a time has consequences in many parts of his life. It makes it difficult, or even impossible, for him to prioritize things because only through comparison can you determine what is more important than something else. When focusing on only one thing at a time, the ability to prioritize simply is not there. An example of this is when my client put a $500.00 ad in the paper, while forgetting that the rent was due a few days later, and then discovering that there was no money left for the rent. He only thought about how useful it would be to put an ad in for his business, but since the rent wasn't due at the same time, he forgot about the rent.

Many times my client tried to make lists of things to do in an effort to create more order in his physical life, but he didn't have very good luck with the lists, either. Distractions kept happening, and the things on the lists remained undone. While studying his case, I slowly started realizing why even lists weren't helpful. Normally, when people make lists, they put the things that need to be done in the future on the list, and they finish whatever they are doing before they go on to the next thing on the list. Medorrhinum doesn't work like that. Because he lives in the NOW, he goes on to the new things instead, and the list ends up as a list of old things that weren't completed. Going back and finishing things on the list doesn't appeal to him because he prefers to live in the now, and right now, something else is happening. Because new things are always happening, he will constantly find himself more attracted to the new, which distracts him from what he is in the middle of, and the old things on the list will never get done. This is also why it takes him several hours to cook dinner, eat and clean up, because he can't hold his focus on one thing long enough to complete it before something else comes up and he shifts his focus to the new. So, in a sense, his focus and distractibility problem isn't caused by an inability to concentrate (like the term ADD, attention *deficit*, implies), but rather by a tendency to focus too intensely on a very narrow area of attention.

In this client's case, I think the most important thing is to understand exactly what the problem is. The problem is actually his focus, not his lack of focus. There is nothing wrong in focusing totally on what you are doing, but at the same time it is important to learn how to deal with distractions more efficiently because that is where his biggest problem is. The main thing he has to work on is how to resist the temptation to jump into new things. This is hard for someone who is adventurous and impulsive because when you get excited about the new, the old completely loses its appeal. However, it is a matter of knowing your weaknesses and cultivating enough discipline to counteract them.

Discipline is not Medorrhinum's favorite thing, in fact Medorrhinum has an aversion to anything that ties him down or restricts his independence and freedom in any way because he likes to have the freedom to live in the moment so he can always go with the flow. If you look up "aversion to responsibility" in the repertory, Medorrhinum is listed in italics. When working on difficult homeopathic cases, I often use numerology to pinpoint someone's core issues and help me understand the case better. In this case, aversion to responsibility is part of this client's numerological "life challenge." In the numerology it states that your life challenge is the most difficult issue you will have to deal with in your lifetime, and if you are able to overcome this challenge, it can become your biggest strength. However, learning to become responsible will not appeal to any Medorrhinum, even though it is, in fact, the best thing they can learn to do for themselves. Learning to channel super focused energy more efficiently, by finding a way to deal with distractions in a more disciplined manner, is an essential key to increased efficiency and the ability to cope with daily tasks. By learning this kind of self discipline, I am convinced that my client's ability to focus can eventually be transformed from being a problem to becoming a potential asset. In an ADD case, this won't be an easy task, but with increased understanding of the nature of ADD, as well as will and determination to change, there is always a possibility that it can be done.

IF I'M PERFECT, I'LL BE LOVED
Natrum Muriaticum

REMEDY DESCRIPTION

Natrum Muriaticum, in its balanced state, is a timid, reserved, mild mannered type. She has a quiet disposition, tranquil and calm, with a reverence for those around her. By nature, she tends to be somewhat conservative with an appreciation for traditional values. She also has a sentimental side, and can be both sympathetic and affectionate.

The original story that goes with Natrum Muriaticum is the story of Cinderella. She is just a dirty servant girl, dressed in rags, dreaming about the prince who is going to marry her so they can live happily ever after. The prince is probably the most unavailable man she can possibly desire, and it takes a lot of magic to pull it off, but the moral of the story is that *it is possible*, and that *it can also happen to you!* So Natrum keeps dreaming about finding the perfect mate and the perfect relationship, never losing hope of finding everlasting love and happiness. Unfortunately, this is also how she sets herself up for disappointment and grief time and time again. In real life, she doesn't have a fairy god mother with a magic wand to help make her dreams come true. She has to rely on her own efforts to make things happen, so it is much harder for Natrum to make her dreams come true, than it was for Cinderella. The funny thing is that if Natrum happens to find a man who *is available* and who does want to be with her, she just isn't interested, or she quickly loses interest, because she intuitively knows that it will trigger her fear of intimacy too much if someone wants to get too close to her. It is much less risky to just keep dreaming about the perfect, but unavailable mate, who can only be hers in her dreams.

The whole dream of finding the perfect mate or relationship is actually a problem in itself. It is a result of unreasonable expectations combined with fixed ideas that stops her from seeing what is actually available, here and now. So, the key to transformation in Natrum Muriaticum is to let go of all fixed ideas, especially the idea that everything has to be perfect because nothing ever is...

However, feeling like Cinderella does nothing for Natrum's self confidence. First of all, she feels confused because she doesn't really know who she is. In the Natrum delusions we find that she may have a sense of duality or a feeling that her head belongs to another, or she may even feel as if she is in a dream. She doesn't always know what is real, and because her sense of self isn't very strong, she may also have a hard time making decisions. This is why Natrums often choose mates who can make most of the decisions in the relationship (Lycopodium is probably her favorite choice of mate, with Arsenicum a good number two), and when she goes shopping for clothes, she loves to bring a girl-friend who can give her a second opinion and help her decide what to buy.

In addition to having a weak sense of self and difficulties making decisions, Natrum also has another problem - she feels ugly inside. She may have acne, which is a constant reminder of her sense of inner ugliness, or she may be dressing with a lack of style, focusing more on comfort than on fashion. Her gestures can be awkward, and she can easily become so self conscious that she can't even bear being looked at. She hates what she sees when looking in the mirror, and she may try to make herself look more attractive with cosmetic surgery or make up, or a more attractive hair color. She wants to be perfect, and tries hard to cover up her imperfections. One can easily imagine how someone like that can become oversensitive to criticism. She can feel offended, even when no one intends to offend her, and she often can't take a joke. Because she is extremely sensitive to other people's rudeness, she can sometimes become so touchy that she even develops a fear of pins and pointed things.

I recently saw a good example of this in the movie "My Blue Heaven." In this movie, the district attorney is most likely a Natrum Muriaticum. She is very conscientious, trying to follow the law and uphold traditional values the best she can. She is wearing a very conservative looking brown business suit with a skirt that covers her knees, and she paired this unflattering outfit with a pair of solid army shoes, which Steve Martin describes as "tragic." (Before she knew that the shoes were tragic-looking, she probably just thought they were comfortable...) In the movie, she is very sensitive to criticism, her feeling of insecurity and indecision is obvious, and she doesn't understand jokes, even though she thinks she has a sense of humor. If you come across this movie, it is well worth watching. Not only is it a very entertaining movie, but it also gives a very clear picture of the nature of Natrum Muriaticum.

A friend of mine once told me another example of how sensitive Natrum can be. He explained that he was simply trying to give his girl friend a compliment, and he couldn't understand why she would take it the wrong way when he was actually trying to say something nice to her! All he said was: "You look really pretty today" and she immediately started wondering if maybe he thought she looked ugly yesterday, instead of enjoying the compliment that he just gave her. The word "today" got him in trouble, even though he was trying to be nice to her because his compliment somehow triggered her insecurity, self consciousness and feeling of inner ugliness.

Both of the examples above show how emotionally sensitive a Natrum can be. In addition, she can also be physically sensitive, especially to music or noise. Music can make her sad or irritable, and she can easily startle from noise. Sometimes Natrum ends up on sleeping pills because she may feel too tense or anxious to be able to fall asleep on her own. I saw an example of this in one of my earlier Natrum cases. The Natrum woman in this case used to startle so easily when trying to go to sleep, that she simply couldn't relax enough to get any sleep at all. In addition, her muscles were also twitching beyond her control because her level of tension and anxiety was so high. After hardly sleeping for several years, she developed such a strong fear of not sleeping that she became addicted to sleeping pills, simply because she felt she couldn't do without them.

Because Natrum hates feeling vulnerable, she does whatever she can to cover up and compensate for her sensitivity, touchiness and lack of self confidence. She may, therefore, present a totally different image to the world, an image of being proud, extravagant and only wanting the best in everything because she deserves it! This, of course, is simply an effort to boost her own confidence and make herself feel more worthy. Because she has high standards and wants everything to be perfect, she can sometimes develop a boastful or critical attitude or become harsh or contemptuous in her expression. She likes to be in control and may become dictatorial and intolerant of contradiction, or she may impose her high standards on the people in her life, expecting them to be perfect, too. The more vulnerable she feels on the inside, the more she has to compensate on the outside so nobody will ever know...

As you can tell, Natrum tends to feel uncomfortable with anything to do with emotions. She is generally much more comfortable with her mental side because living in her mind makes her feel emotionally safe. She is objective and reasonable, and often tends to rationalize her feelings so she doesn't have to actually *feel* her emotions directly. The better she becomes at rationalizing, the sharper her mind becomes. Therefore, many Natrums can easily become leader types. She is intelligent, reliable and punctual, as well as orderly and responsible, and she isn't afraid to work long hours to get the job done. However, Natrum doesn't have a whole lot of stamina. She tends to get burned out and exhausted if she pushes herself too hard, and when exhaustion sets in, she can become both confused and forgetful. Her mind becomes dull and sluggish and she may find it hard to concentrate. Although her memory is normally very good, when she is exhausted, she can't remember what she is trying to say, or what she just read, or even what just happened. In this state, she may become lazy or develop an aversion to work, and she may want to just sit and do nothing. This can eventually turn into chronic fatigue, so it is no surprise that Natrum Muriaticum is one of the remedies that can work well for this condition. In addition, Natrum can also be a good remedy choice in cases where children are slow learning to talk, or they experience difficulties with concentration, learning, or even coordination.

In spite of Natrum's underlying emotional sensitivity, they often come across as very cheerful types, singing, talking, laughing and dancing joyously. Sometimes she laughs immoderately, or involuntarily, or she will even laugh about serious matters. If Natrum's laughter seems to become too excessive, it is often just a cover up for the deep sadness that she tends to hold inside, so she doesn't have to admit how hurt she really feels. She is an expert at hiding her true feelings behind a somewhat "brittle wall" of exaggerated cheerfulness that can potentially crumble or fall apart at any moment. So, whenever someone has a fake smile pasted on their face all the time, or they are laughing more than what can be considered "normal," it is not unreasonable to suspect that a very sad and hurt Natrum Muriaticum is hiding under the overly cheerful façade she presents to the world.

As an example of this, I can mention a Natrum woman who used to call me when she was a little bit tipsy, cheerfully telling me how wonderful her life was, repeating herself over and over, while saying: "It's so good, it's so good, it's... not really so good..." and then breaking down, sobbing loudly. She was trying very hard to convince herself how happy she was, but couldn't cover up her underlying pain, grief and disappointment, no matter how hard she tried. Therefore, we can see why the concept of "positive thinking" really appeals to Natrum; positive thinking is simply an effort to forget her negative thoughts so she can pretend they don't exist. This is also why many Natrums are very good actors, since they are experts in pretending.

There are two main reasons why Natrum pretends everything in her life is great. One reason is that Natrum is lying to herself. She fears that admitting she is hurt is going to make the pain worse. By denying the pain, she is actually hoping it will go away if she can just forget about it long enough. The other reason she pretends is that she is afraid that she will end up getting her feelings hurt even more, if she confronts anyone, or if anyone confronts her. Therefore it is better to pretend that there really is no problem...

This is how Natrum constantly suppresses her emotions to the point where she eventually may have no idea how much old emotional stuff she is actually carrying around. This, of course, is often manifested physically in the form of obesity since the physical symptoms are always a reflection of a person's mental or emotional state. This is also why the diets she tries only work temporarily because she has to let go of the "inner weight" first, before the body can permanently let go of the outer, physical weight, too.

Natrum is so afraid to get her feelings hurt that she also frequently suffers from anticipation anxiety and ailments from bad news. Because she usually chooses to have relationships with more or less unavailable men, or men who have a problem with commitment or intimacy, she is also very susceptible to any kind of deception, grief and ailments from disappointed love. Naturally, she won't admit to anyone how badly she really feels and often hides her pain by pretending to be cheerful and unaffected by what is happening.

Underneath her superficial cheerfulness, Natrum's feelings can be deep, dark and smoldering. She may hate the person who has offended her, and she may wish or plan for revenge. She feels ungrateful, greedy and envious, and she doesn't mind slandering people or being deceitful or sly to get what she wants since she isn't very brave. In the movie "My best friend's wedding" Julia Roberts plays a Natrum woman who is willing to do whatsoever it takes to ruin her friend's wedding and steal her future husband since she has finally decided that she wants him for herself, after rejecting him for years because she was afraid of intimacy. Now that he is not available, she finds him absolutely irresistible, and she *has to* have him back at any cost, through lies, deceit, slander and unsympathetic behavior, regardless of how his future wife feels about it.

This is because nothing is more attractive to Natrum then someone who is unavailable, either physically or emotionally. This is also why many Natrums are especially attracted to married men, or even to womanizers, because there is very little chance that the relationship will last, and by knowing this from the very beginning of the relationship, they can more easily protect themselves from the hurt that is sure to come. (At least it won't be a surprise when it happens). This is also why many Natrums have a hard time deciding who to marry since they want to make sure ahead of time that they are not going to end up getting their feelings hurt again.

Most Natrums are likely to experience many painful relationships in their lives, the first one, of course, is the relationship with the father, who is usually strict, disapproving and critical, and possibly even physically or emotionally unavailable. The disappointment and hurt starts there, and the men she chooses to relate to later in life, just add to the pain she already feels.

This is why Natrums often tend to present a "cold shoulder" of indifference to the world, which is another way she is hiding her true feelings. She isn't indifferent because she doesn't feel anything; she is indifferent because she feels emotionally safer if she can build a wall of ice between herself and other people, to protect herself from more pain. This is also why Natrum picks unavailable men because she feels safer if she can pick men who won't challenge her fear of intimacy. Intimacy happens when you allow someone to get so close that there are no "walls" between you and the other person, and this kind of closeness is way too scary for Natrum, even though her heart, deep down, does desire it. The problem is that she has been hurt so many times before that when she starts a new relationship, it always takes a long time for her to open up and trust a new mate, and if her new mate is moving too quickly for her, she immediately feels scared and pulls back. If he gets too close to her anyway, she will start looking for ways to create space from him so she can feel like she is in control again, at least emotionally. This is why Natrum will tend to pick a fight just when everything is going so well...

Natrum is like a walking time bomb, full of grief, anger and sadness, ready to go off. Often the grief is so deep that she can't cry, even if she wants to. Because Natrum is unable to express her feelings, with words or with tears, she tends to get irritable or angry instead, especially before her menses, after eating, in the morning, or from becoming overheated. This irritability can cause her to become quite difficult to live with at times. Natrums are so full of repressed feelings that the people in their lives can always sense the emotional intensity underlying their cheerful or peaceful façade. However, when Natrum occasionally does express her anger, she can be both furious and violent. She is already carrying so much anger inside that when it comes out; she may overreact about even small issues.

One interesting thing about Natrum is that she also tends to have an issue with God, since God is the ultimate unavailable father figure. Although he has the power to change things, he always seems to let her down, too, and it just isn't fair! He keeps ignoring her, no matter how much she prays, and there seems to be no way to please him! So, Natrum often becomes angry with men in general, including God! Many Natrums have decided that they simply don't need men in their lives any more. They call themselves "Goddesses" and prefer surrounding themselves with like minded women instead, which unfortunately doesn't resolve any of her inner pain or resentment towards men. This is because true transformation and healing can only happen through understanding the issues involved, not by pretending the issues no longer exist...

When Natrum feels angry, sad or hurt, she often withdraws from everyone. She hates it if she thinks anyone pities her, and she doesn't feel better from talking about her feelings, either. She can even become angry or irritable if someone tries to make her feel better. She would rather be alone where she can relax and doesn't have to pretend to anyone. When Natrum feels like this, she may also develop an aversion to certain persons, or to men in general, or even to her own husband or family. She may simply withdraw into aloneness because she doesn't think anyone cares enough to really understand her. She doesn't like any fuss, and she usually feels much better being alone. Although she may feel lonely at times, she still prefers her aloneness because unless she can find the perfect kind of company, she much prefers to isolate herself. Alone, she can at least relax and be at peace with herself!

Unfortunately, Natrum can't easily express her feelings to anyone. Sometimes she isn't able to cry at all, and other times she is only able to cry when she is alone. Once in a while, she may not even be able to stop, once the tears start running, and she may become almost hysterical at times. Thinking about past unfortunate events always makes her feel worse and it doesn't help if anyone tries to pity her, or cheer her up, either. She has a tendency to develop bitterness over time, because she has such a hard time letting go of old pain that she simply can't forget and forgive. Eventually, she may become very negative and complain a lot to anyone who lends an ear.

Letting go of old pain is probably the hardest thing for a Natrum to do. Her thoughts may torment or haunt her about all the bad experiences that she has had and is still holding on to. She can't stop thinking about the past and often blames herself or others for what happened. Sometimes she becomes very confused and doesn't know what to do next. Her ideas tend to become so fixed that it is almost impossible for her to come up with new, creative ideas or solutions to her problems, although that is what really needs to happen.

Natrum is a metal remedy, and metal remedies don't like change very much, unless they happen to be the ones who are initiating the change. This is because Natrum likes to be in control as much as possible. Not only does she like to be in control of her physical environment, she also likes to be in control of other people as well. She feels less vulnerable emotionally when everything is a certain way, which is typical for all the metal remedies. This is why Natrum feels homesick if she is away from home, and this is also why she often has a hard time adjusting to a new relationship after she has lived alone for a while. She likes things to be the way she likes them, and she doesn't want another person to enter into her life and start creating chaos by moving her things around. This is because any kind of change takes her out of her "comfort zone" by triggering her emotional vulnerability.

When Natrum feels emotionally vulnerable, all of her other fears can also be triggered. She may fear that something bad will happen, or she may feel anxious about the future. She often fears misfortune and failure, especially business failure, and her fears are often worse in the morning between 9 and 11 am, even though they can also affect her in the afternoon or at night, or in the dark. She may fear thunderstorms, or she may develop claustrophobia in small spaces, reflecting her need for space, both emotionally and physically. This need for space can also become an issue if she has to be around too many people for too long. As a result, she may avoid crowds or she may withdraw from people, altogether. When walking, she sometimes worries about falling, and she may also worry too much about her health at times. She has a tendency toward hypochondriasis and often fears going to the doctor, since the doctor might discover some kind of scary sickness that she didn't even know she had. In addition, she can also develop fear of death, or fear of being poisoned. All of these fears show how vulnerable she feels on every level. On top of this, we can also add to the list a fear of ghosts, dogs and evil.

Natrum also has a tendency to become impatient about little things and will often do things in a hurry. She is very restless inside, sometimes tossing and turning in bed at night (similar to Rhus Tox). At times, she may even walk in her sleep. If she experiences restlessness or emotional discomfort, or if she is having a hard time sleeping, a walk in fresh air, or dancing, usually calms her down and relieves her inner tension and discomfort.

If we look at the delusions that go with the Natrum remedy picture, we can clearly see how they also reflect Natrum's inner sense of emotional vulnerability. We can see how afraid she is to be hurt, not just emotionally, but physically as well. There are delusions about the house being full of people who are going to persecute her or steal from her, or she may have frightful dreams that make her so anxious that it drives her out of bed. She may even feel so much despair about the future that it seems like she is doomed, and because her mind is so fixed, there is a very strong sense of stuckness in her life, as well as a desire to find someone who can "save" her from her miserable life. (A prince, "soul-mate" or "twin-flame" would be good...) Natrum may also have the ability to see spirits and hear voices. She may even feel like she is seeing dead people or conversing with the spirits. She fears going insane and losing her reason, and in some cases she actually does go insane.

Because Natrum has very low self confidence, she always tries to be perfect in an effort to make herself worthy of people's love or approval. If she still doesn't get her needs met, the grief she experiences can be so deep that she may feel totally devastated. She basically gives up on life and can sometimes become indifferent to absolutely everything. When that happens, Natrum can feel so discouraged that she just wants to be alone. Her discontent is deep, and because she is a dependent type, she can easily become addicted to alcohol or pills in an effort to diminish her sadness and pain, or she may look to religion for support and courage.

At this point, Natrum can become very weary of life and start thinking suicidal thoughts. She is so used to people neither listening to her, nor understanding her, that at some point she may start wondering if it wouldn't be better to just end it all. She may be tempted to commit suicide by shooting herself, and if she does decide to actually go through with it, she probably won't tell anyone in advance how depressed she really feels. It can eventually become an unpleasant shock and surprise to her friends and family when, after she committed suicide, they finally realize how depressed she actually was, and nobody even knew...

NATRUM MURIATICUM IN RELATIONSHIPS

Natrum Muriaticum often comes from a strict family background where she was not encouraged to express her feelings freely. Natrum learned to be withdrawn from an early age, pretending she was fine, to avoid conflict or criticism, so she wouldn't get too hurt emotionally. Natrum's parents usually have high expectations of their children, and often tend to be very critical or disapproving of any efforts Natrum makes. Therefore, she will naturally strive for perfection, hoping that she will be loved eventually, if only she can be perfect enough. She doesn't feel good just being herself because she has learned from an early age that nothing she does is ever good enough, and that her parents still aren't pleased, no matter how hard she tries. This creates dependence. She is so starved for love that she is willing to do just about anything to get it, and her whole life becomes a struggle for approval from others, especially from her parents or, later on, her mate. She is willing to do whatever it takes to make people happy, hoping to get love and appreciation in return, but since she often ends up disappointed instead, she sooner or later puts up an invisible wall to protect her heart. The wall makes it almost impossible for her to experience any kind of intimacy because she won't allow anyone to get too close to her. She is always afraid that she'll just get hurt again. This is also why she usually picks unavailable men, so they won't try to "get behind" her wall, but without intimacy in her life, she won't find the love that she wants either. Therefore, she has a tendency to eventually end up bitter or cynical.

One Natrum man told me that he would always withdraw from relationships with women if he felt that they wanted too much from him (this probably meant that they wanted to get too close to him, which triggered his fear of intimacy). After years of escaping from relationships to avoid getting his emotions hurt, he finally realized that he would never experience the love that he was dreaming about unless he allowed himself to be totally vulnerable again. So when he started his next relationship, he was determined to find enough courage to stay open to the new love of his life, even though it brought up all his old fears. He knew that he had to overcome his fear of intimacy, or he would end up being alone for the rest of his life, which is something he really didn't want, even though he felt less vulnerable on his own. He also didn't feel like having a lot of short term affairs since they always left him with a feeling of emptiness inside, so he knew that facing his fears and changing his ways was the only way to find the happiness he was dreaming about.

However, it isn't just in love relationships that Natrum usually experiences difficulties. Her relationship with her parents can be just as complicated as the next story clearly shows. This is a story of a Natrum woman who was taking care of her mom, who was in a nursing home. Her mom, who also happened to be a Natrum, was unhappy about everything in her life and would greet Natrum with complaints every time she came to visit. Her mother complained about how lonely and miserable she was, how nobody ever came to visit her, and how unhappy she was about it. Natrum was so sensitive to her mom's disapproval that, even though she didn't say directly that she was unhappy with her personally, Natrum could still sense that her mother didn't think she was doing enough for her, and she was continuously feeling guilty about it, wondering how she could possibly do more for her. Natrum also had a full time job and her own family to look after, and the days simply weren't long enough to make everybody happy. Sometimes she would take her old mom home on the weekends, so she could spend more time with her, even though she knew that her husband disapproved and didn't have any patience with her mom's constant complaining. She couldn't express any of her feelings to her mom, of course, since she knew that her mom had never listened to anything she had ever tried to say to her anyway, and she felt really stuck. She felt that it was her duty to be there for her, for as long as she needed her, but at the same time she couldn't help wishing that her mom would finally go ahead and die, so she could get her life back. This was, however, a thought she could barely even admit even to herself because she felt so ashamed. After years of being stuck and feeling guilty for not really wanting to take care of her mom, she gradually built up resentment towards her, and, as a result, her own physical body started showing signs of the stuckness that she felt inside. She developed very painful arthritis in all her joints, reflecting her stagnant state of mind as well as her nonchanging relationship to her mom. Looking at her physical symptoms, it is no surprise that she eventually developed arthritis since she was stuck in this dysfunctional relationship with her mom for about 65 years.

Eventually, her mom did die, and just before she died, Natrum managed to let go of her resentment and come to a place of acceptance and peace about the relationship, which finally made her feel good about herself. She had fulfilled her duty as a daughter, and she could finally breathe a sigh of relief and allow herself to enjoy the feeling that she was "free at last."

It can be very hard for Natrums to change their situations because they are often emotionally or financially dependent on the people who are hurting their feelings or keeping them in bondage. They don't know what else to do, and their ideas and habits are so fixed that they can't easily find a way out of the situation, or a different way of doing things. They have such a strong sense of duty that they can't even imagine not doing what they feel they are expected to do. They tend to pretend everything is fine by suppressing their true emotions, and by accepting what is, rather than doing anything to create necessary change. This is why so many Natrum women end up staying in abusive or emotionally unsatisfying relationships. They hope things will get better over time, or they think they can make it better if only they try a little harder.

This is also why many Natrums become therapists. They feel better about themselves if they can help others, who are also experiencing the same kind of pain as they once were. By reaching out, they are hoping to make people happier, or at least help relieve their pain somewhat, and thereby contribute to making the world a slightly better place to be.

Because Natrum suppresses all of her feelings, she is often emotionally intense in her relationships with others. She can become irritable, critical and difficult to live with, especially before her periods, and she isn't able or willing to let go of old resentments so she can forgive and forget. More than anything, Natrum needs a mate who is willing to listen to her when she expresses herself. She needs to feel supported and accepted, which is something she never experienced as a child. She also needs to feel like her mate really loves and cares about her, and she needs him to show, or tell her this, in many different ways. Although Natrum tends to be withdrawn and aloof in relationships, she actually does need love and reassurance more than anything, even though she has a hard time asking for this directly. Asking for anything isn't easy because Natrum is so afraid of rejection that she would rather not ask at all.

In relationships, Natrum is naturally suspicious, and her trust has to be earned over a long period of time so that she can gradually let go of her defenses and find a way to allow people to get closer to her. She also has to learn how to simply be happy in herself, regardless of what anyone else thinks about her. This is not easy for her to do because her biggest misconception is that she thinks she has to be perfect to be loved. What she has to realize is that this need can only be fulfilled if she can find her inner source of love, rather than always expecting it to come from someone else. Only then can she truly be happy...

WHICH SIDE ARE YOU ON?
Nitric Acidum

REMEDY DESCRIPTION

Nitric Acid is naturally mild mannered, timid and reserved. She may be secretive and sentimental, and often has good ability for philosophy. Her self confidence isn't very strong, but this is a common trait in all the mild mannered types. Nitric Acid is a remedy of the Cancer miasm, which is reflected in her tendency for wanting perfection. She is conscientious about little things and is known to have fixed ideas about how things have to be done.

Nitric Acid can be very affectionate, cheerful and vivacious in her expression. Her sexual desire is usually high, and she may freely enjoy her relationships with men without any moral restrictions holding her back. She is usually friendly and sympathetic towards others; however, her sympathy is a very conditional kind of sympathy. It only applies to friends who have proven, beyond a doubt, that they are also supportive and loyal towards her. If her friends aren't as supportive towards her as she would like them to be, her sympathy can easily turn into a state of anger or maliciousness. You may find it odd, that someone, who is naturally mild-mannered, affectionate and sympathetic, can all of a sudden become the exact opposite, but Nitric Acid has good reasons for her somewhat unusual behavior.

Before we look deeper into why Nitric Acid does what she does, we first have to understand how sensitive she is to all kinds of external impressions. She is strongly affected by pain, as well as sensual, mental or emotional impressions. Horrible things and sad stories affect her profoundly, and she is also extra sensitive during heat and before her period.

Noise is another thing that really bothers Nitric Acid. This includes barking dogs, shrill sounds, voices, and especially male voices. Even music can sound like noise to her, and she may develop an aversion to it. If it were up to Nitric Acid, she would probably want to live in absolute silence if she could. This makes it hard for her to be around other people, since partners or housemates aren't normally quiet enough for her. Maybe Nitric Acid should seriously consider a library job or a cabin in the mountains!

Obviously, Nitric Acid is a bit "on edge." She is very nervous and startles easily from any noise, especially when she is asleep, or about to fall asleep. To understand why Nitric Acid is feeling so nervous, we have to look at some of the delusions that go with the remedy. Three of the most unusual delusions associated with Nitric Acid are: Things may seem longer than they are, or small things may seem to grow smaller, or tall things seem to grow taller. These three delusions indicate that Nitric Acid's perception of reality can be somewhat distorted. It can also mean that her imagination may play tricks with her, especially at night. She often feels apprehension and dread of being alone, and she may fear both evil and death. Any little thing can make her jump, noise, thunder, even touch. She is also fearful when waking up, possibly because she always has a very strong sense of impending danger.

The delusions and scary visions bother her mostly at night. She may have frightful or horrible visions appearing and disappearing. There may be phantoms, ghosts or specters, or she may see actual figures. She envisions herself surrounded by strangers. She must have offended someone, because it seems like she is about to be engaged in a lawsuit. She feels fearful about being involved in a legal process because she is afraid she may have offended some very dangerous people, possibly criminals, and now she will be punished. She can hear their voices and she starts running. She knows that they are coming after her, and that they are most likely intending to kill her. She can already see other dead people, as she is trying to escape. In other words, she is in grave danger, and her life depends upon her ability to either escape or fight off the upcoming danger.

This is the core situation that goes with Nitric Acid. The lawsuit issue also explains why Nitric Acid tends to see things in a very "black and white" way. It is very important for her to know which side you are on. Either you are with her, or you are against her! Either you are her friend, or you are her enemy, and this issue has to be established very clearly. If you are her friend, she'll be very sympathetic and friendly towards you, but if you are her enemy, she'll treat you with a very unforgiving, harsh attitude because there is a very real possibility that you, too, might put her life in danger. From this point of view, we can understand that her harsh and unforgiving manner is simply a survival mechanism. She is reacting to the life threatening original situation, which she is still playing out in her present life, by trying to ward off the impending or imagined danger to the best of her ability.

No wonder Nitric Acid is on edge! Sometimes she feels so anxious that it drives her out of bed, and she doesn't like being alone because she feels weak and defenseless. The anxiety is always worse at night and often comes in paroxysms. Thinking about it also makes it worse. She may feel anxious about the future or about her health, and if she is away from her family, you can expect her to feel homesick, too.

Nitric Acid has a tendency to always look at the gloomy side of things. If there aren't any actual signs of physical danger in her life, maybe the danger she is sensing could be from an impending disease! She may feel like she is seriously sick, even though there are no visible signs of any sickness. The disease, which she is about to come down with, is probably incurable, most likely some kind of cancer, and she doubts that anyone can actually help her recover. In other words, her state is pretty hopeless. (This state of hopelessness and desperation is typical for the cancer miasm). Her anxiety is usually worse during a thunderstorm, especially if the thunder is loud. Sometimes, she just has to hop in her car and drive away, since driving usually makes her feel much better.

Nitric Acid's constant sense of danger also affects how she relates to others. She often suffers from suspiciousness and lack of trust, always wondering if someone is going to take advantage of her or hurt her in some way. Because she is always on guard, she is easily offended and tends to take things the wrong way. She becomes very emotionally involved during debates, even when it is about trifles. Although she is strongly affected by arguments and discords, she still can't stop herself from getting involved.

As I mentioned earlier, Nitric Acid is a remedy from the Cancer miasm, which is reflected in her tendency for perfectionism. In Nitric Acid, the need for perfectionism actually represents survival to her. She only feels safe if everything is exactly so. If anything goes wrong or is out of place, or out of order, she becomes anxious, discontented, displeased and dissatisfied (similar to Arsenicum). This is why she often becomes very controlling in her relationships to others. Her discontent can affect any area of her life, and she may, in extreme cases, feel discontented with everything. If that is the case, she complains a lot and feels very sorry for herself. She may also suffer from greed, envy or hatred towards anyone who has more than she does, and she may feel very unfortunate.

In this state, she may become both cynical and unsympathetic. Her moods can be repulsive, and she may come across as rough, abusive, insulting and rude. She may slander the people she is feeling upset with, and her constant complaints may become a drain on her friends. The problem is that as soon as she feels that someone has overstepped her invisible line between friendship and enmity, it triggers a side of her personality that basically brings out her worst qualities. From being sympathetic, affectionate and mild mannered, she suddenly becomes obstinate, rebellious and contemptuous. She doesn't want to do anything she is asked to do, and she often becomes quarrelsome and dictatorial in an effort to get her needs and desires met. She does this in an attempt to make herself feel safe again, but if her arguing and stubbornness doesn't work, she can also become very angry. She'll either blame herself, or she'll become furiously or violently angry with someone else, even when the anger is caused by something insignificant. Any small sign of contradiction may trigger her wrath. She trembles inside while she is shrieking, screaming and shouting, or she may become spiteful and vindictive, cursing and swearing in her rage. In extreme cases she may even feel a desire to bite.

In some cases, Nitric Acid can also become both hard hearted and cruel. To understand why she doesn't seem to have much compassion towards others, we have to remember what she is trying to escape from, or fight off. She has a strong sense of impending danger that she has to avoid or overcome, no matter what it takes, because in the original story her life depends on it. If she perceives this danger as a threat to her life, it is easy to understand why her behavior often becomes somewhat extreme; it is because she is basically fighting for her life!

If her attempts to express how she feels doesn't give her what she wants, she often ends up embittered and exasperated. In this state, she can develop aversion to certain persons, and may even feel hatred for whoever has offended her. It doesn't matter if the person who offended her was a friend, stranger or family member. The hatred she feels is usually strong enough that she will cut off her connection to that person, possibly for the rest of her life, regardless of whether he is a family member or not.

Nitric Acid is known for being unmoved by apologies, and she may even consider revenge. Again, we have to remember that Nitric Acid can't tolerate any mistakes from anyone, because one mistake was all it took to put her life in danger in the original situation. Therefore, her tendency to be unforgiving also has to be seen as a survival mechanism. Unfortunately, she may lose her friends as a result, and if that happens, she can easily become very depressed. She may feel remorse or blame herself for what happened, even though she doesn't really want to do anything about it. Her grief is very deep, and she often finds it very hard to get over the loss.

In this state of grief, she may find herself in a weeping, tearful mood, or there may be cheerfulness alternating with sadness. She may want company because she really doesn't like being alone, but she doesn't necessarily feel better if anyone feels sorry for her, either. She may experience persistent, disagreeable thoughts that are tormenting her and keeping her in a miserable state. Because it is difficult for her to let go, she tends to dwell on past, disagreeable occurrences more than she should. The more she thinks about an issue, the worse it normally feels. Nitric Acid often struggles with a sense of stuckness in her life, similar to Natrum Muriaticum. (Fixed ideas and a sense of stuckness are typical for all the metal remedies). Her gloomy outlook can also affect her ability to concentrate. She may feel confused, or have a vacant feeling inside. Mental exertion makes her confusion worse. She may even become so dull and sluggish that she has difficulty thinking and understanding. This kind of "brain-fag" also affects her memory and makes it hard for her to remember things.

When she is not happy, Nitric Acid sometimes prefers aloneness. She may become so indisposed to talking that she just wants to remain silent. She doesn't even like to hear the voices of others talking, even in the next room. If someone tries to speak to her, she can become very irritable, especially in the morning after waking up, or in the afternoon.

Nitric Acid doesn't like being so miserable. Although she wants to escape from her misery, she often can't see any acceptable solutions because her perception of reality is too rigid. Out of her sense of stuckness arises a strong internal restlessness, especially after midnight. Her restlessness makes it hard for her to sleep, and sometimes she even talks in her sleep. In the daytime, she may feel an unexplainable impatience and an urge to hurry, which can cause her to become manic or even hysterical at times.

If she can't escape from her misery, she may eventually give up, resign herself, and sink into a state of indifference instead. In this state she can become apathetic towards everything, even towards her own family. Her indifference is totally joyless, and she often sighs deeply while suffering from a level of indecision that keeps her in a state where she is totally unable to change anything in her life. To describe this state I would call it "paralyzing indecision." At this point, her life may become so meaningless that she doesn't even want to go to work. She becomes lazy and starts loathing her life, and at some point, she may even wish she were dead. Although she may become totally suicidal eventually, there is still very little chance that she will act upon any of her suicidal impulses. Her indecision will most likely hold her back, as well as her fear of death and general lack of courage.

NITRIC ACIDUM IN RELATIONSHIPS

Relationships are often very difficult for Nitric Acid. She is sympathetic, friendly and affectionate by nature, but only if she feels safe with someone. She would have to overcome her natural suspiciousness to be able to allow someone to get really close to her. Here, we have to keep in mind that Nitric Acid is on guard, always sensing the possibility of danger or harm in her life. Therefore, she always needs to know which side you are on. Are you in the category of true friend or possible enemy? Are you going to take advantage of her, or cause her harm? Can you, or can't you, be trusted? If she finds reason to believe that you are her friend, she will be very affectionate, sweet and sympathetic towards you, although there is always a suspicious part that will constantly remain on guard, always looking for signs that you may not really be her friend after all. If you make one mistake with Nitric Acid, it is almost impossible to get her forgiveness. She becomes hardhearted and unmoved by your apologies and shows little or no compassion once her trust has been broken.

While working on this chapter, I came across a Nitric Acid client who really helped me understand the psyche of this remedy. The story she told me about her life, before she came to United States, made the whole situation associated with Nitric Acid come alive. This woman was originally from one of the Eastern Block countries in Europe. She told me that when the communists were invading her country, her family had to escape, somehow. They were feeling threatened by the arrival of the communists and feared for their lives. In this situation it was absolutely essential to determine whether someone was a friend or not, since a friend could help them escape, but an enemy could turn them over to the communists. Being turned over to the communists was almost guaranteed to mean harm, torture or even death, so they *had to* know which side everyone was on because their chance of survival depended on it.

Her family needed to get out of their country before it was too late, and they needed help from people along the way to help them escape. They often had to hide in people's basements, and the situation was very scary. She also explained that the biggest problem was that everyone had to choose which side they were on when the communists arrived. Someone, who used to be a friend, could all of a sudden choose to support the communists instead, so everyone had to be considered a potential enemy until their new affiliations had become clear. Her family had to be extremely careful in their associations with people because a simple mistake in their situation could mean the difference between life and death. They could only afford to give people one chance to prove their loyalty. If they found any reason to believe that someone might have changed sides, they could have no further contact with that person because the risk of being turned in was too great. Apologies meant nothing. They couldn't afford to forgive anyone because if someone happened to be affiliated with the communists, they could obviously never be trusted again.

When dealing with survival issues like this, there simply is no room for mistakes, since giving someone a second chance equals the possibility of danger, harm and possible death. To ensure survival, Nitric Acid's family had to pay attention to every little detail since even the smallest mistake could reveal their whereabouts. Therefore, perfection, and a need to be in control at all times, became a survival mechanism in this desperate situation. Their whole focus in their lives became an effort to escape the impending danger.

118

In this situation, we can also understand the relevance of the delusions associated with Nitric Acid's remedy profile regarding legal matters and court issues. If the communists had been able to catch them, they could very well have ended up in court for offending the wrong people by choosing not to support the communists, and this could easily have resulted in disaster, harm and possibly loss of life to everyone involved.

When I heard this story, I strongly felt that this must be the kind of story that the fears, phobias and delusions of Nitric Acid is a reflection of, especially since my client actually needed Nitric Acid for her ailments. After this kind of experience, we can understand how difficult, if not impossible, it is for Nitric Acid to let go of what happened and move on. There is always going to be a feeling that if it happened once, it could happen again. Bad people could start pursuing you, and friends could still turn on you - better be on guard, better be suspicious ...

We have seen, in all the other stories in this book, how we tend to replay the stories associated with each remedy profile over and over, as if the situation is still happening here and now. If the story is no longer happening in "real life," all the feelings and delusions associated with the story are still there. To justify these feelings we start attracting things, situations and people into our lives for the purpose of re-experiencing the same kind of situation again so we can either prove to ourselves that this is just how life is, or we can learn how to resolve the issues and leave them behind. If we are able to resolve the issues, we will no longer attract these kinds of issues again because we have become aware enough that we no longer need those lessons. If, however, we can't resolve these issues, the situation we have created will only strengthen our delusions by proving to us that our perception of life is true and real.

In Nitric Acid's life, this unfortunately means that she will tend to attract people who will put her in some kind of danger, or who will turn on her, or take advantage of her in some way. When this happens in her relationships, over and over again, it makes it very difficult for her to break the old patterns of being on guard, suspicious, hard hearted, cruel, and so on. Based on her past relationship experiences, she can't really trust anyone until they have proven to her, beyond a doubt, that they are worthy of her trust. And, even then, there is always a feeling that it could easily change. To break this pattern of suspiciousness, she would basically have to go against her past relationship experiences, take a leap of faith, and actually trust someone for no reason at all, even though there is no guarantee that she is not going to be deceived or harmed in the process. Unless she is able to do this, her suspicious nature will always stop her from feeling truly intimate or close to anyone, and her relationships are likely to always be complicated, maybe even scary, and very rarely of a permanent nature. Nitric Acid has been through so many scary experiences that it has become almost impossible for her to trust anyone. To overcome this perception of reality, she, somehow, has to realize that the danger is over, and it is finally time for her to take a deep breath of relief and just let go. She needs to put all the danger behind her, and she needs to learn to relax again...

THE GREAT CONQUEROR
Nux Vomica

REMEDY DESCRIPTION

We don't normally think about Nux Vomica as someone who is timid and reserved, careful or cautious, but it is the unusual combination of qualities like cautiousness and audacity (courage) that actually makes Nux such an excellent leader. One Nux client told me that he always tried to be as careful as possible before doing the dangerous, or reckless, things that he loved doing as a child. This is very different from the cautiousness we see in other remedy types, since it is more like an inner feeling that can't be seen by observing the child in action. This inner sense of cautiousness helps Nux determine how to do something dangerous or risky, and still remain safe.

If we look at Nux in a situation of war, courage and cautiousness has to go hand in hand if he wants to improve his chances for survival. Courage without cautiousness would be nothing but stupidity, and Nux is far from stupid. This is why many military generals are often Nux since they have the ability to keep their men safe in dangerous situations, and still get the job done.

Nux is a natural leader who loves being in charge. He perceives his reality as if he is a king, and he can sometimes be vain, proud, selfish and independent. He doesn't ask for anyone's advice, unless he really needs it, which is almost never. Nux has a powerful presence and talks with a certain air of superiority, which easily commands respect from people. At the same time he is also both social and vivacious, he knows how to flatter the people he wants to influence, and he is often both fun and entertaining to be around.

Nux is naturally charming and optimistic. He likes company and has a great appetite for life. He is passionate, his sex drive is generally high, and he loves excitement. Therefore, he often ends up overdoing it on sex, parties, drugs and alcohol. The remedy Nux is often a good choice for people who are addicted to alcohol in company with others, and also for people who use it to relax after a stressful day at work. Nux is also one of the main remedies for hangover, whether the hangover was caused by too much sex, food or alcohol the night before. In addition, it can also be used to help addicts who experience delirium tremens when trying to quit drinking.

Nux is generally an ambitious, zealous type who knows what he wants. He is very capable with a sharp mind and a strong inner drive that helps him achieve his goals, no matter what it takes. He has very high standards in everything he does, and he is usually hard on both himself and the people in his life. Nux can be restless, impulsive and impatient, and almost always in a hurry because he feels like time is passing too slowly. He likes order because he hates wasting time looking for things, and it often doesn't take much to upset him. In fact, Nux can be extremely critical of others, almost to the point of contempt. He can even become so self righteous in his views that he sometimes feels as if the whole rest of the world is full of only idiots.

Nux has lots of physical energy and loves working. He fears poverty and usually feels better when he is making good money and accomplishing his goals. His bright and clever mind is full of new ideas, and he is often willing to take many risks to achieve his goals. Because Nux is optimistic, impatient, impulsive and willing to take risks, he can easily develop a passion for gambling, which can get both him and his family in trouble very quickly.

Actually, Nux doesn't really need an excuse to get himself in trouble. The fact is he thrives on confrontation. Because he perceives reality as if he were a king, he also behaves like a king and likes to be treated that way. He is obstinate and headstrong and often resists the wishes of others. He is often defiant and quarrelsome, too, with a tendency to contradict and slander. He nags and reproaches others, and he can be rude, vindictive, malicious or even spiteful if the situation requires it. Nux is also capable of being sly and deceitful in order to accomplish what he wants whenever it suits him. As a king (or queen), he doesn't see any problem with having double standards and breaking his own rules when necessary, even when he expects others to follow the same rules. He does, however, have a big problem with anyone who is not playing fair. Because he has a very strong sense of justice and fairness, deception and injustice is probably one of the worst things that can possibly happen to him. This is because, in the original story, he was actually deceived or betrayed by one of his closest friends. His honor was wounded, he was disappointed, his business was affected, and he lost his position and probably also his house and his love.

In history, we often see examples of this when great warriors, who have just won a battle, are betrayed by a close friend or a relative (like Julius Cesar was betrayed and assassinated by his adopted son, Brutus). This also explains why Nux is so affected by discord between relatives or friends. It triggers emotions from the original situation of betrayal or deceit by a close friend, relative or business associate. As a result, Nux often feels anticipation anxiety because he has a hard time trusting the people in his life. He subconsciously expects something equally unpleasant to happen again here and now.

Nux also experiences jealousy strongly at times. If he is betrayed by someone who has taken his place, he may react with jealousy, violence and possibly even a desire to kill the person. The purpose of Nux's jealousy is to get his lost position back. Nux has many delusions that also reflect this issue. In the Nux profile we see the delusions that someone has gotten into his bed, that there is no more room in it, or that someone has sold his bed. This, of course, means that someone has taken over his position. Then, there are delusions that he has been insulted, and that he is away from home, or that someone has taken his bed and thrown him out of his home. We can see why Nux would be jealous and feel like killing; he needs to "get his bed back," or get back whatever was taken from him, including his position as king.

Because someone betrayed him in the original story, Nux is always full of worries. He fears that something bad will happen (again...), something horrible, or some kind of misfortune. He is anxious about his future and about business in general. He feels vulnerable and insulted after losing his position, and he is worried that people are laughing at him or mocking him. He fears people's opinions and can easily develop a fear of people, fear of being approached, or a fear of being in a crowd. He may even become paranoid enough to think that he is about to be persecuted or pursued by enemies.

This is why relationships are very important to Nux, especially family relationships. He needs a place where he can rest and feel safe, so when he finally does settle down, he can be quite warm and affectionate towards his wife and children, especially if he isn't working too much. He has a soft and caring heart behind the strong, capable image he presents to the world, and sometimes he shows sympathy and compassion, as well as anxiety for others.

The truth is that Nux is generally much more sensitive than he would like to admit to anyone. He is often deeply affected by hearing horrible things and sad stories, and he is also very sensitive to all external influences, like light, music, odors, pain, pollen and noise. He startles easily from noise, and he may feel tired or oversensitive after eating. In addition, Nux can also become anxious about his health and develop a hypochondriacal mania where he compulsively starts reading medical books. He doesn't like the sight of blood, and he fears impending disease (interesting, since he doesn't mind going into battle). He may feel like he is already sick and refuse to go to work, or he may fear going to the doctor. If he really is sick, he may fear that he will never recover from his illness, and he may even think he is about to die, or that he actually is dying.

When Nux feels vulnerable, he has a tendency to become scared. He may have frightful delusions or terrible dreams. Everything seems unreal, as if he is in a dream, and he may fear going insane and losing his reason. If something goes wrong, he may feel guilty and blame himself for what happened, and sometimes he actually does go mad.

We see an example of this in the movie "The Last Samurai," where Tom Cruise plays a Nux warrior. After his men ran away and left him to fight the enemy on his own, he was hurt in battle and captured. While he is in the process of recovering from his wounds, he has terrifying dreams about battles, and he just wants to drink himself unconscious. He feels so badly about what he has done in his life that he has completely lost his will to live. After staying with the Samurai people for a while and learning about their way of life, he chooses to become one of them and is finally able to regain his dignity and honor.

When Nux has been hurt or betrayed, the grief affects him very deeply. He may be sighing, moaning, groaning, whining and complaining from wounded honor, he may feel so inconsolable that he may not be able to cry at all, or he weeps to the point of hysteria. If he has been betrayed or deceived by someone he knew, he may feel very depressed and gloomy, and he may also develop sleeplessness caused by a rush of thoughts from stress, grief or disappointment, especially in the evening in bed. His moods can be very changeable, from cheerful to sad, repulsive or ugly and he may be in indecision about what to do. His behavior can become both confused and chaotic, or even childish at times, but physical contact usually makes him feel much better.

Nux can normally handle a lot of stress, probably better than any other remedy type, but when it gets too much, even for him, he will eventually withdraw from people just to get a break. He may want to be alone because company and consolation aggravates him too much. He often becomes angry if he is interrupted or expected to answer questions, and he can eventually develop an aversion to everyone in his life, even his own family and children because he just feels like escaping from it all.

When Nux feels this kind of discontent, he can also become discouraged or even disgusted with everything. He may feel so suspicious of everyone that he just wants to sit in his room, silently brooding over his misfortunate situation. In this state, he may even feel estranged from his own family. Little things upset him very much, and he easily responds with anger.

Anger and irritability are common Nux traits because Nux is generally too high strung and too tense for his own good. All his nerves are on edge, and there is a strong sensation of inner tension in his body as well as his mind. The irritability is just a natural reaction to the added stress he feels when the system is already in a state of overload. Nux therefore uses anger and irritability as a release mechanism when tension builds up too much, but the anger doesn't necessarily make Nux feel better afterwards. The anger can also trigger various ailments and can even add to the stress that he already feels.

When Nux is stressed, it is almost impossible not to make him angry, especially in the morning. He becomes angry if he makes mistakes, if he is contradicted by anyone, or if he is even spoken to. It is best for the people in Nux's life to stay far away from him when he is in an angry, irritable mood because you can't cheer him up no matter what you do. Nux is like a rubber band that has been stretched too tightly, and is almost ready to snap, so watch out!

Nux is famous for his angry outbursts. He may curse, swear, scream or shout. He may become so furiously, or violently angry that his anger turns destructive and he may want to break things or even strike someone if necessary. He is revengeful and often hates the people that have offended him (and if he attracts betrayal into his life, he may have good reason to). There is often a strong desire to kill, and even a fear of killing, especially with a knife, which shows that deep down Nux fears that his anger can get really out of control.

It is important to understand that anger isn't really a natural state for a Nux to be in; it is actually just a survival mechanism Nux uses when the stress in his life is too much and he needs a way to release his pent up tension. The problem is that if the stress levels are too high for long periods of time, and Nux keeps pushing himself, anyway, even though he needs a break, he eventually ends up totally exhausting himself. In the beginning of this chapter, I mentioned that Nux tries to achieve his goals no matter what it takes. The problem with this is that he will eventually end up making himself sick, if he doesn't stop and take a break when his body needs it. In addition to physical ailments, pushing himself too hard can also lead to exhaustion, or burnout, which isn't an easy thing to reverse.

When Nux becomes exhausted, he gradually starts becoming more and more dull and sluggish, which may eventually lead to difficulty with thinking, concentration, or comprehension. He can become forgetful and confused and he sometimes makes mistakes while speaking or calculating. When Nux reaches this level of exhaustion, he just wants to sit and rest and may completely lose interest in working or doing any kind of business. In addition, he may also become weary of life in general. He may desire death, even to the point of wanting to commit suicide, but he often lacks the courage to actually do it. In some cases, Nux will turn to religion for comfort. He may feel anxious about his salvation or loss of faith and can turn to either western or eastern religions to look for answers to soothe his soul.

125

NUX VOMICA IN RELATIONSHIPS

Nux Vomica is a natural leader type, who loves being in charge, both at work and in personal or family relationships. There are many different types of Nux leaders, some more dictatorial than others, but they all have in common the fact that they like making decisions on their own, and they don't like being contradicted or told what to do by anyone else. If a Nux isn't in charge, the person who is in charge has to be another Nux, or at least someone Nux can respect, or it isn't going to work. Nux prefers to find work where he can be in charge, or work for himself, because he isn't happy if he has to work under anyone else's leadership. He will express his discontent very clearly, and either end up getting fired or rising to the top where he can be the boss.

The reason why Nux likes to be in charge in relationships makes perfect sense from a Nux perspective. Nux isn't just smart; he or she has a very quick mind and can often assess a situation accurately almost instantly. Nux behaves, and perceives reality, as if he were still on the battle field where his survival depends on his ability to accurately assess a situation and quickly make decisions on his own without consulting others. This is also why Nux hates being told what to do by others because if his survival (on the battle field) depends on him being right, and someone questions his decisions or even worse, tells him he is wrong, it triggers his (survival) fears and he responds with anger or irritability.

Unfortunately, Nux does the same thing in his personal or work relationships, too. He can quickly decide what a situation requires, and he makes decisions without even thinking about asking his boss, partner or mate how he, or she, feels about it. This can easily get him in trouble with his boss or mate, who may think he is selfish, dictatorial or disrespectful. Nux doesn't mean to be selfish, it just doesn't occur to him to ask for anyone else's input when he can instantly see what needs to happen in a situation on his own! He doesn't realize that someone else may see it from a totally different perspective, and that he or she might like to have their opinion heard, too, even if they eventually end up agreeing with Nux.

One of my Nux clients used his ability to assess a situation to his advantage on his job. He worked as a car sales man for a big company and had enough freedom that he was able to do things his own way without getting in trouble with his boss. I asked him what he does when someone comes in to buy a car, and he told me he just tries to help them. I asked how, and he explained how he instantly figures out what they want, what they need and how much they can afford. (He identifies the target, straight to the point, true Nux style). Once he has gathered all the information he needs, he suggests the perfect car for them, and the customers often end up buying it, even though it is most likely a different car than what they originally had in mind. My Nux client isn't trying to fool anyone. He just has a natural knack for picking cars that really suit the person's situation as well as their wallets. He is honest, fair and sincere, and his clients feel comfortable buying from him. He has been salesman of the month several times and really enjoys his work.

The only problem he has had so far was when he discovered that another sales person had talked to one of his customers six months earlier and now wanted him to share the commission of the sale he had just made, since they had both spent time talking to the same people. As far as the Nux salesman was concerned, six months was a long time ago, and since he was the one who actually closed the sale, he didn't feel like he should have to share his profits with the other person. Salesmen spend a lot of time talking to people, but it only pays the bills if they are able to close the sale. Nux closed the sale and didn't feel like the other sales person had anything to do with it. He was working on his own and felt that he needed to get paid for what he did. This shows how Nux thinks. He likes working for himself and doesn't consider himself "part of a team."

Another Nux client (woman) was very unhappy working in a local restaurant. The owner of the restaurant kept hiring new people to manage the place and cutting down on my friend's hours, which she was quite upset about. One manager after another turned out to be unsuited for the job, and my friend had to come back and help out time and time again after each manager got fired. The owner of the shop couldn't see that my Nux friend was the one who really should be in charge of the place, and Nux grew more and more frustrated and irritable. I finally had a word with the owner, who is also a friend of mine, and told her she should give Nux a chance to manage the place. She followed my suggestion, and a month later she called and told me that everything was working unbelievably well. She told me how surprised she was to find what a great manager Nux ended up being. Nux is happy to finally be in charge, she is not irritable any more, she is a good boss, and all the workers are happy with the arrangement. She has eliminated all the chaos and nonsense that was previously happening, and the owner of the place can finally relax, knowing she can trust Nux to take care of things when she isn't there.

These examples clearly show why a Nux can be the perfect person to run a business or get a job done effectively, but we can also easily imagine how these same traits can get Nux in trouble in his, or her, personal relationships. In personal relationships, Nux is better off if he can find a mate or partner who honors his position as king (or queen), and lets him be in charge and make most of the decisions. He definitely doesn't like having to consult with his mate before making decisions or being told what to do in any way. (Nobody tells the king or queen what to do!) Nux doesn't mind having a strong, spirited mate to share his throne with where they are both independent and each make decisions for themselves, but this kind of relationship is less common. Usually, Nux's mate, or partner, ends up in his shadow and wisely accepts his position as king of the castle.

WANTING FAME AND FORTUNE
Phosphorus

REMEDY DESCRIPTION

Phosphorus perceives reality as if she were someone of high rank, some-one important, distinguished, rich (nobility comes to mind). She can be proud, critical or dictatorial in her views if she feels that she isn't being appreciated or supported enough in the right way. A beautiful Phosphorus friend of mine who loved to mix and mingle with the rich and the famous, always managed to find extremely wealthy boyfriends who would treat her the way someone of high rank deserves to be treated. Since she never had much money in her own pocket, finding someone else with money was an easy solution for her.

Phosphorus is timid, mild mannered and patient by nature. She doesn't like conflict and seriousness, and she prefers to withdraw during uncomfortable circumstances. She can be calm and meditative, although she chooses not to get too serious even about meditation. She easily becomes bored and drained if anything tends to get too heavy in her life; and she much prefers to keep every-thing light and fun all the time. Phosphorus is a Tubercular remedy, which is a combination of Psora and Syphilis. If Psora dominates the picture, you get a Phosphorus who is quick, bright, focused and intelligent, who learns and under-stands things easily, and who remembers well and has abundant ideas. If the Syphilitic tendency dominates the picture, you get a Phosphorus who has a hard time focusing, understanding, thinking and learning, with deficient ideas, slowness, dullness and brain-fag. This kind of Phosphorus has a weak memory. She tends to forget what she was about to do or what she just read, she often has to think long and hard before she is able to answer even simple questions, and there is an aversion to thinking because too much mental effort can easily drain her energy.

One of the most characteristic traits of both types of Phosphorus is their sensitivity to all kinds of external impressions. They are sensitive to odors, touch, light and noise, as well as sensual impressions, beauty, sad stories and other people's emotions. Phosphorus easily feels what other people are feeling, and often starts feeling the same way without knowing why. If someone is sad, frightened or happy, Phosphorus will act like a psychic sponge and soak up the feelings, as if they were her own. She is very impressionable and has no sense of personal boundaries which can create separation between herself and others. This issue often causes problems in her relationships.

Phosphorus doesn't have a strong sense of self, which is one of the reasons why she doesn't have any sense of personal boundaries. She is very confused about who she is. According to the Phosphorus delusions, she may have a sense of duality, or she may feel as if she is in a dream. Familiar things may seem strange to her, and she has a hard time knowing what is real and what is not. This perception causes chaotic, confused behavior and lack of self confidence. She often feels helpless and doesn't know what to do, which affects her will to do anything. Phosphorus loves to be around other people, especially if they give her a stronger sense of who she is. She craves affection and emotional support, and she is very good at getting her needs met.

It is hard to ignore a Phosphorus. Besides being physically beautiful, with big eyes, lean body, silky skin and shiny hair, she also has a cheerful, charming, bubbly, excitable personality that makes it very easy for her to make friends. Her lighthearted quality, chattiness and contagious laughter, make her irresistible to others and fun to be around. The metal Phosphorus bursts into fire when exposed to oxygen, and the Phosphorus personality also reflects this unstable quality. Phosphorus tends to become over-excited over little things, which is often followed by complete exhaustion or burn-out.

Phosphorus doesn't like being alone. She has a strong sense of isolation, as if she were on a distant island (core delusion). Aloneness brings up all her fears, and she avoids it as much as possible. She is always anxious that something bad is going to happen to her friends or relatives because of the possibility that she could end up being all alone. She worries a lot, even though her anxiety is often causeless. She has a deep inner sense of being unloved, and to compensate for this feeling, she is affectionate to others, hoping, and even demanding, that they should give her affection in return (similar to Pulsatilla, who is also trying to compensate for feeling forsaken, but Pulsatilla is less demanding and often more manipulative).

Phosphorus is sympathetic to the point of clairvoyance. She knows what other's feel, even if they are physically far away. She likes being dependent on others who will tell her what to do, since she needs a lot of reassurance and suffers from too much indecision when she is on her own. Because Phosphorus is dependent on others, she may end up doing things opposed to her intentions, similar to Sepia. She often compromises what she feels in an effort to receive attention and sympathy in return.

Phosphorus usually has a strong sexual drive and often has lots of relationships. In spite of the fact that Phosphorus has many friends and easily ends up in relationships, she doesn't necessarily know how to form intimate connections with others. She still feels isolated, even when she is around other people.

When the relationships in Phosphorus' life don't work out, it affects her deeply because it brings up her original feeling of being unloved and isolated. She is a very emotional type who experiences strong feelings of fear, disappointment, grief, despair, jealousy and hatred, especially towards the men in her life. Phosphorus feels jealous if she isn't the most beautiful person in the room, which reminds me of the evil queen in Snowhite. As long as her magic mirror tells her she is the most beautiful woman in the land, she feels great, but when Snowhite becomes more beautiful than her, she orders the huntsman to take her out into the woods and kill her!

When Phosphorus' relationships break up, she often feels beside herself with grief. She dwells on what happened, complaining, moaning and looking for sympathy from her friends. Consolation always makes her feel better; in fact, she craves it so much that she can become extremely demanding of her friends at times. Her moods often change, alternating between cheerfulness and sadness. Phosphorus is, however, a pretty resilient type. She tends to recover fairly quickly after a brief period of grieving.

Because Phosphorus has a weak sense of identity and doesn't always know what is real, she often blames herself when something goes wrong. Sometimes she even accuses herself of doing things she didn't do. She feels guilty, like a criminal, and thinks that she will be pursued by the police, or that she will be murdered, robbed or poisoned. Her lack of boundaries makes it hard for her to have an objective, realistic view of life. In some ways Phosphorus deals with life as if she were still a child. She can be very innocent, optimistic and hopeful about things, and therefore she sometimes ends up being deceived. This can in turn make her both suspicious and secretive.

Phosphorus is a passionate type, who gets offended easily and can become very upset over little things. She can also be stubborn and angry and stick to what she wants. She can become furiously angry and expresses herself with a passion, scolding, cursing and swearing whenever she feels like it. She doesn't worry about following any rules and does whatever it takes to get what she wants. She doesn't mind being malicious, spiteful, vindictive, rude or violent if necessary. She screams and shouts and may even feel like killing the person she is angry with. Trivial things can aggravate her anger, especially if it triggers her basic feeling that she is not getting enough love, support or reassurance from her friends or family. When this happens, she'll either end up in a rage, or she will totally withdraw from everyone. (Again, we can refer to the evil queen

131

in Snowhite – every day she was asking the mirror "Who's the fairest of them all?" because she needed daily reassurance that she was the one, and this is what Phosphorus needs to know as well. Phosphorus' magic mirror is, of course, the people in her life).

When Phosphorus doesn't feel enough love or support from the people in her life, she can sometimes withdraw from company altogether. She doesn't feel safe around people, and doesn't want to talk to anyone. She can even develop an aversion or indifference to her own family, children and dearest friends. She feels estranged from her family and may attempt to escape, but if she does escape, she develops homesickness. Again, we can see how the delusion that she is on a distant island applies, and get a sense of her basic underlying feeling of being unloved and isolated.

Aloneness is very hard for Phosphorus. It brings up all her fears, and she is pretty much afraid of everything. She is affected by storms, thunder, lightning, rain, and fire. (Remember how the evil queen died? She was chased by the seven dwarfs up the mountain until she found herself on top of a huge boulder. As she was standing there, a lightning bolt suddenly struck the rock, and she fell to her death. No wonder Phosphorus is still afraid of lightning!)

One Phosphorus friend of mine, ended up under her living room table, hugging her dog, when she found herself alone during a horrendous thunderstorm. She was totally terrified by the intense flashes of light and the crashing sound of thunder right above her head, desperately wishing that she wasn't alone! (Again, it is interesting to note that Phosphorus is one of the main remedies to give to someone who has been struck by lightning! And, it is also one of the main remedies for someone who has been put into a deep sleep, not by a poison apple, but by anesthesia!)

Phosphorus' anxiety is often worse in the morning and in the evening, especially around twilight and in the dark. This is when her imagination takes over. The fear is felt in the stomach, and it can often be overpowering, almost to the point of panic. She can also experience fear of insanity at times, which is something I think all the more unstable emotional types have in common.

In addition to having fear about her mental health, Phosphorus also tends to develop fear about her physical health, especially the possibility of heart disease and cancer. There are ailments from anticipation, before going to the dentist or physician, and fear of doctors. Phosphorus has a tendency toward being a hypochondriac, and often exaggerates her symptoms in the doctor's office. She may be doubtful of her recovery, but she can easily change her mind about that if someone tries to cheer her up (consolation ameliorates).

When it comes to practical issues, Phosphorus doesn't really understand how to manage money and often finds that she has less money in the bank than she thought she did. Unless she can find a rich boyfriend who can take care of her financially, this can easily lead to anxiety about the future and fear of misfortune and failure. She wants to work and often talks about business, although she can be a bit scattered at times. She doesn't have a lot of self discipline and has a tendency to lose her focus, while still thinking she is working hard. She can, however, be both fastidious and industrious when she wants to be, and she often works very quickly.

Because Phosphorus isn't very good at managing money, she often gets herself into financial trouble by being too generous with her friends. When Phosphorus realizes that her money is gone, she naturally expects her friends to be equally generous with her. Either she will find someone who will simply give her the money she needs, or she will borrow the money from her friends. In most cases she does intend to pay them back, but she may not have any idea how, and she often ends up not paying them back at all.

Phosphorus just isn't that interested in business issues. She may develop an aversion to work, simply because it might be too serious and structured for her, and she needs more time for fun and "going with the flow." She tends to trust that things will somehow, mysteriously work themselves out, and she can be charming enough that someone usually ends up rescuing her when she needs it the most.

Phosphorus has a great imagination, which can be a problem for someone who doesn't know what is real. She often has a feeling that something will happen, and that something could come creeping out of every corner. One Phosphorus girl was so afraid to go to bed at night that she became an expert in jumping from the door right into her bed so she didn't have to step on the floor. She was sure the devil was under her bed, just waiting to grab her ankles and pull her straight to hell. Therefore, it is no surprise that going to sleep alone, in the dark, is the hardest thing for Phosphorus. Her imagination is too active in the dark, especially after going to bed, and this causes sleeplessness and makes it tempting for Phosphorus to use sleeping pills. One Phosphorus woman, who lived alone, had to use sleeping pills every night, in addition to having the TV on all night in her room. She also used to have recurring dreams of suffocation, and she would sometimes wake up in the middle of the night in complete panic.

Phosphorus has a tendency toward addictive behavior. Her intense delusions and fears, which affect her sleep and make her exhausted during the day, are the main reasons why she often ends up addicted to alcohol, sleeping pills and other allopathic medications (poison apples...). She also tends to become discontented, discouraged and disgusted with everything when her relationships aren't working out, and pills and alcohol can be a great temptation which quickly becomes a habit that can be hard to kick.

When Phosphorus is unhappy, she may sigh and weep a lot, which makes her feel better. She may become weary of life and desire death, but she also fears death, so she isn't likely to actually kill herself unless she accidentally overdoses herself with alcohol or pills. She is more likely to reach out to her friends when she feels badly since she always feels better when someone keeps her company, especially at night. She may even overdose herself slightly if she thinks it will get her more attention from her friends or family by doing so. Phosphorus just hates being alone and will do whatsoever it takes to get attention in order to avoid aloneness altogether if possible.

PHOSPHORUS IN RELATIONSHIPS

Phosphorus loves being in relationships. Deep inside, she feels unloved and isolated, so she will do almost anything to find someone who can keep her company in order to avoid these uncomfortable feelings. Therefore, she always surrounds herself with as many people as possible, especially people who appreciate her, pay attention to her and tell her how beautiful she is.

Phosphorus is normally very charming and can easily make friends, but she still has a hard time creating intimate relationships. There are a few different reasons for this. First of all, she expects her relationships to always be exciting and fun, and she very much dislikes seriousness and conflict, which is also a natural part of relationships. She prefers relating on a light, but somewhat superficial level, and then wonders why she can't create a deeper connection to anyone. Because she knows that the connection isn't as deep as she would want it to be, she needs constant re-assurance that she is beautiful, and that her partner loves her. Although she is usually very affectionate in relationships, her affection isn't always given from a truly loving space. Subconsciously, she is hoping that the more affection she showers on her partner, the more affection she will receive in return. This is, in fact, what she actually expects him to do, even though she may not openly express it to him. The partner often feels this underlying expectation, anyway, and doesn't always reciprocate her display of affection. This makes Phosphorus feel drained and depressed, and eventually she will either withdraw from the person who is not reciprocating her affection, or she will become very angry towards him and start demanding his attention in a very controlling way. If she really wants him to pay attention to her, and he won't, she can even make herself very sick. Fibro-myalgia is a good example of a Phosphorus ailment that has the potential to create a lot of attention in her life, and for that very reason, it is also very hard to cure because who wants to lose all that attention? If, however, she pushes the issue too hard, or starts raging because she is not getting the attention she wants, her mate often ends up leaving her because there seems to be no end to her demands, and he just has to get away from her to find relief. This is often "the story of her life," and she finds herself alone, heart broken and feeling unloved, time and time again.

Phosphorus tends to create what I call "high maintenance relationships." If you want to be friends with a Phosphorus, she does expect a lot from you in return. One Phosphorus woman, I used to know, often left messages on my answering machine, asking me to go and get things for her at the local store and bring them to her, since I lived closer to the store than she did. Another Phosphorus woman used to call and ask me to bring her bottles of homeopathic remedies simply because she was tired and didn't feel like getting into her car. This woman was also addicted to all kinds of allopathic medicines, and she used her homeopathic remedies in much the same way as she used her allopathic ones. She had no regard for following my instructions, which made it virtually impossible to manage her case, and I finally had to break off my relationship with her, which put her into a nasty rage. She told me then that every therapist she had ever worked with had done the same thing to her, and that she felt totally abandoned by everyone. She didn't realize that her tendency to constantly self medicate with a mixture of everything she had on her shelf, basically, made it impossible to work with her. She simply thought she was exercising her rights as a client, and couldn't see why I made it such a big deal out of it! She had no clear personal boundaries, and therefore, she couldn't understand the boundaries that needed to be present in the relationship between client and therapist, either.

This same woman would often call her friends any time, day or night, and ask them to come over and spend hours of their time with her because her fears were out of control. She had no idea what a burden or a drain, this was on her friends, and when they eventually withdrew from her because they needed a break, she would become horribly angry and often complain about how much energy she was always giving people without ever receiving anything in return. This is a very common Phosphorus issue. The fact is, they do give a lot of love and attention to their friends, but there is usually an ulterior motive behind their giving that others can often sense. Their main purpose for giving love to others is to receive love in return, and this unexpressed, underlying expectation often makes others feel uneasy about the whole situation. Phosphorus has adopted this kind of strategy simply because she is good at it, and it works. The more they give to others, the more they expect others to give back to them. They need constant reassurance from everyone in their lives about how beautiful they are, and how much they are loved and appreciated, and they are most likely unaware of how demanding this can seem to their friends in the long run.

Another Phosphorus woman who had terminal cancer, went back to the town where she grew up when she found out she was about to die. She didn't get along with her own family, which is often typical for a Phosphorus, but luckily, she had many friends she could count on. She moved in with an old boyfriend and told everyone she knew that she was dying, and that she needed their help. Before long, all her friends, as well as the rest of the community, were offering whatever they could do to help. Someone would bring her free wood and make fires for her, someone else would cook her food, make fresh vegetable juices or do her dishes, she was offered free massages on a regular basis and she also had friends who would come and give her a bath, wash her hair and clean her bed whenever it was needed. Sometimes people would even spend the night watching over her so she didn't have to wake up scared. As I looked at the situation, I asked her if she thought all those people were helping her get well, or helping her stay sick. She looked at me shocked and said: "What do you mean?" So I told her I could see how much she loved all the attention she was getting and I asked her if she was willing to give it all up. I told her she was only getting this much attention because she was sick and that all that attention would disappear if she actually became well. So, I asked her again: "Are you willing to give it up?" She got very much disturbed by my question and said she needed time to think about it. Unfortunately, she wasn't willing to give up any of the attention she was getting. This was what she had wanted her whole life. For the first time in her life, she felt totally loved and cared for, and she would rather die than give it up. So, needless to say, that is what she did...

My feeling is that Phosphorus needs so much attention from others that almost no amount is really enough because she hasn't learned how to love and appreciate herself, yet. This is why she goes from one relationship to the next, always searching for what she can't find in herself and hoping to find it in the right kind of company. This is also why Phosphorus often ends up with lots of loving pets in her life since the pets don't mind giving her the unconditional and constant love and attention she craves. The key for Phosphorus, to resolve her issues, is to stop looking for love to come from someone else, and instead, look inside for her inner source of love. This is, of course, the last thing any Phosphorus wants to hear, but nevertheless, the only way to find true and lasting fulfillment.

IF I'M GENTLE AND SOFT, I'LL SURVIVE
Pulsatilla Pratensis

REMEDY DESCRIPTION

Pulsatilla Pratensis has a feminine and soft quality. She is mild, yielding, submissive and timid. A Pulsatilla child may be so timid and reserved that she may hide from strangers, although she usually warms up to them after a while. There may be a sense of selflessness or weakness of will, and her confidence may be lacking. She has a hard time saying no, and sometimes her speech is hesitating or wandering. She may take on tasks that she doesn't really feel like doing because her main concern is to please people. If we look at someone's mental state as a survival mechanism that helps us survive our childhoods, we can see how Pulsatilla has chosen to be soft and yielding as her survival mechanism (if I am soft enough, I will survive!)

Pulsatilla is a cautious type. Because her confidence isn't very strong, she becomes careful, conscientious and fastidious. It isn't the kind of fastidiousness where she feels compelled to keep things orderly and neat all the time, it is more of a "fussy" fastidiousness which manifests itself as pickiness about little things. Because she does things slowly, she often has a tendency to be late for her appointments. However, you can usually trust her to do things right if she has a job to do, since it is important for her to please the people she works for so she doesn't risk losing her job. She is very sensitive to any kind of disharmony, both at work and at home, and she has a tendency to worry a lot about both business and domestic affairs.

Pulsatilla is a sensitive soul. Because she cares so much about other people, she can become profoundly affected by hearing horrible things and sad stories. She is also very sensitive to heat, and most of her complaints are better in fresh air. Noise is another thing that often bothers Pulsatilla. It makes her startle easily, both in her sleep and while awake.

By nature, Pulsatilla is sweet, sympathetic and affectionate. She has no problems expressing her affection to others since she is warm emotionally and finds it easy to hug, kiss or love the people in her life. Her sexual drive can be quite strong, and she may sometimes flatter others to make them feel good, especially if she thinks they will give her affection in return. (This is different from Phosphorus, who both expects and demands that people return her affection and who gets angry if they don't).

It is often be fun to be around Pulsatilla, even though she can also be quite demanding at times. She has a charming, playful, cheerful, optimistic disposition. She is a very emotional type, and it is easy to bring her to laughter or tears. She often becomes very excited, impulsive or impatient, even over little things. Her emotions seem to be very close to the surface, and since they aren't suppressed or intellectualized, she tends to behave somewhat childishly at times. Therefore, some Pulsatillas seem to get stuck at the stage of teenage girl, and the idea of marriage may seem unendurable if she doesn't feel totally ready to become a grown woman, yet.

There is also another side to Pulsatilla, which is less obvious than her sweetness. There may be selfishness and egotism under her cheerful, affectionate personality. She gives a lot to others, but in return, she wants affection and attention, and she may turn quarrelsome, difficult, obstinate or critical in order to get it. She may become intolerant of anyone's contradictions and can sometimes be proud, manipulative, impulsive and fearless, if necessary, in order to get her needs met. At times she may even go ahead and just do whatsoever she wants, regardless of the wishes of others. She wants what she wants, and the word "no" may not mean very much to her.

There is a sense in Pulsatilla that we are dealing with a person of high social rank, someone who doesn't totally understand the value of hard work and money. She may be spoiled, since there is a tendency for greed and envy, and she isn't always grateful for what she has. She may be full of desires for this and that, and she would love for someone to just give these things to her. If she is lucky enough to get others to pay for whatever she wants, she may not even want to know anything about money. She often doesn't mind frivolously spending money that is given to her, and she may even develop a passion for gambling.

As I mentioned above, Pulsatilla can be quite manipulative or sly when she wants something. She may try bargaining, lying or even stealing if she finds it necessary. This is a more hidden and unsympathetic side of the Pulsatilla nature. It shows how she has a talent for getting her needs met by gentle manipulation hidden behind a sweet smile, or by being sly, or even by persistently whining and complaining until she gets her way. (This, too, is different from

Phosphorus who tends to go into a rage when she doesn't get what she wants. Pulsatilla chooses to do things in a much more subtle and gentle way).

There is also a different type of Pulsatilla who isn't as spoiled or manipulative as the type described above. This kind of Pulsatilla may be ambitious and even have an aptitude for finance. She may have a well developed mind with easy comprehension, good memory and an abundance of new ideas. She may be very capable, although she often has difficulties making decisions, and she is definitely not a leader type.

The fears that go with the Pulsatilla remedy profile, also confirm that Pulsatilla is a person of higher class. There is despair of losing her social position and fear of high places, which shows that her position is not fixed. She is worried about what others may think or say about her since their negative opinion can affect her position (she could fall down to a lower level as a result). She also fears being humiliated or neglected. She has a tendency to easily feel offended and doesn't always take jokes very well. In addition, she also has a strong fear of poverty, misfortune and disaster. She doesn't feel totally capable of taking care of herself, and her fear may be so overpowering that she can get heart palpitations at times. She may feel fearful or anxious, even inside her house, and she often worries about simple household matters.

Because Pulsatilla tends to depend on others for support, she often suffers from anticipation anxiety, especially about future and health. She has a tendency for hypochondriacal worry and may develop a mania for reading medical books. Or, she may have a sense that something bad is going to happen. She is very affected by bad news, and she may worry about her business failing, or about losing her job, since both could easily result in a loss of social position and poverty.

In addition, Pulsatilla is also very sensitive to deception, which can cause her a great deal of grief or humiliation if it happens. She is sensitive to insult and disappointment, and she can easily become jealous, aggressive or even hateful toward others if she feels emotionally hurt, or if she doesn't get her needs met for some reason. (Pulsatilla's jealousy mainly has to do with losing her position, while Phosphorus' jealousy has to do with someone being more beautiful than she).

When trying to get a feeling for what the situation is that goes with the Pulsatilla picture, we have to look at a combination of fears and delusions. We already know she is afraid of losing her social position, possibly because that is what happened to her in the original story. In addition, there is also apprehension and dread, as well as ailments from grief and aloneness. Her main issue is the delusion that she is completely alone in the world, and that she is doomed, forsaken and away from her home. We also see the delusion that there is some-one in bed with her, a naked man. Therefore, my feeling is that Pulsatilla must have lost her lover, her home and her social position. She blames herself for the loss of her lover and feels like she has neglected her duty or done something wrong. She is angry with herself and feels guilty and sad. It is as if heavy, black clouds have enveloped her.

After losing her lover, Pulsatilla becomes inconsolable with grief. Even though she is submissive by nature, she may start developing suspiciousness because she doesn't know who to trust. Her suspiciousness can sometimes increase to the point where she may even consider everybody to be her enemy. She can feel so beside herself that she doesn't want to go to work, and she may not even want to get out of bed. She has a tendency toward monomania, talking about the same things over and over, while whining, complaining and crying. All her emotions are close to the surface, and she does not suppress or hold anything back. She weeps and sobs loudly and has a definite tendency to be-come hysterical. She can even faint from hysteria. Once she starts weeping, it is hard for her to stop. She weeps so easily that she may not be able to control herself at all. Sometimes she weeps when answering a question or describing her condition or situation, and in some cases her weeping may alternate with laughter. The weeping may be causeless, joyful or sad, and it is often worse before her periods. She weeps when she feels humiliated, and she may even weep in her sleep. Weeping always makes her feel better, so the saying "there is nothing like a good cry!" must have been made up by a Pulsatilla

Basically, there are three things that always make Pulsatilla feel better: weeping, open air and affectionate company. She needs someone to keep her company so she doesn't have to be alone, preferably someone who will listen to her complaints and hopefully hug her, hold her or caress her while listening.

If Pulsatilla can't change her unfortunate situation or get over her sad-ness, she can easily sink into a state of deep depression, gloom and despair. Again, her mental state is always worse in hot weather and around the time of her period or menopause, and she always feels better when walking in open air. If the condition becomes permanent, Pulsatilla may eventually change from her normally outgoing personality to the exact opposite. She may develop an aver-sion to talking to anyone and will just sit, very still, sighing deeply once in a while.

It is hard to imagine that sweet, outgoing Pulsatilla can become so silent, introspective and withdrawn, just sitting there, staring ahead, not wanting anything to do with anyone. Natrum, Ignatia and even Aurum come to mind, and at this point it may be difficult to differentiate. Pulsatilla's thoughts are persistent, especially at night. There is a rush or flow of thoughts that wander from one issue to another. She may develop sleeplessness from having too many thoughts, or her thoughts may seem to vanish into thin air.

Pulsatilla has never had a strong sense of identity or self. When she experiences emotional turmoil and distress, she becomes very confused and tends to have more delusions. She may have a sense of duality, or a sense that she is divided into two parts. Strange things may seem familiar, and it feels as if she is in a dream. Because she often doesn't know what is real, her confusion makes it hard for her to make decisions, and as a result, her behavior can become somewhat chaotic at times.

In the Pulsatilla remedy picture we also find many anxious delusions. In her delusions she is surrounded by strangers. She sees people, possibly criminals or enemies, who may be pursuing her. She feels obliged to scream and attempts to escape. She looks around and sees that the world is on fire. She can see the flames, and she can also see big eyes looking at her. There are animals, too, black cats and dogs, insects and bees. If her delusions scare her enough, she may even develop a fear of real dogs.

Generally, twilight and evenings aggravate all her mental symptoms. She is afraid of the dark, and she can see images just by closing her eyes. There may be phantoms, specters, ghosts and spirits, and she may even see black forms in her dreams. The visions can be so horrible that she strikes at them or holds up a cross. She may also have religious delusions, where she sees the devil and is afraid that he may take her away. She is afraid of evil and she often fears aloneness and death. She feels better if she can sleep with someone, or if she can at least sleep with the light on, and she has a strong desire for change!

If Pulsatilla becomes too fearful and vulnerable, she may even develop a fear of people in general. If she finds herself in a crowd, her fear may become so strong that she just wants to escape. She can develop a fear of eating (anorexia) or of losing her reason and she may also suffer from claustrophobia in narrow places (too stuffy for her to breathe). Her anxiety and uneasiness is always worse in the dark. She may be so anxious when going to bed in the evening that she may have a hard time falling asleep. Sometimes the anxiety drives her out of bed, especially if she wakes up from frightful dreams in the middle of the night.

The most peculiar thing about Pulsatilla is that all her symptoms are usually better in open air, and worse in warm, stuffy rooms. She needs to loosen her clothing and open the windows, or even better, go for a walk outside to feel better.

Besides being affected by warm stuffy rooms, Pulsatilla is also often affected by hormonal changes before her period and around the time of menopause. Her anxiety can also be affected by too much mental exertion, which also tends to affect her ability to think. She feels dull and sluggish and often finds it difficult to concentrate. At times, she can even develop a strong aversion to reading or other mental work, especially if her mind is overloaded, and her sense of brain-fag becomes exhausting. In addition, her memory can also be affected by stress. She may develop a weakness for expressing herself, or a weakness for remembering words or names. Sometimes she makes mistakes speaking or spelling, or she may even go completely unconscious, especially in a crowded or warm, stuffy room. The unconsciousness can be transient (passing out for a few moments), or she can actually go into a coma.

Pulsatilla is often very restless. The restlessness is worse at night and in the morning after rising. Sometimes she finds herself tossing about in bed, especially when the room is too hot or if the bed covers are too warm. She often has a hard time sleeping, and the restlessness can easily drive her out of bed.

Not only is she restless, but Pulsatilla can also become very irritable, especially in the morning on waking. She may become irritable when questioned, and she may feel easily offended. There is irritability with sadness and the irritability is always worse in a warm room. Her moods can often be quite repulsive and her irritability can sometimes turn into anger.

When Pulsatilla is angry, she may not even want to talk to anyone. Her anger may have been triggered because of something that was said or from having to answer questions when she doesn't want to talk. When Pulsatilla is angry, her face turns red and at that point she can become quite furious: shrieking, screaming and shouting in anger, even though the anger doesn't make her feel good. She often feels frightened or sad after that kind of angry outburst, and the whole thing will most probably end in tears.

Pulsatilla can also become rash or hasty when she is upset about something. She may do things as fast as she can, almost getting a bit manic at times, but she doesn't feel good after hurrying either. The anger and rashness only appears when Pulsatilla feels far off balance since she is usually much sweeter by nature.

If, however, Pulsatilla doesn't consistently get her emotional needs met, she can eventually become quite discouraged, discontented and dissatisfied and she can develop an aversion to almost everything. Sometimes she blames herself for what is wrong, and other times she feels disgusted with everyone else. She may eventually become so lazy that she will have no desire to go to work, or she may develop an aversion to the opposite sex and even to company in general. It is rare that Pulsatilla develops aversion to company, but it can happen. If she is upset with her own family, she may still treat others nicely, but not her own family. She may even pretend she is well when she is very sick, because in this state, she doesn't really care about anything. She may become so indifferent that she doesn't even care about business affairs or the opposite sex. This is a very joyless state where Pulsatilla can become tempted to use alcohol or drugs to make herself feel better. She drinks from sadness, indifference and weakness of character, and she may eventually become a drunkard, or even go insane, as a result of some old grief or humiliation that she simply can't get over. The tendency toward insanity is worse around the time of puberty or menopause. There is also the possibility of insanity from fear of losing her position, as well as the fear of losing her lover. Even if she does go insane, there is still great restlessness, and maybe even a desire to travel. If alcohol doesn't appeal to her, she might decide to turn to religion for comfort instead.

Pulsatilla can become very religious. She may do a lot of praying since she is often full of fears about her salvation. Her religiousness can sometimes be narrow-minded and rigid, even to the point of fanaticism, and she can easily work herself into a frenzy often getting too excited for her own good. Her point of view can turn a bit eccentric, and her religiousness is often just an attempt to compensate for her personal doubts. She may doubt her soul's welfare, and she may even doubt her own ability to recover from whatever she is suffering from. She feels vulnerable and anxious, and if she isn't well cared for in this dimension, she hopes to get her needs met through religious worship instead.

If she still doesn't feel comforted, she may become so weary of life that she starts having suicidal thoughts instead. She thinks about committing suicide by drowning, poisoning, or even by shooting herself. She may find herself in a weeping, tearful mood, loathing both life and work. Pulsatilla craves love and attention, and if she doesn't get it, she may not see much reason to stay alive. She is psychic enough to know if death is coming, and she may either welcome the thought of it, or feel anxious about it. Because Pulsatilla can be hasty, impulsive, courageous and fearless, there is a definite possibility that she could go through with a possible suicide attempt. If, however, someone knew of her state, they may be able to talk her out of it, since Pulsatilla usually feels better when she has company who can help lift her spirit. And, of course, a good cry or a hug always helps!

PULSATILLA PRATENSIS IN RELATIONSHIPS

From the beginning of Pulsatilla's life, she is usually very attached to her mother. She loves to have physical contact with her as much as possible, and she doesn't handle separation well. Pulsatilla children don't like sleeping alone.

They are afraid of the dark, and often insist that their mothers lie down next to them when they go to sleep. It is not unusual to see a Pulsatilla child who is nursing at 3 or 4 years of age because they refuse to use a cup for drinking. Weaning a Pulsatilla can easily become quite a battle of wills since she will stubbornly resist and make her mother feel awful. I remember one Pulsatilla child who refused to quit nursing. She was 4 years old, and her mother was totally exhausted from nursing too much. She also insisted on sleeping between the parents in their bed every night. Needless to say, she wedged herself between them in more ways than one. Anytime the husband wanted her to sleep in her own bed so he could have some time with his wife, Pulsatilla's protests and whining quickly put a stop to any attempts at marital intimacy.

The Pulsatilla child doesn't want to share her mom with anyone else, and she will do whatever she can to make it hard for others to connect with her. She wants all her mom's attention for herself, and she is willing to fight to keep her position if necessary. I saw this clearly one day when I went to see one of my friends. I needed to talk to her about some important issues, but her Pulsatilla girl made it almost impossible to carry on a conversation. As soon as we started, she wanted juice and a bagel, and when the bagel was served, it had the wrong kind of cheese on it, so her mom had to make it for her again. She ate a few bites and then went looking for a toy that she couldn't find, and she started crying hysterically because she had to have it RIGHT NOW! Her mom had to go and help her find the toy, and when she tried to continue our conversation after finding it, the girl made sure she stood between us so I couldn't see her mother's face. She had to tell her mom something, very urgently, but when she got her mom's attention, she couldn't remember what it was. When I asked her if it was alright to talk to her mom for a few minutes more, she told me "NO!" We did eventually finish our conversation, but it took a lot of time and effort, as well as endless interruptions.

One of the worst things that can happen to a Pulsatilla child is having a younger brother or sister. Her position as her mom's favorite child will be threatened, and she will have to share her mom's attention with her new sibling. She will feel very jealous about this new situation and will do whatever it takes to get her position back as her mother's favorite child. One Pulsatilla girl suggested to her mom that they put her new brother in the trash, so they could get rid of him for good. She couldn't see any reason to keep him since he was crying a lot and taking too much of her mom's attention away from her. In other cases, the normally gentle, sweet and mild mannered Pulsatilla child can become quite aggressive towards the person who threatens her connection to her mom. Her aggression can be aimed towards the father, siblings or her mother's girlfriends, or if she has become the "teacher's pet," she could become mean toward anyone else that the teacher also likes.

I have seen many examples of this kind of behavior. A Pulsatilla girl may slam the door to a room open, even though she knows that her baby sister is possibly playing behind it. When her sister gets slammed in the door, she can always pretend it was an accident although she knows very well that it wasn't. One Pulsatilla girl used to play with a smaller girl from the neighbor's house, and I observed how she spent a lot of time trying to convince the smaller girl how much bigger she was, and how she was more capable, stronger, better, prettier, more popular, and more helpful to her mom than the little girl. She had obviously earned her position as the best and most lovable, and wanted to make sure nobody else would threaten her place.

I also watched the same girl trying her best to please her mom by helping her around the house. She was helping her mom in the kitchen cooking, cleaning or folding laundry, frequently asking for praise. She felt very proud of herself for being her mom's favorite helper, and her mother spent a lot of her time giving her attention, help, guidance and affection. Naturally, she couldn't handle separation from her mother well. She tried going to both preschool and kindergarten, and after just a few days in each place, she decided she would rather be at home with her mom.

Pulsatilla's two biggest fears are of losing her position and of abandonment. She compensates for this insecurity by being affectionate, devoted, mild-mannered and sweet, as long as she gets her needs met, but if she doesn't get what she wants, she will whine, complain and manipulate until she gets her way. She wants instant gratification and often has a jealous or selfish attitude, sometimes giving others the impression that she is spoiled. The reason why she behaves like this is her strong need for emotional security and affection.

As Pulsatilla becomes a teenager, she will finally have to let go of her mom before she can create a family of her own. The core situation that goes with Pulsatilla is a situation where she has lost her lover and is continually grieving for her lost love. When she starts becoming interested in finding a mate of her own, it will automatically trigger her fear that she may lose her lover for some reason, and she may become extremely worried and also clingy. She is afraid of abandonment and aloneness, and she compensates for this fear by being as affectionate and loving as she can, so she won't end up alone.

Pulsatilla craves affection and needs a mate who can give her the physical affection as well as the reassurance she needs so she can feel emotionally secure. She is devoted to her loved ones, and her mild mannered personality won't challenge a man's lack of confidence. In fact, she is so utterly feminine in her ways, that she will often attract the exact opposite, a mate who is, or wants to be, very strong, masculine and protective. (And if he isn't as strong as he would like to be, Pulsatilla is still so feminine and helpless that she makes him feel masculine and capable anyway). This is why Pulsatilla often ends up with men who like to be in charge in the relationship. She doesn't mind, since she has a hard time making decisions for herself and she needs a strong man in her life. Pulsatilla is generally easygoing, impulsive, spontaneous and fun to be around. She is innocent, excitable and absolutely adorable, which makes it easy for her to find a mate, although she may have difficulty deciding which one she likes better.

In relationships in general, Pulsatilla hates disharmony and displays of aggression, and she tends to be submissive and avoid conflict as much as she can. This is why Pulsatilla can be very tolerant of abusive relationships as well as dictatorial mates. She often picks a Lycopodium mate who will take good care of her and make her feel safe, even though he may be way too cold for her emotionally. And Lycopodium loves Pulsatilla because she is submissive, looks up to him and lets him be in charge without questioning his authority.

When Pulsatilla is upset, she will cry, or bang the cabinets in her kitchen, maybe even smash a plate or two, but she won't easily go and directly confront the person she is having a problem with. (And this is exactly what Lycopodium likes about her!) If she is pushed far enough, she will eventually express how she feels, and she may even scream and shout doing so, but it doesn't happen very often, and it doesn't make her feel good afterwards.

Even though she may not feel happy in her present relationship, she won't even think of leaving it because she can't bear starting over on her own. Even the idea of leaving is sure to trigger her core issues of losing her lover and feeling abandoned and alone again, which is something she will try to avoid at any cost. So, she tends to stay in the same relationship for a long period of time, regardless of how unhappy she may be with her mate.

THE PULSATILLA MAN

When treating children, it is not unusual to find both Pulsatilla girls and boys, but Pulsatilla is a constitution that can change into other remedies as the child grows older. This is why Pulsatilla is not as common in women as we tend to think, and it is even less common in men. However, I did recently have one interesting encounter with a Pulsatilla man. He came to me because he was in the process of going through divorce, and he wasn't coping well with the stress of the transition. When I asked him what was bothering him the most, he told me it was hard for him to be on his own, and to have to make rational decisions. He told me his wife had always taken care of the bills, paperwork and other practical things that required rational thinking and that he was more of an intuitive, emotional type. He was having a hard time doing these things for himself now. Trying to fill in his divorce papers stressed him out so much that it felt like his brain was freezing up, and he simply couldn't do it. He was in a state of complete exhaustion because he couldn't sleep at night, and he told me the worst time of the day was after midnight, 1 or 2 am. I sensed a certain childishness about him when he told me how lost he felt now that his wife was leaving, and at one point in the interview he almost panicked and needed both of the windows in my office opened. He was able to calm himself only after he deeply breathed in the fresh, cool air from outside.

In some ways, this was an unusual presentation of Pulsatilla. He told me he was never really close to his mother. Both his parents were strict, overprotective and expected a lot from him. He told me how his father had always wanted him to be less soft spoken, and how he was trying as hard as he could to behave in a way that would fulfill his parent's expectations of him. The result was that he completely lost his sense of personal self, and he became so shy that he felt totally isolated. He felt that the world, and the people in it, was too harsh for him, and he developed such a fear of people that he simply couldn't get himself to reach out to others. So, he ended up a loner, desiring company but not knowing how to overcome his shyness so he could connect to others.

It must have been extremely difficult for him to be a Pulsatilla child in a family who wasn't warm emotionally. Pulsatilla needs a warm emotional atmosphere and a strong connection to the mother, more than anything else, because it creates emotional security. Because he wasn't getting these needs met in his family, this man had to find other ways to make himself feel safe. He told me he liked sleeping under heavy bedding because the pressure of the bedding made him feel more secure. He also told me that he sleeps on his back with one hand across his forehead because the pressure of the hand on his head also makes him feel safe.

We usually think of Pulsatilla as someone who is helpless, cute and adorable, and who has a talent for getting people to take care of her. However, a man with the same qualities wouldn't necessarily attract the same kind of help and support that a woman would because we expect men to be more masculine and to be able to take care of their own needs. We expect them to be independent, practical, rational beings that don't need help from others to feel secure. Because this man wasn't at all like that, he simply didn't know how to overcome "the gap" between himself and others. He felt so forsaken and isolated that he was in a state of total hopelessness and helplessness, feeling that he was all alone in the world, and that nobody was there for him (Pulsatilla's core delusion).

When he left my office, one of his tires had gone flat, and my husband helped him put the spare on. He was so grateful for the help he received, that he spontaneously gave him a hug, instead of just shaking hands as a "thanks."

Even though he was shy and found it hard to connect with people, the hug he offered still shows his affectionate and spontaneous Pulsatilla nature.

Because we are all conditioned to think that men should be a certain way and have certain masculine qualities, a Pulsatilla man simply doesn't fit this picture at all. He can therefore end up as a very troubled Pulsatilla that doesn't necessarily show the normal picture of what we think a Pulsatilla is like, and we may have to pinpoint the correct remedy by using physical and general symptoms in addition to the mental and emotional ones.

ALWAYS COMPROMISING
Sepia Succus

REMEDY DESCRIPTION

Sepia Succus is a mild mannered, timid, absent minded type who spends a lot of time buried in thought. She is introspective, meditative, and loves to day dream and theorize. Naturally, she is calm and serene, with a tendency to be critical and serious. She can also be vivacious and passionate when she feels good, but it is easy to get on the wrong side of her because she tends to be overly sensitive to many things. Her self confidence isn't very strong, and because she has a tendency to be too serious, she can easily feel offended about little things. She fears being humiliated, laughed at, mocked or embarrassed and therefore often suffers from anticipation anxiety which can make her want to completely withdraw from others. In addition, Sepia is also profoundly affected by horrible things or sad stories. Too much excitement or strong emotions usually affect her deeply, and besides being emotionally sensitive, she is also affected by cloudy weather, sensual impressions, odors and noise. She startles easily and can sometimes become sad when listening to music.

Sepia is restless and impatient and often feels like she has to hurry. Although she can be very picky about little things, she is not too fastidious, unless she needs to be for some reason.

Work is important to Sepia. She is afraid of poverty and always feels better when she is making money or accomplishing something outside the home. She is very concerned about her position in society and fears losing this position.

Unfortunately, Sepia tends to have a pessimistic outlook on everything. She may be anxious about the future, especially if her business fails or if she loses her social position for some reason. There are delusions about being poor, and about the possibility of being robbed, and there is a feeling that she is very unfortunate, and that she and the rest of her family will probably starve, so if she does lose her social position, she is in great despair.

Because Sepia is worried about being poor, she sometimes becomes greedy or envious of others if she doesn't accomplish what she wants. She is very stubborn about what she wants, and she is definitely not happy if anyone contradicts her. By nature, Sepia is defiant and has a tendency to argue back. She is suspicious, mistrustful, and can sometimes be secretive, deceitful or sly in order to get her needs met. Because she is not very courageous, she prefers to avoid confrontation completely, if possible.

Sepia is an independent type, but at the same time, she is also very sensitive to the expectations of others, and this is actually her core problem. Because she is so full of cares and worries about her domestic affairs, she often ends up compromising what she wants for what her family wants. It is important to Sepia that she keeps her family happy first, even if it means that she doesn't get to do what she wants a lot of the time. So there is always this conflict between Sepia's need to be independent, her desire to work, and her family's needs. Sepia has a hard time saying no and always ends up doing things she doesn't really want to do while putting her own desires on the "back burner." She eventually ends up feeling weak, empty and exhausted with a strong desire for something in her life to change, but she doesn't have enough energy to actually do something about it.

The reason why Sepia often compromises her need to be independent for her family's needs is because she doesn't want her mate to reject her. In Sepia, there are ailments from disappointed love, scorn or just disappointment in general. She is also very sensitive to deception and grief. She tends to hold on to the memories of sad happenings from the past and often hates the people who offended her, similar to Nat Mur. There is also a feeling, deep down, that she is not loved or appreciated enough by her parents, friends or husband, which makes her feel very sad. In this state, she will either complain about the people in her life, or she tends to become hypercritical.

Sepia's continuous compromising in relationships eventually leads to confusion, exhaustion, and potentially, serious physical ailments, like stroke, diabetes and colon cancer. When she is confused or exhausted, she often doesn't know what to do and tends to feel as if she is in a dream; she may not know what is real, and everything may seem strange to her. Her confusion, anxiety or anger is usually worse in the morning, and sometimes she becomes so discouraged that she may not even want to get out of bed.

When Sepia gets confused, her brain feels dull and sluggish, concentration becomes difficult, and she may become unable to read. She makes mistakes in speaking, misplacing words or using the wrong words. She tends to feel that relationships are too much of a hassle, and eventually prefers to be alone, even though she may actually fear being alone, too. She may develop an aversion to company and often feels confused or irritable when spoken to. At this point, she just wants to be quiet and be left alone. She may become fearful of going outside, and she may just want to hide under a big rock like a squid, with a black cloud of ink around herself.

If Sepia's family members don't honor her need to be left alone, she can eventually become totally indifferent and develop an aversion to everything in her life, including her children and husband. She feels estranged from her family, her affection is stifled, and she becomes irritable after coition. If it goes too far, she may even become completely averse to coition. At that point, she wishes she could escape from her family and children, but if she does end up leaving, she quickly develops homesickness. Again, there is a contradiction of will.

The problem isn't really that Sepia is unloving, she simply becomes too exhausted to put out any more energy toward other people, and she feels a need to withdraw in order to replenish her own energy. So, although she may seem emotionally cold or indifferent toward her loved ones at times, her indifference is just an expression of the exhaustion she feels after trying to fulfill everyone's expectations of her for too long.

When Sepia is exhausted, she doesn't have any energy left for work, either. She may feel an aversion or indifference toward work, or she may totally lose all ambition and develop a delusion that she is seriously sick so she doesn't have to do anything. If this doesn't work, and if Sepia's wish to be left alone still isn't honored, she can easily become furious, or even violently angry. When she is angry, her body often trembles, and she will either suppress her anger, or express herself rather harshly. She is easily upset by little things and tends to hold on to old issues from the past for too long. However, open conflict usually doesn't make her feel good, either, since she is very affected by the energy of anger, regardless of whether it is her own, or it is coming from others, so she will try to avoid open conflict whenever possible.

After compromising too much, Sepia eventually becomes discontented, displeased and dissatisfied with everything. She has a strong need to be understood by the people in her life and often feels very upset if they don't understand her. If she is not understood, she can become critical, faultfinding, harsh, abusive, insulting, malicious, spiteful, vindictive, and quarrelsome. She often shrieks, screams and shouts. Her moods can alternate between anger and anxiety since she easily becomes frightened and often feels anxious when thinking about something unpleasant. She may feel anxious about real or imagined disease, or about thunderstorms, and eventually, she becomes totally exhausted from too much worry. The interesting thing is that even when Sepia is exhausted, she usually feels better from strong physical exertion, like dancing or brisk walking, although she may have to force herself to do so if her exhaustion is too much.

Sepia can become very depressed about her unfortunate situation. When that happens, she usually feels better after a good cry, but not from any kind of consolation. She may become hysterical and sob loudly, or her crying may become involuntary, or causeless. At times, her sadness may even alternate with involuntary laughing. She often cries and sighs when telling of her sickness, she enjoys complaining about her situation, and she usually feels better if someone holds her.

Sepia has many fears and delusions. She fears disease, doctors, insanity and death, and she may feel despair about ever recovering. She may even feel like she is dying, and she is often afraid to be alone. Her fear of aloneness is another reason why she compromises in her relationships. In her perception of reality, it is better to compromise, than to not have any people in your life. Therefore, compromise has basically become Sepia's survival mechanism, but this kind of compromise has a high price.

One of my Sepia clients was asked by a dying friend to take her place and raise her son after she passed away. Since it was her dying friend's last wish, Sepia, who was a single mom at the time, couldn't say no, simply because she didn't know how and probably also because she needed someone to take care of her and her children. As soon as the friend died, she married her friend's husband, a man she didn't even like very much, so she could raise his son, who, in her opinion, was nothing but "a fat monster."

11 years later, her body had completely deteriorated. She went from being "fit as a fiddle" to having diabetes, colon cancer and a series of little strokes, and when I saw her, she needed a deep breath from her oxygen bottle just to be able to get both of her feet over the threshold of the entrance door! She had kept her promise to her dying friend, but her sickness was the price she paid for the sacrifice she made against her own will.

At times, Sepia can become very depressed, gloomy, and indifferent about her situation. She just can't seem to find a way to be in relationships without always being forced to compromise. Her misery and exhaustion can eventually become so overwhelming that she totally loses her will to live. At this point, Sepia can either turn to religion for comfort and courage, or she may start thinking suicidal thoughts or wish she were dead. However, it isn't likely that she may have enough energy to actually kill herself, in which case she will simply remain stuck and withdrawn, hoping that her unfortunate situation will somehow, miraculously, change by itself.

SEPIA SUCCUS IN RELATIONSHIPS

To Sepia, relationships are mainly a burden. A perfect partner, from Sepia's perception, would be a partner who could be responsible for his own happiness and not expect it to come from her. If Sepia could find a partner who would support her independence and allow her to fulfill her heart's desire, without asking anything in return, especially sexually, it would be a dream come true. But most Sepias always end up with mates who expect more from them than they are willing to give. One Sepia client said it very simply; "You meet a man and you think he is nice, but then he changes!" This woman's favorite book, which she read from cover to cover, was called: "I hate you, don't leave me!" This very short title contains the core of Sepia's problem; she doesn't want her mate to leave her because she is too dependent on him for whatever reason, so she has to keep compromising to make sure he doesn't leave, and she hates him for having to do so!

The reason why relationships are so hard for Sepia is the fact that Sepia wants more for herself than just being a mom or a caretaker. Sepia fears poverty and always feels better when she works. She is often ambitious and likes making money because money equals independence. Because she wants more out of life than just washing dishes and changing diapers, there is always an inner conflict between her relationship duties versus her desire to pursue her own needs or interests. She may have a strong need to do something more creative, or pursue a specific career, even if it is just on a part time basis. She likes the feeling of accomplishing things, and she often has strong creative urges and abundant ideas for future projects she would like to carry out, if only she had enough time. At the same time, she feels that she is very much needed at home, especially if she has small children. Because she is a responsible type, she does whatever she can to fulfill her duties at home first, or she may even try to do both and eventually ends up feeling totally exhausted and drained. This is what triggers Sepia's darker side. Either she withdraws and develops aversion to her family members, or she starts expressing her discontent harshly to the people around her.

It is no fun to be around a Sepia who has compromised too much. She is very miserable: complaining, weeping, nagging, or screaming. She becomes irritable or indifferent, and she just wants to be left alone with no expectations put on her, and nobody talking to her. One Sepia woman told me how she would sometimes feel so exhausted that she would constantly postpone things she needed to do because she couldn't bare the thought of doing anything or of even talking to anyone. She was too exhausted, and she just wanted to be left alone without anyone expecting anything from her. Sometimes she didn't even return her phone messages or answer her emails because she just didn't have enough energy. Sepia is a remedy made from cuttlefish juice, and this is what the cuttlefish likes to do, too. When life is too much, it likes to sit alone under a rock and hide behind a big, black cloud of ink, hoping nobody can see it.

Sepias often feel depressed about their situation. On one hand, they can't stop compromising, even when they feel that people are expecting too much from them, and on the other hand, they often can't say anything about it, either, because they are too hypersensitive about what people expect from them. So, they always end up doing what they don't want to do, and this creates resentment towards the people who are making demands on them.

A good example of this is post partum depression, which is a common thing, especially in a career woman who has had to change her lifestyle drastically after having a baby. An independent woman could easily experience motherhood as a shock, especially if she was totally unprepared for the level of surrender needed to take care of a newborn baby. In a situation like that, it is common for women to feel resentment towards the baby, which is something a few doses of Sepia can help to resolve.

Sepia is naturally independent, but not independent enough to do what she wants without also considering what would make her family happy. Sepia feels guilty if she becomes too selfish, and she often blames herself when things don't work out. One Sepia woman got pregnant so easily that she ended up with 4 children very early in her life. She was an independent type who liked doing "her own thing," but she kept having babies and started feeling stuck and tied down. Between diaper changes, night time feedings and her husband's insatiable appetite for sex, there wasn't much time or energy left for pursuing her artwork, nurturing her spiritual needs or finding ways to replenish her constant lack of energy. After her last baby was born, she felt that she needed to simply get away from it all. She decided to follow her heart and go on a spiritual quest, and as soon as the baby was old enough, she went on a trip to see her spiritual teacher in order to nurture her soul and find her connection to source again. She felt guilty for leaving all her children behind, including the new baby, but she never had any time to nurture her own needs, and she *had to* have a break! She was gone for a month, but when she came back again, she was full of inspiration and had a new zest for life. Although both her children and her husband resented her for a while, they were ultimately better off having a happy mom again.

A more extreme version of this is the issue of sexual abuse. One male Sepia client was sexually abused as a young child and the experience filled him with such horror, that he was never able to get over it. Being sexually abused is worse for Sepias than for any other constitution, because they already have core issues about being forced to do things against their will, and core issues are always painful and affect people deeply.

Although Sepia often feels exhausted by the needs of her children or mate, she is usually a good mom and tends to raise psychologically healthy children. Because she values her own independence, she doesn't usually interfere with her children's independence either. She is often supportive and encouraging when her children want to pursue their own interests, and she allows them a lot of freedom to explore because she isn't overly protective.

It is common for a lot of women to enter into a Sepia state around the time of menopause, even though they may not be Sepias constitutionally. Natrum Muriaticum is one of the remedies that often turn into Sepia around this time. From a homeopathic perspective this makes sense because Natrums are very duty bound and tend to build up resentment towards the people they are trying to please. Eventually, they may start becoming more independent and develop a desire to pursue a career of their own after raising their children. They may finally feel that it is time to nurture their own needs, and this is often when Sepia symptoms starts showing up. Sepia is more independent than Natrum, but she is still very concerned about keeping her family happy, and she often feels the conflict between family needs and her own needs.

The issue of compromise often ends up ruining Sepia's relationships, so it is a very important issue to address. If the people in her life expect or require her to compromise too much, she may even become physically ill as a result, or she may come to the conclusion that she is actually better off living alone. A better conclusion would be the possibility of dealing with the issue of compromise in a way that allows her to be independent without feeling guilty. If she could find a way to state her needs and get her partner to understand and support her in fulfilling those needs, she could find her happiness again and the tension in the relationship would be greatly reduced. Getting her partner's support is very important to her because it will help her validate her needs without guilt or a sense of selfishness and it will also help her stop compromising, thereby reducing her feeling of resentment.

STUBBORN AND INDECISIVE
Silicea Terra

REMEDY DESCRIPTION

Silicea Terra is naturally a mild mannered, timid, reserved type with a quiet, yielding disposition. She is careful and cautious, likes being told what to do by someone else and often respects and admires the people around her.

Silicea doesn't like seriousness. She can be as light hearted as Phosphorus, but she usually has more intellectual depth. She is generally optimistic, cheerful and affectionate, easily excited and loves having fun. Her sex drive can be high, and she knows how to flatter people. Because Silicea is a dependent type, she needs a strong reliable mate, and, luckily, she knows how to attract one.

By nature, Silicea is a sensitive being. She is sensitive to mental impressions, horrible things and sad stories, and she is often haunted by persistent thoughts, especially about unpleasant subjects. Therefore, she doesn't easily let go of things. Silicea is also sensitive to touch and noise and she startles easily. Loud thunderstorms scare her, and she is so sensitive to touch that she may eventually develop an aversion to touch or even a fear of pins or pointed things. (This also reflects how "touchy" she is emotionally). In addition, Silicea doesn't always sleep well, either. She may stay awake from a rush or flow of thoughts, or she may do things in her sleep, like whimpering, walking, laughing or talking loudly.

Silicea is naturally cautious and timid. In addition, she is obviously also a very delicate, refined and somewhat fragile person who doesn't have a strongly defined sense of self. She often feels confused about her identity, and sometimes she feels as if she is in a dream. There is a sense of duality, and also a strange feeling of the body being divided in half. According to her delusions, she sometimes feels as if the left side doesn't belong to her, her head seems too large, or she feels like she is in two places at the same time.

Confusion about identity and difficulty knowing what is real is something you can expect in all the more sensitive types. They don't have very strong personal boundaries that can give them a sense of separation, which is something that is necessary for developing a strong sense of self. Therefore, Silicea often suffers from a lack of confidence. She is a mental type who prefers to hide how capable she is intellectually. Instead, she hesitates and holds back timidly, giving others the impression that she doesn't know what to do, even though this is not so. The truth is that when Silicea holds back, timidly, she does this from a lack of confidence, not from a lack of ability (this is similar to what some Lycopodiums also do).

Irresolution or indecision is another thing you can also expect to find in someone with a weak sense of self. Silicea usually has a hard time making decisions, or even keeping her promises, because her will is so weak that she much prefers to have others make the decisions for her instead so she doesn't have to worry about the consequences of her choices. This is why Silicea tends to be a dependent type.

The remedy Silicea is a Tubercular remedy, similar to Phosphorus. The Tubercular remedies are influenced by both Psora and Syphilis. If the Psoric influence is stronger, the person will have a clear, active and objective mind with abundant ideas, a love for theorizing and a good ability for intellectual depth. If the Syphilitic influence is stronger, Silicea can become dull and sluggish with difficulty thinking and comprehending. This explains why some Siliceas are quick, bright and intelligent, while others are slow, dull and sluggish. However, both types of Silicea have a tendency to feel exhausted from too much mental exertion since she doesn't have much stamina mentally or physically. Therefore, she often finds concentration difficult if she has been studying or reading too much, and she sometimes develops an aversion to reading and may even lose her ability to read altogether because of mental overload. When she experiences this kind of brain-fag, she also tends to become forgetful while speaking and frequently makes mistakes, often using the wrong words. She may have difficulty expressing her ideas when writing, and may eventually become totally unable to write anything since writing also makes her feel too tired. The truth is, Silicea isn't really interested in any kind of mental effort. Because her stamina is so low that she can only do a little bit at a time before she becomes exhausted, she tends to postpone everything until the next day if possible. Needless to say, she is often late on her assignments since just thinking about the effort it will take can be enough to exhaust her and tempt her to postpone the whole task.

So far we have seen how Silicea is a timid, dependent, mild mannered and cautious type with a lack of self confidence. She often has a hard time making decisions, but when she actually does make a decision, she can become as hard as flint (reflecting the quality of the mineral Silica) and stick to her views with extreme obstinacy. Her ideas can become very fixed, and she may defend her views fiercely by scolding or by becoming surprisingly quarrelsome. She can even become haughty, self righteous or contemptuous, if she finds it necessary, and she will defend her position in a way that no one would expect from a mild mannered, timid, reserved type. At this point, she can also become both critical and intolerant of contradiction, or even violently angry when crossed. She may lose her self control completely, and start screaming and shouting in abusive or insulting ways, and this surprising combination of traits is very characteristic for Silicea. Her proud, stubborn attitude combined with a somewhat fragile and refined quality indicates that Silicea also is a person of high rank, similar to Phosphorus and Pulsatilla.

Silicea's tendency to be extremely fragile, delicate and refined makes me think of the story of "The Princess on the Pea." (The funny thing is that many of my Silicea clients have told me that their parents used to call them "the princess on the pea" when they were children). Like the princess in the story, Silicea definitely looks like a princess with her slim, beautiful body and graceful movements. She also has a certain attitude, or air of nobility, about her, in addition to her fragile and delicate nature. In the story of "The Princess on the Pea," this quality alone is the sign of a true princess.

For anyone who doesn't know this story, here is a very short version of it. In this story, the prince was looking for a true princess to marry, and although there were many princesses to choose from, nobody fit his criteria of what a true princess really was. Finally, one day, a beautiful woman knocked on the door of the castle in the middle of the night and asked for a place to sleep. Although she looked like a princess, the queen first wanted to test her to determine if she really was a true princess, or not. She put a pea under 10 mattresses, and 10 down duvets, and told the girl to sleep on top. The next morning, she asked how the girl had slept, and the girl told her she hadn't slept at all. She was black and blue all over because the bed had been so horribly uncomfortable. When the queen heard this, only then did she know for sure that the girl really was a true princess because only a true princess could be so sensitive that she would be able to notice a small pea under all those mattresses.

Because of Silicea's sensitive and delicate nature, little things are often very important to her. She is anxious and conscientious about trifles, and blames herself whenever anything goes wrong. Silicea has a strong sense of guilt and remorse, which also goes with the delusion that she has done something wrong. The reason why she is so concerned about little things, and so willing to defend her views in spite of her natural shyness, is because she is desperately trying to keep up a certain image to the world. And, this brings us to the original situation that goes with Silicea.

In the original situation, she may have been someone of high rank, possibly a princess, and everything about her is very refined. She is conscientious about little things because she is always worried about her public image. She is afraid to appear in public, she fears that her gestures are awkward, and sometimes she can't even bear to be looked at. Some day she is expected to take over the position as queen, and she strongly feels the need to create and uphold an image worthy of her future position. Her need to uphold this image makes her extremely nervous and tense every time she has to do something in public because she is afraid that if she ruins her image, she'll prove herself unworthy. This gives her anticipation anxiety, especially before examinations or tests, where her performance will be judged, or before public engagements, where she is the focus of everyone's attention. This is also reflected in the story of the "Princess on the Pea" where the old queen has to test her first, to see if she is worthy, before she is allowed to marry the prince. If she hadn't passed the test, she wouldn't have become the future queen, so it is no wonder she always feels nervous, anxious and apprehensive before going through any kind of tests.

Leaving the fairy tale behind, we can easily imagine what a real princess would feel like in public with people watching her every gesture. She is scared! What if she does something awkward? What if something goes wrong? What if she can't keep up her image, which is an image she has to uphold at any cost, as if her survival depends on it! (Actually, her position as princess or queen depends on it, but to Silicea, it feels like her survival is only possible if she can keep her position). She would much prefer to hide in the shadow of someone else and get no attention at all. At least then, she wouldn't feel judged or have to worry about making mistakes all the time. This is also why Silicea is so timid when she has to appear or speak in public. She is so afraid of failure that she prefers not doing anything because she is sure that everything she does will fail and if it fails, her image will be ruined, and if her image is ruined, she is doomed. Therefore, she prefers to not work at all, just to avoid the possibility of failure. And not only that, she doesn't really have the energy to work, anyway. After all, she is a princess, and princesses don't really have to work, or even do any kind of housekeeping. Being lazy and frivolously squandering money fits the image of being a princess much better. A princess doesn't have to worry about money issues, because she is supposed to get all her needs taken care of by someone else, someone who will deal with those kinds of issues in her life.

So, what happens then, if Silicea isn't able to keep up her image to the world? What if she didn't pass the test, or fulfill the expectations which had been put on her, and she had to leave the castle and take care of herself? The idea of this possibility scares her very much. She simply wouldn't know how to survive, and she could easily develop fear of the dark or anxiety about the future, or even about her health! This is why she has to try to keep up her image, no matter what, so she won't ever have to experience being on her own.

In the Silicea remedy profile we see that she also has a fear of falling, which doesn't just mean a fear of physically falling. This fear also symbolizes her fear of falling from her position of royalty.

To Silicea, losing her position would be nothing less than a disaster! Not only does she not know how to take care of herself, but she would also feel vulnerable to all kinds of horrible things since she has no idea how to really be on her own. Who knows what could happen to her? Perhaps someone would walk up behind her, or next to her, or someone could get into her house, or someone could intend to injure her. There could even be criminals, thieves or robbers who would try to take her possessions. Her imagination is strong enough to envision all kinds of frightful images and horrible visions of the bad things that could possibly happen to her, and that is why she'll do anything in her power to avoid this possibility.

The delusions that go with each remedy profile always tend to reflect different aspects of the original story that has long since been forgotten on a conscious level. In this story, the princess did lose her position and her home. She found herself on a journey, alone, homesick and full of cares and worries. She felt beside herself, almost hysterical, and she desperately wanted someone to be with her, hold her, and make her feel safe. On her own, she often feels sad, depressed and gloomy. She thinks that she may have been deceived by a friend, and her moods may change often. She complains in her grief, and at times she feels very discouraged, discontented or even disgusted with everything in her life. At this point, she may have no desire to be around other people. She is inconsolable, and there is nothing anyone can say to make her feel better. She doesn't want to talk to anyone and she may even develop an aversion to being spoken to. She becomes irritable if anyone still speaks to her, and her symptoms are often worse during menses.

A Silicea who has been betrayed, or lost her position, will often become both suspicious and impatient. She will feel an internal restlessness, maybe even a manic feeling at times. She is in a hurry to get back to her old position again, and she may even feel greedy or ungrateful when thinking about the way things have turned out. She doesn't really know what she wants, but if she sees something she wants or needs, she doesn't mind just taking it, simply because she feels that she deserves it. Therefore, Silicea doesn't mind being deceitful or sly, if that is what it takes for her to get what she wants, since she isn't very brave. She doesn't mind bargaining, lying or being dishonest or hypocritical, if there is a chance that it will help her get her position back, and if she becomes desperate enough, she can even go insane. She may want to kill whoever deceived her, or she will just sink into indifference or a state of deep apathy, where nothing matters to her anymore. At this point, Silicea may turn to alcohol for relief, or possibly to religion for courage and support. If, however, the situation doesn't improve, she may become both weepy and weary of life. Because life no longer seems to have any meaning to her, she may start desiring death instead. She may feel like she is dying, she may have a sensation of death (clairvoyance), or she may become suicidal and think about killing herself by drowning, or by throwing herself from a height. However, it isn't very likely that she will actually go through with it because she won't be able to make up her mind, and she'll probably end up postponing the whole issue, anyway.

The combination of indecision, stubbornness, fixed ideas of how things should be, as well as the tendency to postpone things, often gives Silica a peculiar feeling of stuckness and inability to create any change in her life. She craves change, even though change scares her more than anything, but the fear of losing control and of not knowing what is going to happen if something changes, holds her back. The feeling of oppression and stuckness, with desire for change, is a reflection of the Tubercular aspect of Silicea, since Tubercular remedies often have a strong feeling of oppression or stuckness, as well as a great desire for change. So, the lessons Silicea is here to learn has to do with learning to be on her own, trusting her own abilities more, and also with learning to become flexible and open to change, none of which is easy for her to do.

SILICEA TERRA IN RELATIONSHIPS

The best mate for Silicea is a leader type who is willing to take charge and provide for her, so she can keep up the standard of living she is used to. She often expects her mate, or parents, to provide for her, since she is a bit of a princess. She likes being dependent on others and prefers not to have to work to support herself. She also likes being "in the shadow" of her mate, where he gets the public attention and she doesn't, so she avoids being judged by anyone. Silicea prefers to be alone, rather than attract any attention to herself, so she is more than happy to let her mate get the attention instead. That way she doesn't risk ruining the image she is trying to uphold. Silicea is usually timid and irresolute in relationships, and doesn't mind if her mate is in charge and makes most of the decisions, except of course, if she has already made up her mind about something. If that is the case, she can be unbelievably stubborn, and doesn't let go of the issue, no matter what happens.

One of my Silicea clients presented a strong image of being a spiritual person with a very open mind. He told me he had overcome all his childhood issues and, therefore, refused to talk about anything from his childhood. He suffered from horrible migraines for 30 years after exposure to asbestos (a silica compound), and he wanted to explore what homeopathy could do for his condition. He didn't mind telling me about his physical symptoms, but any questions about his mental, or emotional state, made him tired and irritable. Once he even got up in the middle of the consultation and told me he had to leave because he couldn't handle that much thinking. This is when I started wondering why he actually came for a consultation in the first place, when he didn't want to answer any personal questions which were relevant to his case, but it all started making sense as the case progressed.

I gave him Silicea for his headaches based mostly on his physical symptoms, and the fact that the headaches initially appeared after exposure to asbestos. The most peculiar thing about the headaches was that they were always improved by any kind of heat, hot wraps, hot water, hot tea, even heat from the sun! This all pointed towards Silicea.

He took a dose of Silicea 30c and experienced a horrible aggravation for a couple of days. I told him to wait until the aggravation passed and then dose himself on an as needed basis, with a follow up in a month.

After a month he came back and told me he didn't know if the remedy had been doing anything at all. I asked if he was still doing his allopathic pain and sinus medicines, and he told me he had stopped all that. He still insisted that the remedy didn't have anything to do with it, and he couldn't tell if the headaches were still there or not. I found this statement very strange, since his headaches were often serious enough that he frequently ended up in the emergency room, so why was he not able to tell if they were gone or still there?

At this point I was confused and didn't really know where to go next. However, I don't usually give up on a remedy unless I have tried it in at least 2 different potencies, so I decided to try Silicea 200c. On the next follow up he told me that he had taken a dose when his head was hurting. I asked if it had any effect, and he said he couldn't tell. I asked again if the pain had improved at all during the last month, or if it had remained the same or worse. He still couldn't answer. I also asked if the frequency of the headaches had changed in any way. Again he said: "I don't know, I really can't tell." I told him to try a dose of the 200c weekly for a while, and see what would happen, and on the next follow up, I found that he had stopped taking the homeopathic remedy and resumed taking all his old allopathic medicines again. He told me that my remedy didn't work, and that his headaches were just as bad as they had always been. I told him then that I simply couldn't help him, and he answered happily with his arms crossed in front of his chest: "No, that's right! Your remedies don't work for me!"

At that time a friend of mine confessed that this client hadn't actually come to me on his own initiative, rather she had convinced him to come and see me. My personal feeling is that he came to see me so his friend wouldn't judge him or think him closed minded. This was so important to him, that he was willing to pay my fee with his hard earned money, just to prove that homeopathy couldn't help him. This also explains why he didn't show any personal interest in homeopathy, or have any motivation to cooperate with me while taking his case, and he didn't seem to have any interest in actually using the remedy I suggested, either. He had been doing allopathic medicine for his headaches for so long that he felt comfortable with doing what he was familiar with since he was convinced that nothing was going to cure his condition anyway. He was annoyed to have to answer personal questions that could challenge his image of being spiritually advanced and open minded, and he kept telling me not to feel bad if I couldn't help him. Finally, I understood! He didn't actually want my help! He only wanted to be able to say that he had tried homeopathy, and that it didn't work for him, and then go back to what he was doing in the first place! (This case was from my earlier days as a homeopath. If someone like that came to see me now, I would simply tell the person to come back again at a later time when they were more ready to work with me.)

This case shows the quiet stubbornness that goes with Silicea. When Silicea's mind has been made up, the ideas can be absolutely fixed. No matter how convincing your arguments are, she (or in this case, he) will quietly stick to what she feels, regardless of whether she is right or not. This is one of Silicea's biggest problems in relationships, too. Once she makes up her mind, you don't have to bother arguing because you are just going to waste your time. This lack of flexibility can make Silicea a bit of a challenge to live with.

Another challenge for Silicea is the combination of indecision and stubbornness. A male Silicea client was so depressed that he had almost lost his will to live because his life was so stagnant that he just couldn't stand it any longer. He told me that this has been a pattern throughout his life. He "gets into a groove" and when he gets tired of it, he can't seem to find a way out. He had a history of changing jobs and short lived relationships, and it was always the same story. Once he was familiar with something, and there were no more challenges, the feeling of stagnancy would creep in again and make him feel that life was totally meaningless. In the interview I found that he had a brilliant mind and could produce fantastic ideas on the spur of the moment, but he always ended up talking himself out of things, or simply postponing them. His critical nature combined with a lack of self confidence and indecision made it impossible for him to move forward. In addition to indecision, we can add stubbornness, resistance to change and a tendency to postpone, and we end up with total stagnancy. Changing the external circumstances only made him feel better until the newness wore off again, and by the time he came to me for a remedy, he had seen that this was a pattern that wouldn't go away by a change of scenery. I decided to give him Silicea, and after I described the remedy picture to him, he started feeling very cautious. He wanted a very low potency to start with, and at first, he couldn't even decide if he wanted to take the remedy or not. What if it was going to change him too much? There were many things that he liked about himself, and he wasn't sure if it was worth changing, or if he would be better off staying with his old, familiar self. This shows how hard it is for Silicea to embrace anything new, even though they may be miserable with their present situation.

This issue often shows up as a general lack of spontaneity in Silicea's relationships. Because Silicea's ideas are fixed, she doesn't easily adapt to any spontaneous suggestions from the people in her life, and this can easily become a continuous source of conflict, especially if she has chosen a more spontaneous type for a mate. Maybe she will choose a mate who is very different from herself because she instinctively knows that she needs to loosen up a bit and learn how to let go, but that is usually easier said than done for someone who resists change and is naturally stubborn and cautious.

HUMILIATION AND LACK OF RESPECT
Staphysagria

Staphysagria is extremely sensitive to any kind of insults, real or imagined, as well as rudeness, reprimands or injustice. He always tends to take things the wrong way because of what you said, or the way you said it, or the attitude he was able to hear in your voice, or the energy behind your words. He is so sensitive and conscientious about little things that it doesn't matter if you meant to insult him or not. He just *knows* that you are trying to insult or offend him, and if he feels that way, there is nothing you can do to convince him otherwise. This kind of hypersensitivity is characteristic of all the plant remedies, but especially so in Staphysagria. Staphysagria is particularly sensitive to insults because he is trying to uphold his dignity at any cost, as if his survival depends on it.

Dignity is a huge issue for Staphysagria because he is naturally a proud type. Originally, he may have come from an honorable, dignified background. Although he may be poor at the moment, and you may not be able to see how dignified he really is, he'll be more than happy to enlighten you. Don't you know who I am???? Staphysagria loves talking about his own greatness. He feels that he is so much greater than everyone else; he just doesn't know why they can't see it and treat him with the respect he deserves. Staphysagria doesn't even mind lying about his greatness if necessary, and he often appears obstinate, disobedient and critical of others. This is where Staphysagria differs from Sulphur, who is another proud type with very high thoughts of himself. Sulphur doesn't care if anyone else thinks he is great, while Staphysagria's feeling of greatness very much depends on whether others can see it and appreciate it in him, or not.

Looking at the ailments and delusions that go with the remedy, the same issues are reflected there. Being insulted, humiliated or embarrassed is the worst thing that can possibly happen to Staphysagria. He is so afraid to lose his position in society that he often develops fear of high places, or fear of falling, and he has to maintain self-control at any cost, so he doesn't end up doing something that can hurt his reputation or position. If he is insulted by someone lower than himself, he can't even allow himself to react at all. If he reacts, the risk of losing his dignity is too great, so he prefers to suppress all his feelings, instead, in an effort to preserve his image and reputation. His self confidence is so dependent on what others think of him, that, in a sense, he is actually dependent on the people who insult him! Therefore, he makes such an effort to try to please others that he can completely lose his sense of self in the process. (This is why Staphysagria is a cancer remedy since cancer has to do with suppression of the self).

To understand where Staphysagria is coming from, we first need to look deeper into why he perceives his reality the way he does, and we also need to see if we can figure out why everyone insults him, even though he bends over backwards to please them. What exactly happened to Staphysagria when he was a child?

You'll find that most Staphysagrias had very strict upbringing. Most likely, he had controlling, disapproving parents who would punish or insult him if he ever expressed his discontent about anything, so he learned at an early age to avoid confrontation and keep things to himself. He became such an expert on guessing what others expected from him, even before it was voiced, that he became totally clueless about his own wants or needs because that wasn't where his focus was. However, this kind of suppression can have serious consequences for Staphysagria. One of the problems is that the more he compromises his own needs in relationships to others, the more resentment he builds up inside. In addition, he doesn't have a lot of energy or stamina when it comes to doing things. He often finds it difficult to concentrate, since his mind can't handle much mental exertion, and he may develop an aversion to reading, writing or concentration in general. At the same time, he feels that it doesn't really matter whether he knows how to read or write well, because he believes that he is such a great person that he deserves to be respected anyway, without having to do anything to earn it. This is the reason why the people in his life often perceive Staphysagria as a "good for nothing bum," since he is often lazy and doesn't want to do much. So, naturally, this is one of the first insults Staphysagria hears as a child, and it often comes from his mother, who can be extremely ambitious (and frustrated) on his behalf.

Because Staphysagria's mind can't handle much mental exertion, he tends to give up easily. His mind goes into overload from too much mental stimulation, and this can happen from studying, reading and writing, and also from conversation, emotion, humiliation or masturbation. His mind is often dull with a lack of ideas, and he may also have difficulty thinking and comprehending. Because he has a hard time concentrating, his thoughts tend to vanish while speaking, or if he is interrupted. His memory is weak for places, and for what he has read, and he frequently makes mistakes in speaking, writing or math.

Mathematical calculations or algebra are often a bit of a mystery to Staphysagria. He may even find it hard to measure anything accurately because he tends to be dyslexic and mix up the numbers. Even the thought of doing math can be enough to fill him with a sense of horror, so that is another thing he will do whatever he can to avoid.

One Staphysagria man wanted to learn cabinet making from a local cabinet maker who had more work than he could handle, and who was willing to teach an apprentice. He lasted about three days before he got fired because he kept making mistakes measuring and cutting the wood. The cabinetmaker, who valued accuracy and perfect workmanship, simply couldn't afford to have that much wood wasted. So Staphysagria proved himself to be good for nothing, and the cabinet maker had no choice but to fire him since he didn't do the job right. I have seen similar things happen to several other Staphysagrias, too. They want respect and appreciation, but they don't make enough effort to get it, and when they suffer the consequences of their own lack of effort, they resent people for not giving them the respect they feel entitled to.

Staphysagria's lack of stamina and inability to do things properly, combined with a general lack of will power, often leads to laziness and a desire to just sit around and do nothing. What is the point of doing anything if nobody will appreciate his efforts anyway? He might as well daydream instead!

Staphysagria loves daydreaming. In his dreams everything is perfect. Nobody can tell him that he did something wrong, or that what he did wasn't good enough. This is so appealing to Staphysagria that he prefers dreaming about what he is going to do, rather than actually doing it. Sometimes the dreams and fantasies feel so real that Staphysagria can't tell what is actually real, or what is not. He may think he has completed a task that he hasn't even started, and he can spend days dreaming about the future and just frittering away his time. In his dreams and fantasies his mind is clear and his ideas are abundant. He is often sleepy and dull in the daytime but experiences a rush of thoughts and mental clarity at night which often causes sleeplessness. He tosses and turns in bed, and his thoughts frequently dwell on sexual matters or great plans for the future.

Naturally, you will find that Staphysagria's relationships to women are often complicated as well. Because he is an affectionate type and his sex drive is strong, he loves *the idea* of seducing a woman. Therefore, he often flatters women any way he can in an effort to seduce them. But, at the same time, he is also afraid of rejection, humiliation and embarrassment, and, therefore, he may prefer to hold back, suppress his sexuality and enjoy his fantasies instead. This is why dating on the internet appeals so much to Staphysagria. He can fantasize about all the beautiful women he is connecting with, but he doesn't actually

169

have to meet any of them in person, so there is no risk of rejection, insult or embarrassment. In fact, on the internet, he can have as many girl friends as he wants, since none of them will know about the others. That way, if one of them turns him down, there will always be others...

Because Staphysagria doesn't like the possibility of ruining his reputation, he is often timid, cowardly and yielding in his relationships to women. He has an effeminate quality that makes him seem more like a boy than a man, which may or may not appeal to the women he is trying to seduce. It is almost as if his female energy is too strong compared to his male energy. Perhaps the reason for this is that he has suppressed so much of his anger and aggression that the rest of his male energy has also been suppressed. Therefore, his inner male and female balance has been disturbed, and the result is that he doesn't come across as very masculine. His energy is more that of a boy, than that of a man. The problem with this is that a boy, who doesn't feel confident around women, has a greater chance of attracting a mother figure than a lover, which is actually a big problem for someone who has a bad relationship to his mom. Attracting another mother figure into his life, makes Staphysagria feel confused, restless and uncomfortable and only adds to the problem that he already has with women.

If Staphysagria actually does end up having sex with a woman, he often experiences peculiar ailments after sexual excitement, coition or sexual excesses. Sex seems to make him restless, forgetful, irritable and even hypochondriacal, since the pressure of trying to perform in bed is another situation with great possibility for humiliation and embarrassment, especially if his erections are unreliable. Therefore, Staphysagrias are always worried. They are worried about having their reputation ruined, and they are worried about losing their position in society. They are worried about being humiliated and having their honor wounded, and because they don't feel at ease around women, the idea of marriage and commitment may seem unendurable. Staphysagria worries about the future and fears the possibility that his family will starve, and he often feels extremely confused about whom to marry, and whether they should have children or not, since he doesn't trust his ability to care for a family.

He also has the delusion that his wife will run away from him. Subconsciously, Staphysagria will try to make this delusion real by behaving in a way that makes it virtually impossible for the relationship to survive, unless he is married to a saint, which is not really likely. It is easy for him to do this, considering the fact that he isn't really motivated to provide for his wife very well, or even to do much else to contribute to the relationship. He would much prefer it if she provided for him, instead, so he could just have an easy life and not have to grow up and be responsible. (This is why Staphysagria often ends up with a very responsible mate, like a Natrum Muriaticum, an Arsenicum or even a Carcinosin, or he tries to find himself a rich girl friend so he never has to worry about money again).

When, or if, his girlfriend or wife does leave the relationship, it affects Staphysagria very deeply, so deeply in fact that he may never be able to get over it. He may be totally consumed with disappointment, jealousy, grief and resentment, and he may not be interested in talking about anything else for years to come. (Staphysagria's jealousy has to do with someone else, who is more highly regarded than himself, taking his place and getting the respect that he feels he should have had).

When looking at the ailments and delusions that go with Staphysagria, we can easily see how he feels about his misfortune. Someone has criticized him rudely and treated him unfairly. He either feels like everything is his fault, blaming himself for creating the situation and losing his dignity, or he totally blames somebody else for everything that has happened. Either way, he feels disrespected and humiliated, yet again, and is sure that someone is out to "get him." His health will start to fail, sickness will come, and someone will probably even murder him. Therefore, Staphysagria feels extremely sorry for himself if someone he cares about dies or leaves the relationship, or they simply don't want him in their lives anymore. He tends to dwell on old grief and offenses from long ago, and keeps going over the issues again and again in his head. He hates those who have offended him or hurt his feelings, regardless of whether they had reason to, or not. He thinks about how things used to be, and feels jealous, unfortunate and ungrateful about his present situation. He pities himself and complains to anyone who lends him an ear.

When Staphysagria is feeling sorry for himself, he cries easily, especially when talking about his unfortunate situation. The interesting thing is the fact that talking about it actually makes him feel worse, but still, he can't stop doing it. There is almost a masochistic quality to Staphysagria where he starts receiving pleasure from the pain, grief and resentment he is feeling, and therefore becomes unable or unwilling to let go of it. In his bleak perception of reality, he is incapable of seeing the possibility that he may have had anything to do with what happened, and he will hate anyone who carefully suggests that he was actually responsible for creating part of the situation he is suffering from. In fact, he may not even know how angry he really is until someone suggests that he was partially responsible, and then it all comes to the surface.

This is because Staphysagria is so good at suppressing his anger that he may not even know that it is there most of the time. The reason why he does this is the fact that if he were to express it openly, he may risk losing control of himself, and therefore also risk losing his dignity in the process. He is so afraid of losing his dignity that he would rather hold everything inside than lose his self control and risk humiliation. But, even when the anger is suppressed, you can easily see the signs of anger, red face, trembling, weakness...

Because Staphysagria takes everything personally and perceives insult even when no one intends to insult him, we can easily imagine how everything that happens to him adds to the anger he already feels. The more anger he has bottled up inside, the harder it is to stay calm, and eventually, the inner tension becomes too much. Staphysagria simply can't hold back any more, and his anger becomes explosive when the tension is finally released. Therefore, he is often totally overreacting to something insignificant, and all of a sudden he is furiously raging. When that happens he can be harsh, abusive, insulting, quarrelsome, vindictive and cruel. He simply doesn't know how to handle the energy of anger in a constructive way because there is too much of it that comes out all at once and also because his anger has deep roots into the past. Not only is he verbally abusive when he gets angry, but he can also get physically violent and destructive to people or things in his environment. He may throw things at the person he is angry with, or he may want to break things or hit someone. He may even become violent enough that he feels like killing someone or setting things on fire.

One very sweet natured Staphysagria told me that he would become violently angry only once every few years, but when the anger came out, it was so strong that it scared him. He couldn't stop himself from smashing things, or pulverizing bricks outside his house, and he felt extremely uncomfortable about this part of himself.

Staphysagria can often be both greedy and ambitious. He likes nice things, but he doesn't necessarily want to put in the effort it takes to get what he wants. The truth is, Staphysagria wants an easy life, where people look up to him and things come to him effortlessly. He doesn't really want to grow up and take on any serious responsibilities, so in some ways, there is definitely a boyish "Peter Pan" quality to Staphysagria. He can be impatient and impulsive and would love to win the lottery, or inherit a fortune from a rich relative. He doesn't mind taking what he wants, if the opportunity presents itself, and he can easily develop a passion for gambling, since gambling also represents an opportunity for easy money. And, while we are talking about easy money, let's not forget about the temptation of using credit cards...

One Staphysagria male told me that he has made most of the money in his life through gambling, and now he is about to realize his most exciting dream, to open his very own bingo place! As a Staphysagria, he couldn't have picked a more suitable business for himself. He has found investors who are willing to put up all the money it takes to get his new business started, and soon he will finally have the opportunity to build a reputation for himself without having to put in too much physical effort to make it happen.

Not all Staphysagrias are lazy, though. There are some Staphysagrias who are hard workers, and who don't mind the responsibility and effort it takes to create the kind of reputation for themselves that they want and feel that they deserve. This type will, most likely, attract fewer insults than the lazier type, and as a result, they are possibly suppressing less negative emotions as well.

If Staphysagria isn't able to keep up his reputation or his dignity, he tends to develop aversion to the people in his life. People represent insults, and insults make him feel worthless, so if nobody respects him, he is better off alone. He feels discontented, displeased and dissatisfied about everything, and often feels very discouraged and sorry for himself. The more he thinks about his misfortune, the worse he feels, even consolation and kind words make him feel bad. He becomes doubtful and suspicious towards people, since he often feels misunderstood and doesn't know who to trust. When he finds himself in this negative frame of mind, he can easily develop an aversion to being spoken to as well as indifference to everything and everybody in his life, including his work.

Staphysagria often feels tempted to escape from his family, since he feels so out of touch with everybody, but if he does escape, he often ends up feeling homesick since he can't handle the aloneness well either. This is when Staphysagria tends to look for other kinds of escape, like alcohol or pot, which dulls his pain and makes it easier for him to avoid his emotional issues. (This is also why a lot of Staphysagrias tend to get very addicted to smoking cigarettes). Because Staphysagrias always try to avoid dealing with their pent up emotions for fear that it will bring up even more pain and discomfort, they often become addicted to drugs and alcohol because they always prefer looking for the easy way out.

When sadness and depression are bogging Staphysagria down, he may also turn to religion for comfort. Trust, faith and forgiveness appeal to him very much, because it doesn't involve any doing or growing up on his part, and there is no risk of humiliation, either. However, if even religion can't help him get over his sadness, he could easily end up becoming suicidal from all the pain he still feels inside that he simply can't get over.

As you might have been able to tell by now, Staphysagrias perceive their reality in a very subjective way, based on what they *think* is real, which could easily be part imagination and part fact (but they often don't know which part is which). They think they are greater than other people, but very much misunderstood, they think they are insulted and unappreciated, whether it is true or not, they think about sex, or work or future, without making any physical efforts to accomplish anything, and they think about death and suicide. However, there is a big difference between *thinking* and *doing*, which Staphysagrias often aren't very clear about.

When Staphysagria starts thinking about death, he may also fantasize about killing himself by drowning, shooting or by throwing himself from a height, but because he is very afraid of death, and he also has a cowardly disposition, there isn't much of a chance that he will actually go through with his idea of committing suicide, even though he does desire death simply because it represents an escape from his miserable life.

STAPHYSAGRIA IN RELATIONSHIPS

Staphysagria is often yielding, timid and easy going in relationships, at least as long as nobody insults him, but for some reason, Staphysagria always attracts insults and humiliations more than any other remedy type.

As a child, Staphysagria quickly learns to suppress and avoid anything that has to do with conflict since conflict usually equals insult and emotional pain, which he is trying to avoid at any cost. Staphysagria often becomes an expert at avoiding conflict and discomfort in relationships by learning to guess what other people's needs are, even before they are verbally expressed. They focus so much of their attention on what others expect or want from them that they often don't even know what their own needs are. In fact, their own needs don't even matter, as long as they can keep their dignity intact and hopefully receive the respect they require in return. Unfortunately, this isn't usually what happens.

Staphysagria's first relationship is to his mother, and this is often where the problem starts. One Staphysagria boy was highly dyslexic and couldn't figure out which way the letters had to go. He didn't do well at school, and his mother was not happy. She took the boy to one psychologist after another to see if anyone could help. He went through every kind of test to find out what was wrong with him, and he continued to go to different kinds of therapy for years since his parents were hoping the problem could be fixed somehow. His main feeling throughout his childhood was that he was faulty, something was wrong with his head, and he was stupid compared to his sisters. He felt humiliated, unappreciated, and preferred daydreaming rather than working hard since he couldn't compete with anyone anyway. This of course, added to his mother's frustration, and she started telling him that he was a good for nothing, lazy bum who would never amount to anything unless he would make an active effort to change his ways. Even though his mother was right in many ways, and her intentions were good, scolding and criticism were not the best way to inspire or encourage her son to make more of and effort. In fact, her criticism had the exact opposite effect.

Even when the boy did make an effort to change, he still felt that there was no way he could possibly please his mom. No matter how hard he tried, she kept insulting him because he wasn't doing as well as his two sisters. The boy eventually ended up hating his mother, although he could never express his feelings to her directly. Instead, he eventually transferred his hatred for his mother onto every woman he tried to have a relationship with later in his life. He wanted to please women, but whenever his attempts to please failed, he would break out in a furious, intimidating rage which was often out of proportion to the current issues.

Besides anger issues in relationships with women, there were also three other issues that were creating problems for Staphysagria. As soon as the women in his life started resembling his mother, he would lose all interest in being sexual with them. After all, who wants to make love to his mother, or to someone who reminds him of his mother?

The second issue, which is also typical for Staphysagria, was a total avoidance of any emotional issues in general, which manifested itself as lack of communication about anything serious or unpleasant, or as a desire to escape, either physically or through the use of drugs, whenever his mate wanted to have a serious talk.

And the third issue was the issue of laziness and the desire to have an easy life where he didn't have to contribute hardly anything to the relationship. This, of course, would make the women in his life accuse him of being a good for nothing, lazy bum, just like his mother used to tell him when he was a child, which, eventually, would lead to the end of the relationship since all the women in his life, sooner or later, ended up resembling the mother he still hated so much. These patterns went through all of Staphysagria's relationships with women, regardless of who he chose to be with.

The only way these patterns can be changed is if Staphysagria begins to understand that respect has to be earned, and that he has to be willing to do something to earn it. The Staphysagrias, who do decide to grow up and be responsible and hard working individuals, don't receive the amount of insults that the lazier types receive, and they are therefore often healthier psychologically. The other option, of course, is for Staphysagria to simply be happy with himself as he is, and to stop trying to please others in an effort to get them to respect him or think that he is great. He has to understand that he is already great, in his own way, regardless of what anyone else thinks about him. All he has to do is accept himself and learn to be happy with who he truly is.

Another interesting thing about Staphysagria is the fact that he doesn't mind talking about emotional issues, in fact, a lot of times he loves talking about his emotions. But, he carefully avoids actually *dealing* with emotional issues or taking any responsibility for working through his problems (again, there is talking versus doing something). Because Staphysagria is dependent on the person who insults him, he is totally incapable of actually confronting this person directly, since his psychological dependence prevents him from risking the consequences of such a conflict. This is why it is so hard for him to let go or change his ways, and this is also why it is difficult for him to create a truly intimate relationship with anyone. He is carrying so much garbage from the past that it becomes almost impossible for him to simply allow someone to come close.

If Staphysagria wants to learn to resolve all these old issues, he has to, first of all, understand how he, alone, is responsible for creating his own reputation. If he wants respect, he has to be willing to do what it takes to earn it, through hard work, instead of just expecting people to respect him for no reason whatsoever. Respect doesn't happen by trying to please others, but by being the best he can be. He has to also let go of the idea that his happiness is going to come from other people's praise, and simply learn to be happy about what he is doing, regardless of anyone else's opinions. This can possibly happen over time through a combination of psychotherapy, a high potency of homeopathic Staphysagria as well as a willingness to do what it takes to break through the destructive patterns. Not an easy task, especially for someone who is so hypersensitive to criticism that he may not even be open to any kind of therapy, but if he can find, within himself, enough willingness to change, anything is possible.

WHY AM I HERE?
Thuja Occidentalis

Thuja Occidentalis has a strong sensation of being frail, fragile, easily broken (brittle, made of glass). This makes Thuja oversensitive to everything ("touchy"). Thuja feels that the world is too harsh for him, and this makes him fearful because he doesn't really feel safe anywhere.

Because Thuja feels fragile inside, he easily develops fear of touch, and fear of others approaching him. He is afraid someone will bump into him too hard, or say something harsh to him. Because Thuja doesn't feel at ease around people, he may develop an aversion to company, and a feeling that he is pursued by enemies. He is worried about every little thing, and can easily become a hypochondriac.

Thuja suffers from a very weak sense of self. He is confused about his identity. He feels like he is in a dream where everything is strange; it feels like his soul is separated from his body, or too big for his body. His boundaries are weak, and he may even get a sense that there is an animal inside his abdomen. He can't easily tell what is real because he is not totally present in this dimension. Thujas mind is so confused that he often develops a fear of insanity, too. He just doesn't understand this place, and he doesn't feel at home here.

Language is another area that Thuja has a hard time with. His memory is weak for words, and he may have difficulty expressing himself accurately. He often makes mistakes calculating, speaking and writing, and his brain becomes easily overloaded. It is very difficult for Thuja to think clearly and make independent decisions, but once a decision has been made, he tends to stick to it stubbornly.

One reason why Thuja has a hard time concentrating is because he is easily distracted and tends to forget what he was doing, or what he was about to do. Sometimes he is totally absorbed in what he is doing, and other times he is absent minded and forgetful. Sometimes his mind is clear and his ideas are abundant and other times he doesn't have any ideas. Sometimes his thoughts vanish while he speaks, and he tends to answer slowly, hesitating, trying to find the right words, or he doesn't feel like talking at all. No matter how hard Thuja tries to do something, time usually passes too quickly, and he doesn't easily accomplish as much as he would like to. When that happens, he often becomes very upset.

Thuja is not very stable emotionally. His moods easily change from one extreme to the other. He tends to be oversensitive and may act out his strong feelings rather than talking about them. He is a cautious, suspicious type, who is offended easily and can be both weepy and tearful at times. He doesn't like quarrels or confrontations because he often becomes too much affected by other people's anger. This is interesting, considering how angry he can also get.

Thuja's ideas are often fixed, so he can't handle change or surprises well. Anticipation anxiety is common because he prefers to know ahead of time exactly what is going to happen. If something doesn't go according to Thuja's preconceived ideas, he can easily become hysterical and fly into a temper tantrum with shrieking, screaming and shouting. This can apply to adults as well as children.

Little things are often very important to Thuja. He can get extremely upset about little things because he often isn't able to see that they are simply trifles. He can't always tell what is wrong or decide what is important and what is not, so when something goes wrong, Thuja often judges himself harshly. He may blame or hate himself, and he doesn't easily let go of unpleasant things from the past.

Thuja is a very complicated remedy, full of internal contradictions. He tries very hard to hide his weakness and sense of frailty. He often compensates for his weak sense of self by behaving exactly opposite to how he feels inside, and he can sometimes be very difficult to be around. He likes to be in control and is often extremely obstinate, headstrong, contrary and quarrelsome. If he doesn't get his way, his behavior can be both ugly and abusive. He can be impatient, irritable, hurried, restless and passionate, and he doesn't mind being deceitful and sly, either, to make sure he gets his way.

Religious affections are common in Thuja, because Thuja feels more at home in other dimensions. Some Thujas have clairvoyant abilities and are able to see and even communicate with spirits, while others just show an interest in the metaphysical realms or religion in general. Some Thujas develop religious delusions, like despair of salvation or fear of evil, or they may get a feeling they are under superhuman control. Because Thuja's ideas tend to be fixed, he can be quite fanatical in his views.

Thuja often has a hard time coping with life in general, and he can easily develop anguish, indifference and aversion to everything from work to company.

His will is weak, and he may feel discontented, displeased, discouraged and disgusted with everything. He becomes easily depressed, bored and sleepless, tossing and turning in bed. He may eventually become so weary of life that he just wants to die, and he sometimes feels a sudden impulse to kill himself.

Thuja often feels very tired of being on the earth plane because everything is such an effort here and also because he doesn't cope well with anything. He doesn't really understand how anything works in this dimension and didn't really want to be here in the first place. He often has a stronger connection to other realities and longs to go back to dimensions where he can feel more at home and at ease.

THUJA OCCIDENTALIS IN RELATIONSHIPS

Thujas are often troubled beings who don't have an easy time in relationships with other people. Because Thuja feels fragile, oversensitive and is easily offended, he prefers to either be alone, or around mild mannered people who are careful about what they say or do to him.

Thuja likes to be in control, even though he often has a very hard time making decisions. He doesn't always cope well with tasks that need to be completed in a timely manner, especially if he is interrupted, and he may need help coping, prioritizing and managing his time. However, the help has to be offered in a very gentle way, not to aggravate his obstinate and somewhat quarrelsome nature. Thuja can be extremely hard to please, because everything has to be exactly so, and he can be quite a challenge to live with.

Change, transitions and surprises are often hard for Thuja to deal with. He always feels better if he knows ahead of time what is going to happen. He enjoys stability, predictability and familiar routines and surroundings, since familiarity makes him feel safe.

I had one case with a Thuja child who was experiencing difficulties after his parents went through divorce. He had a very hard time with the transition and started digging his heels in. He became obsessive about little things, extremely stubborn and controlling. Things had to be done in just the right way, or he would have a full blown temper tantrum, screaming with frustration. Little things would aggravate him. He could take a bite of his sandwich, but if the tomato fell out, the sandwich would be ruined, and he would throw it across the table and have a fit. He also had a very hard time making decisions. He was picky about food, and he knew what he didn't want to eat, but he wasn't able to decide what he did want to eat. He just didn't seem to be able to think clearly.

His memory for words also started deteriorating. He would either ramble away a mile a minute, or he would talk so slowly that you had to keep waiting for the next word. He had a hard time expressing his thoughts and became hypersensitive to any kind of criticism. He couldn't concentrate on even simple tasks, and needed 20 minutes just to get his shoes on in the morning. At school he often didn't get recess. By the time he was ready to go out, the others were coming back in again. He also became extremely anxious about trying anything new, and at the same time he was so bored he couldn't stand being alive. He was very difficult to live with, feeling offended about everything and having a very low tolerance for the normal frustrations of life.

His parents realized that a Thuja child has to be treated in a different way than other children. They learned that life became easier for everyone if he was allowed to be in control of anything that didn't affect others, like what he would like to wear or eat, or when he would like to eat, or when he wanted to do his homework, or how he wanted his hair, or even when he wanted to go to bed. His mom made a deal with him, that he could be up as long as he wanted, as long as he was in his room, not disturbing anyone, and as long as he was able to get up and go to school the next day. Because he couldn't handle change or surprises well, his parents learned to give him several warnings ahead of time before something was going to happen, and they also learned to give him enough time to get ready so he wouldn't feel rushed when he needed to go somewhere. Lots of gentle hugs and positive attention made him happier and easier to be around since he didn't respond well to any kind of punishment. In addition to these adjustments in his environment, an occasional dose of Thuja 10M made a huge difference in his ability to cope with life in general.

Another Thuja client was a traveler who happened to find me between her journeys. One of the first things she told me was that she felt like her body was made from broken glass because her hips, sacrum and joints kept popping, snapping and cracking. The feeling of being made out of glass is one of the symptoms associated with Thuja, but it is rare to actually hear anyone describe themselves that way. She explained that she never felt like she was totally in her body, and sometimes her body felt hollow inside. She often felt uncomfortable about being a woman, too, because she didn't like the attention you get from having hips and breasts. Because she never felt really at ease being in this dimension, she became very shy around people and didn't want anyone to look at her. She had no real sense of self and often felt better being on her own.

When I asked her what she was doing in her life, she told me she had no goals. She never even made any plans; she just traveled around and trusted that she would somehow be in the right place at the right time. She lived her life as if it were a great spiritual journey, full of surprises and challenges that she could learn from.

An interesting thing about this case was her feeling of inner ugliness, and the way she dealt with this issue. A feeling of inner ugliness is common in most women, but the normal way women deal with this issue is to hide their perceived ugliness by dying their hair, shaving their legs and dieting, and by enhancing whatever they perceive as beautiful with make up and fancy clothing. However, my Thuja client had a totally different approach. She was hiding her beauty to the best of her ability while exposing her perceived ugliness (she had very hairy legs); so that people would start realizing that there was beauty, even in ugliness. She called herself a contrary and said that her core issue in life was a sense of being an outsider, of not belonging anywhere and of not feeling comfortable in her body, or in this dimension. I gave her Thuja 200c, and she experienced intense depression for a few days. Then her mood lifted, and she started feeling better than she had ever felt before...

The female Thuja client had no interest in any long term relationships. She was simply too fragile and too confused to want to be closely involved with anyone. Some Thujas, however, do end up in relationships at times, even though they don't usually have an easy time relating to others. In the movie "A beautiful mind," the main character, who is most likely a Thuja, told his friend that he had found a girl who "contrary to all probability finds me attractive." He felt so alienated from people in general that it came as a great surprise to him that a beautiful girl actually wanted to be with him, and it was her unselfish love, persistence and patience that made the relationship possible.

Thujas are often loving and sweet as long as their needs are met by someone who is patient, gentle, and considerate, who, preferably, doesn't expect too much from them in return. They need someone who doesn't rush them, who can help them cope when they are having difficulties, and at the same time allow them to have it their way as much as possible. A Thuja needs someone in his life who will help make his time in this dimension a little easier for him, someone who can make him feel like he is no longer a stranger here and who can give him a sense that he actually does belong.

PART THREE
RELATIONSHIPS
Predictable Patterns

Relationship Means Something Complete,

Finished, Closed.

Love is never a Relationship;

Love is relating.

It is always a River, Flowing, Unending.

Love Knows no Full Stop;

The Honeymoon Begins, But it Never Ends.

The Book of Wisdom
Bhagwan Shree Rajneesh

WHAT IS LOVE?
Arsenicum Album and Staphysagria

This is the story of the relationship between Arsenicum Album (woman) and Staphysagria (man). To understand the issues in this relationship, we first need to take a look at each person's past history, since the past often contains valuable clues about why the relationship is the way it is right now.

Staphysagria and Arsenicum had known each other for several years before they got together as a couple. Staphysagria started working for Arsenicum's father when he was quite young. He helped him run bingos and made most of his money doing that. He loved running the bingos, but he told me that he didn't feel that running bingos was a very great example for his children (a valid Staphysagria concern). He would have liked his life to be better, but it didn't quite turn out the way he had hoped it would.

When telling me about his past, he explained that he had been married twice before he got together with Arsenicum. He was very committed to his first wife, and they had 2 children together, a son and a daughter. He was working 20 hours a day and making lots of money, but he didn't have much time for his family. Some of his income wasn't totally legal, and he ended up getting busted. That is when he found out that his wife had been having an affair with another man for over a year. She asked for a divorce and left with both the children. Staphysagria didn't contest the divorce. He gave her what she wanted, which was pretty much everything, and now he doesn't even get to see his children. This was a very painful experience for him.

After some time he married again, this time to a rather large woman who he thought would make a good mother. Staphysagria really wanted another child since he had lost his other two, and he did eventually have a son with his second wife. Again, he was committed to the relationship. He put his new wife through nursing school and tried to find other kinds of work for himself, since she didn't like him running bingos. One day, suddenly, she also left. She took his son with her and never came back. This brought back old wounds from his first marriage, and he turned to alcohol and pot in an attempt to drown his pain and lighten his depression.

He never tried to get his children back from either of his previous wives because he felt that the children needed their mothers, and he didn't want to be selfish. Some people may think that he just abandoned his children, but if anyone suggests this possibility Staphysagria feels very angry and hurt. The pain he feels about losing his 3 children is so deep that he doesn't know if he will ever be able to get over it.

Arsenicum is a very successful therapist who works with people's personal problems. She is good at making money, and she likes helping people in need. She became involved with Staphysagria after her father hired him to paint her house, and they got along so well that he just ended up moving in with her. Arsenicum and Staphysagria had known each other since they were both very young, and Arsenicum already knew all about his previous divorces and the loss of his children.

As a therapist, it was tempting for Arsenicum to try to get him to reestablish contact with his children. Staphysagria didn't appreciate being told what to do and often got very angry about the whole situation. Arsenicum felt intimidated by his anger and verbal abuse, but since it isn't in her nature to back off when she thinks she is right, she couldn't stop pushing the issue. Staphysagria couldn't let go of his old pain, and Arsenicum couldn't let go of worrying about him and wanting to help.

When I started working with this couple, Staphysagria's anger and Arsenicum's tendency to worry were the first issues we dealt with. I gave them both remedies in high potency, and pretty soon they both became more "easy going." As time went by, the dynamics of the relationship started changing slightly. The main issue right now is the issue of energy exchange in the form of love and money, in other words, who contributes what to the relationship.

Arsenicum has always been the main breadwinner. She feels the pressure of being the sole earner because she can't really allow herself to take time off when she feels exhausted. Staphysagria is good at many different things, but he doesn't have any specific skills. If Arsenicum wants to talk about this issue, Staphysagria is not very happy at all. He doesn't like conflict and doesn't like talking about anything unpleasant, which is typical for all Staphysagrias. The fact that Arsenicum is articulate and brilliant at arguing doesn't help the situation any either. She can easily argue circles around anyone, and Staphysagria isn't that good with words. He would much prefer to avoid the whole issue, since he can't compete with Arsenicum anyway.

This is frustrating for Arsenicum. If she feels that she can't get through to him, she sometimes insults him by saying she can make more money in a day than he can make in a week. This upsets Staphysagria more than anything, and he often responds by becoming stubborn, arrogant, vindictive and verbally abusive, and eventually, he even threatens to leave the relationship. This, of course, worries Arsenicum very much and triggers her fear of being abandoned. Because she is so exhausted from working with people's problems all the time, she feels that she needs a nurturing, loving relationship with her mate to balance the chaos she deals with the rest of the day. The problem is that Staphysagria doesn't usually reassure her or express his love for her enough to put her mind at ease.

Arsenicum feels like she is always the care taker in her relationships, and she often feels used by the people around her, her clients included. She is worried that if she becomes weak, everyone will disappear. She feels like she is giving too much and often feels a little run over by the people she is trying to help. Sometimes she feels righteous indignation when people take advantage of her or don't appreciate the help she is giving. She worries so much about other people that it often interferes with both her life and her relationship to Staphysagria. The interesting thing is that when her patients are doing well and don't continuously call for help, she doesn't feel needed, which also worries her. It is almost like she is dependent on other people's crisis to feel worthy.

After putting all her energy into caring for others, and helping people in crisis on a daily (or even nightly) basis, Arsenicum often tends to become totally drained, weak and exhausted. Even the money she makes in the process can't compensate for the energy she is putting into her work. What Arsenicum really wants and needs is someone who can take care of her after she has taken care of everyone else. Someone who really loves her and isn't afraid to show it. Someone who can shower her with gifts and complements, and give her back some of the energy she feels she is wasting on people who don't appreciate it. So, this is basically what she expects from Staphysagria.

Staphysagria knows and feels what she expects from him, but he doesn't find it easy to fulfill her expectations. He explained that he felt emotionally "robbed" by his past relationships, and this has made him "pull back" in a way that negatively affects his present relationship to Arsenicum. He told me that he will do anything Arsenicum asks, which fits the mild and yielding Staphysagria personality profile, but he doesn't shower her with love or gifts. He often doesn't have enough money to buy her gifts, and he usually doesn't think about initiating any show of love. Staphysagria loves Arsenicum dearly and feels that she probably does deserve more affection than what he is offering (delusion that he is not good enough), but he describes himself as "self-consumed" and explains that he has had to build up an armor to protect himself from more emotional pain.

From Staphysagria's past relationships we already know how much emotional pain he is carrying and also how hard it is for him to let go of this. It simply isn't in Staphysagria's nature to put himself in a situation again where he might risk more rejection, humiliation, insult, embarrassment or emotional discomfort. Staphysagria views women as mysterious beings who are difficult to please and who makes no sense to him, and he much prefers to take a passive role in the relationship so he doesn't get himself into trouble. Unfortunately, Staphysagria's passive role in this relationship does get him in trouble with Arsenicum, anyway.

Arsenicum, who naturally feels unloved, deep inside, doesn't understand why it is so hard for Staphysagria to show more love towards her. She loves him, and she wishes he could love her the same way. When he doesn't measure up to Arsenicum's high expectations, she tends to insult him. She'll tell him she can do better, she can find a better guy, and she can have a better life with someone else. From Arsenicum's point of view, Staphysagria just isn't doing enough to contribute to the relationship neither monetarily nor emotionally.

Here we can see how Stapysagria's lack of open affection towards Arsenicum triggers her core issue of feeling unloved, and when she becomes defensive and starts to insult Staphysagria, it triggers his core issue of not feeling good enough. Staphysagria doesn't want to be responsible for ruining Arsenicum's life. He is sorry for who he is, but doesn't feel like that is something he can control. Staphysagria's main reaction, when he finds himself in this kind of situation, is to lash out viciously or to escape. To preserve his dignity, he often feels his best choice is to pack his bags and leave the relationship, since he knows he can't measure up in an argument with Arsenicum anyway. Arsenicum, who is a therapist, thinks that everything needs to be spoken about so the issues can be resolved, but to Staphysagria talking equals more emotional pain, which he is trying to avoid at all costs. If Arsenicum pushes the issue, Staphysagria feels like escaping from the whole situation. This is when Arsenicum desperately tries to get her point across and often ends up insulting Staphysagria in the process, which only makes things worse.

It is important to understand why Arsenicum insults Staphysagria. She doesn't insult him because she wants him to leave, she insults him because she wants him to stay! Arsenicum believes that she will only be loved if she can convince someone that she is right, so by insulting Staphysagria she is hoping to get the point across clearly enough that he will come to his senses again. The problem is, the harder she pushes, the more he will avoid her and be tempted to leave the relationship, which is something they both have to understand and become more aware of if they want their relationship to last.

Recently there has been another new and interesting development in their lives, which can also possibly have a negative affect on their relationship dynamics. Staphysagria is in the process of starting a new business that could potentially bring in huge amounts of money. So far, Arsenicum has provided most of the money in the relationship while complaining about Staphysagria's lack of ability to make money. Because she had more money and was providing physical security for both of them, she felt that there was a subtle dependency in the relationship. Since all Arsenicums know, deep down, that they don't always treat the people in their lives as nicely as they should, they also know that there is a definite possibility that, one day, their loved ones will feel that enough is enough and decide to leave the relationship. Staphysagria's financial dependence on Arsenicum made her feel less anxious about this possibility. If, however, Staphysagria finally starts making big money, this can easily change.

Staphysagria is very excited about this possibility for several reasons. He will be able to contribute more money to the relationship and take some of the burden off Arsenicum. He will be able to do well for himself and regain his dignity. He will finally become worthy of people's respect, and he may even be able to shower Arsenicum with gifts. Unfortunately, the situation isn't as simple as it looks.

At first, it looks like this will make both happy. Staphysagria gets respect, dignity and money, and is able to contribute more money to the relationship, and Arsenicum can allow herself to work less and receive gifts that will prove to her that Staphysagria truly loves her. But the problem with the new situation is that if everything works out for Staphysagria, he will end up becoming financially independent from Arsenicum. It is very scary for Arsenicum to have a financially independent mate because it triggers her fear that he will leave the relationship, simply because he can, and then she will be left alone. This is a classic Arsenicum fear, and the normal reaction, when this fear is triggered, is to look for a way to make it impossible for her mate to leave. She can either find another way to make her mate dependent again, or she can make herself so needy that her mate has to take care of her.

I saw an example of this in a relationship between an Arsenicum man and his more independent mate. He would get deadly sick, instantly, every time she even thought about leaving the relationship. The message he was constantly giving her was: "Don't leave me, I am very sick and I will surely die soon!" This strategy worked for several years until his mate finally said: "I don't care!" and left anyway. And surprisingly, when nobody was there to take care of him anymore, he miraculously recovered his health in a fairly short amount of time and started taking care of himself, instead.

There is a very real possibility that a similar thing could also happen in this relationship. Staphysagria is just about to become financially independent, and if he succeeds, his success will almost certainly trigger Arsenicum's abandonment issues. In that case, it becomes even more important for Staphysagria to keep reassuring Arsenicum of his love for her because if he doesn't, she may instantly believe that he will start a life on his own as soon as he is no longer dependent her for money. And, as soon as that thought enters her head, she may desperately try to convince him to stay, whatever it takes! She may even have to insult him to get her point across! But, unfortunately, this method never really works... And if it doesn't work, her only other option is to make herself dependent on him, instead, by becoming sick, or by having some kind of accident...

It is obvious that something has to change between them if they want their relationship to survive. The good thing is they still want to be together, even though the relationship gets a bit rocky at times, but if they really want to change what is happening between them, they both need to become more aware of why they do the things they do so they can find ways to let go of these old patterns, especially the pattern of insulting someone in an effort to get a point across! It is also important for Arsenicum to understand why Staphysagria is choosing to stay with her. He is with her because he loves her, not because he needs her, and she has to understand that love and neediness are not the same thing, in fact, the two has nothing to do with each other. (And, of course, the issue of money shouldn't even be mentioned when talking about love, since money and love has nothing to do with each other...)

The only time Staphysagria threatens to leave the relationship is when Arsenicum insults him, so if she wants to reduce the possibility of him leaving, she simply *has to* stop insulting him. It doesn't matter whether or not she is right about something, or if she can justify her insults. She simply has to stop doing it, or I can predict, with great certainty, that he will eventually leave the relationship. At some point, she has to see for herself that her way of trying to convince him to stay, by trying to force him to see things her way, is nothing but an old pattern that has lost it's usefulness in this reality.

If she can understand the reason why she argues the way she does, by reading more about it in the remedy profile that goes with Arsenicum, she might be able to understand that what she is doing is just an old pattern which is based in the core fear that goes with the remedy itself. It will take a lot of trust to let go of this strategy, but the rewards will make it worth her while because her relationship to Staphysagria will improve as soon as she stops insulting him the way she has done up to now.

Another problem in this relationship is the fact that Arsenicum is an expert at arguing, and Staphysagria simply isn't that good at expressing himself verbally. This always gives Arsenicum an advantage when they argue, and Staphysagria immediately becomes defensive and stops listening to her. To overcome this issue, it might be helpful if she simply mentions to Staphysagria what she wants to talk to him about, later, and then gives him plenty of time to prepare himself for the upcoming discussion. This way, Staphysagria gets to think things through, ahead of time, so he doesn't feel so "put on the spot." This won't be an easy thing for Arsenicum to do because she is often a very impatient type, but if she can do it, Staphysagria will most likely be less defensive if she gives him enough time to think things over before he has to express himself verbally.

For Staphysagria, my suggestion is to try to put his fear of rejection and insult aside, and see if he can find the courage to express more affection towards Arsenicum, since this is such an important issue for her. It isn't easy to please an Arsenicum, since they are always very picky about things. They have high standards about everything, and if something isn't exactly right, there can easily be trouble... But nevertheless, Staphysagria still needs to at least make an effort to express his love for her more. If he does, Arsenicum will feel better and hopefully stop being so hard on him, in fact, she *has to* stop being so hard on him, or it isn't going to work!

It is vitally important that Arsenicum understands how scary it is for Staphysagria to let down his protective armor and allow himself the vulnerability of having to openly express his feelings to her. Therefore, she should never judge or criticize any of his efforts to please her, even if he doesn't do things the way she would have wanted them done. In other words, both these people need to understand their own, as well as each other's, core issues, and based on this knowledge, look for the courage to break some of these old patterns that go with their remedy pictures.

Looking at the Arsenicum remedy picture, we can see how Arsenicum basically feels unloved and weak. She feels dependent on the people who are taking advantage of her, in this case her clients. She often makes herself available day or night, well beyond the call of duty, and in return, her clients give her money (rather than love or appreciation), which she can use to create physical security for herself. (Here we can see how money can be used as a substitute for love, but because it isn't the real thing, no amount of money can ever fulfill the desire for love).

Physical security is more important to Arsenicum than emotional security, but this doesn't mean that Arsenicums don't also care about emotional security. They actually do want both, but physical security is easier to create, control or demand. This is why Arsenicums tend to be nice to the people they think they need in their lives, even though they know well that the very same people are actually also taking advantage of them.

Another mysterious Arsenicum trait is their tendency to insult people to get their point across in an argument. In this story, Arsenicum was insulting Staphysagria to make him stay. This makes no sense to anyone who isn't an Arsenicum, unless we look at the Arsenicum profile again. Arsenicums are still responding to their reality as if they have been unjustly accused of something they didn't do, and as a consequence they were pursued, attacked, robbed,

191

injured and almost died. If they had been able to convince their accusers, that they were right, and that others were wrong, they could have been able to avoid the consequences that happened. This is why Arsenicums have become experts at arguing, and they can't relax until the people in their lives are convinced that they are right. This is also why Arsenicums are not concerned whether anyone gets hurt or insulted in the process, because if it takes seemingly callous behavior to get the point across, then so be it! Whatever the situation requires is what will happen. In this relationship, Arsenicum's technique, which often works well in other situations, has the completely opposite effect on Staphysagria. The harder she tries to convince him, the more he feels like getting up and leaving the relationship, so this is one issue she needs to work on changing.

Because Arsenicum and Staphysagria are committed to the relationship and to each other, they are both willing to work on their core issues to make the relationship better. I believe that awareness is the first step towards creating the understanding needed for permanent change to take place, and I also believe that anything is possible. We just have to recognize the old patterns each time they appear and simply stop and acknowledge that it is just an old pattern. After stopping, we need to think about other ways to respond instead of just blindly reacting in an unconscious way, and we have to find courage to take the jump into the unknown and try something totally different. Core issues are hard to change, but when we focus on changing only one issue at a time, it doesn't have to be an overwhelming task, and the rewards as well as the spiritual growth that results will make it well worth the effort.

SOME TIME LATER...

Before Arsenicum read the relationship story I had written about them, she jokingly told Staphysagria that if his bingo took off, and he started making lots of money, she might have to break her ankle, like she did once before, so he wouldn't be able to leave her. This statement clearly shows Arsenicum's fear, that if Staphysagria became too independent financially, he would no longer want to be with her. She was amazed to read my story after she said that, only to realize how predictable these patterns really are. Now that she has become aware of the issue, she no longer has to break her ankle to get her mate to stay. All she has to do is stop insulting him and trust that he actually does love her, even if he doesn't need her money any more, and she even gets to keep her ankle in one piece!

INDEPENDENTLY TOGETHER
Kali Carbonicum and Nux Vomica

This is the story of the relationship between Kali Carbonicum (woman) and Nux Vomica (man).

Kali and Nux met over 10 years ago. Kali described herself as mild mannered, serious, shy and timid, but added that she can be independent, spontaneous and fun-loving, too. As a child she grew up on a farm where the family was the basic social unit. She had a good relationship with her mother, who had a nurturing and encouraging personality. The parental values she learned from her were very idealistic. They should all live in peace and harmony, and everyone should be cheerful and easy going. The family members kept the atmosphere peaceful and tried to avoid conflict, since conflict didn't really work within their value system. Kali's father was a strict disciplinarian whom she didn't feel particularly close to. He had his own set of values and didn't mind causing a disturbance in order to assert his authority. Kali felt more attracted to her mother's values and eventually adopted them as her own.

Kali was used to always being part of a group, since her family loved to do things together. There were often family outings, picnics, re-unions, and lots of fun and playtime with siblings and friends. The family members depended on each other for support, and this was something you could always count on. She referred to her family as "the tribe", and explained to me that once you are a member of "the tribe", you can't do anything to get out of it. Even if you do something that the family disapproves of, they would rather pretend it never happened than consider the possibility of disowning someone.

Nux came from a totally different kind of family background. He was the only child in a family where his mother struggled with alcoholism, and his father always worked too much. He experienced a great deal of physical and emotional abuse from his mother, which he responded to by withdrawing into the basement where he could get away from conflict and be creative. Nux had a good relationship with his father, who taught him many things. His father was the bright and skillful manager of a local plant, and probably another fellow Nux, which explains why they got along so well.

INDEPENDENTLY TOGETHER Kali Carbonicum and Nux Vomica

At school Nux was a grade A student with a special interest in science and math. His memory was so good that he could remember both words and things with photographic accuracy. After finishing school he got a job as a research scientist. The job was challenging, and he loved it. He especially liked the fact that no one interfered with what he was doing most of the time, which is the perfect kind of job for a Nux. He described himself as a loner, not a team worker, who liked being in a position where he was working on his own. He also told me how he needs to have order in his life so he doesn't have to waste time looking for things. Since he has photographic memory, he just takes mental "snap-shots" of his environment, and he immediately knows where everything is, as long as nobody moves things around. That way he can be super efficient and accomplish huge tasks in a very short time.

Nux's energy level was always very high, and he was extremely disciplined. He worked long hours every day, but still found time to exercise 4 hours a day, before and after work. He even ran marathons when the opportunity presented itself until he eventually injured his back and had to be more careful with physical activities.

Because Nux was living a very active life, it was no surprise that he eventually became interested in meditation. At first he was doing TM (transcendental meditation), so that he could learn how to relax, but as time went by, he became more and more interested in the spiritual aspects of meditation. At the time when he met Kali, he was ready for a totally different kind of life.

Kali had lived a much less disciplined life than Nux. She had traveled around the world by herself, she had been the creator and owner of two different businesses, and she had been self-employed most of her adult life. Whenever she didn't enjoy where she was at or what she was doing, she moved on to something else. This was a new concept to Nux. He realized that he didn't have to stick with a high stress job if there were other things he would rather do, so he quit his job and started focusing more on the deeper aspects of life. Meditation was important to him, and he explored it with the same level of dedication and passion that he used to put into his research.

Kali was a fellow meditator, which really appealed to him. At this point in his life he felt that a relationship could only work if it was based on spiritual practice, and Kali felt the same way. She also liked the fact that Nux was very straight forward. They enjoyed interesting conversations together, and Kali felt that there was potential for real friendship, which was probably the most important thing to her. Because she is primarily a mental type, she was happy to find someone she could have a strong mental connection with, but she also enjoyed the fact that he was emotionally available.

Their friendship grew, and since they both wanted a committed relationship, they decided to get married about a year after they first met. Their wedding vows reflected the spiritual nature of their relationship, where they promised to help each other awaken and also to suffer together. However, Kali told me that Nux was the one who included "suffering together" in their marriage vows. She was never interested in suffering, but jokingly added that Nux introduced her to it!

They both kept up their meditation practices, which meant slightly different things to each of them. Kali enjoyed the process of meditation and the daily sense of peace she felt after going within. She also enjoyed the group of people she was associated with, feeling a strong connection to like minded people who were all moving together towards higher levels of consciousness. Nux was slightly more ambitious than Kali, hoping to achieve certain levels of consciousness through daily practice, although he knew well that those levels can only happen through ultimate surrender when the time is right. He explained how meditation was teaching him patience, which is probably the hardest thing for a Nux to learn. Hours, days and weeks of sitting silently eventually mellowed him out and loosened his fixed position, so he became less rigid and critical. He is still a loner who doesn't like to be told what to do, so once in a while he experiences conflict with other associates in the group, but this is to be expected from any Nux who joins a group. Maybe a little more meditation will mellow out that part of him, too.

In their personal relationship Nux and Kali had to learn to live together in spite of their differences, and they found very simple ways to cope. One of the first differences they discovered was the difference between Nux's need for order, and Kali's messier living conditions. When someone has a strong need for order, they simply can't handle living in chaos. In a Nux it will create inner tension and irritability, so when they decided to move in together, this was the first issue they had to address. They agreed on an arrangement that worked really well for both. Kali was to keep the main part of the house neat, but in her own room she could keep things as messy as she wanted. With this solution they both got their needs met. Kali would only get herself in trouble is if she moved something in the neat part of the house, and she didn't return it to the same place after she was finished with it. Nux expected everything to still be in the place where he saw it last, and he was not happy if the had to go looking for anything.

During the course of their marriage, this issue kept changing. Nux has become messier and less obsessed about order, and there have been times when they have even changed roles. Over time, Kali also noticed that Nux's photographic memory only applies to his tools and things that are important to him. When it comes to things that he has no interest in, Kali can be more orderly than he is. This role change is very healthy, because it deepens their mutual understanding and reduces tendencies to judge.

Another difference they were soon to discover was their difference in temperament. Nux is impatient, fiery and irritable, with a tendency to become mean. Kali is more patient and mild mannered, although she can be irritable and quarrelsome, too, especially around the time of her periods, or while going through menopause. Nux is often annoyed about little things, like when things are moving too slowly, or when he has to waste time looking for something. Kali is more annoyed when something doesn't make sense to her. If Nux wakes up irritable in the morning for no specific reason, Kali can become very critical. This doesn't fit the values she learned from her family, where everyone should be happy, cheerful and easy going. If she decides to point out to Nux that his negativity and irritability isn't in his best interest, and that he would be happier if he tried to slow down and be more "easy going," it aggravates Nux's irritability even more. Kali is more stable than Nux emotionally, and she doesn't totally understand where all his inner fire is coming from. However, if Nux decides not to take her unsolicited advice, she can get into a terrible mood.

The solution to this problem was also simple. She learned to leave him alone in the morning and allowed him to be grumpy, even if he shouldn't be. She would just go about the day, focusing on her own things, and Nux's irritability would eventually pass without any conflict. The energy of his anger still affects her, but she has learned that it is better not to add fuel to the fire.

In addition to the different temperaments, there was also a difference in speed and spontaneity. Nux is always quick, Kali prefers to move slowly. Nux gets impatient and irritable when Kali moves too slowly, and Kali resists and feels anxious when she is being rushed. Nux makes decisions on the spur of the moment, Kali prefers to think things through and plan things properly before she jumps into anything. Nux is more impulsive and reckless, Kali is more cautious. Nux can easily handle change; Kali prefers to ease into new things slowly. Kali can be stubborn about how she likes things to be, and she may even tell Nux what to do. This doesn't work, of course. Nux is "the king," and nobody tells the king what to do. However, if Nux tells Kali what to do, that may not work either, since she can quietly and stubbornly stick to whatever she is doing, regardless of how convincing or persuasive Nux may be. She may not argue back, but she doesn't let anyone "push her around" either. She knows what she wants, and this can be a source of frustration for Nux, since he can't easily convince her to change her mind.

The solution to this problem is also very simple. If Nux tells her ahead of time what he wants to do, she can prepare herself and be ready when the time comes. This way Nux doesn't have to wait, and Kali doesn't have to feel rushed.

And, of course, they have to stop telling each other what to do, since that doesn't work anyway.

The last issue that this couple has had to deal with is their differences in social needs. Nux is happy chit-chatting with anyone he meets, while Kali feels extremely uncomfortable with casual small-talk. Kali feels better when she can connect deeply with other like-minded souls. Nux is independent and more of a loner, while Kali is dependent and loves being part of a group. In their personal relationship, Nux doesn't really understand why Kali needs so much together-ness and support, probably because Nux has enough self confidence that he personally doesn't need anyone's support. This is hard for Kali, who is used to being part of a family where everyone depends on each other. Nux sometimes gets the feeling that Kali depends on him for her happiness, and he isn't willing to play that part in the relationship. He may even tell her to go and "get a life," which hurts Kali's feelings and is very difficult for her to hear. She does have a life, but her priorities are different than his. Kali needs the support of her husband more than the support of anyone else because he is the one closest to her. If he isn't available to fulfill those needs, she connects with her friends instead. She has willed herself to become more independent, but it doesn't always feel very good. This is Kali's core issue, and core issues are always the most difficult challenges to try to change.

There are many interesting things about this relationship. First of all, the two people in the relationship have very different personalities. In terms of compatibility, they are probably polar opposites in many ways, even though they do have things in common, too. When people attract their polar opposite as a mate, it is often because it provides a bigger opportunity for personal growth. In this case, it is obvious that they have learned things from each other. Nux is becoming more patient, mellow and tolerant. He quit his high stress job and has found more time to explore the deeper, spiritual levels of life. Kali is learning to be more independent, which is hard for her, but it is admirable that she is able to move beyond her core issues. Nux is learning to work with someone who values togetherness more than independence, and Kali is learning to leave someone alone when they need space. When it comes to all of these issues, they have both had to learn more tolerance of each other's differences, and as a result they have learned to overcome many of their issues successfully. One of the things I noticed about this relationship was their lack of blame, at least during the interview. Kali later admitted that she does have a tendency to blame Nux, since she doesn't always agree with him, or understand their differences, but she is trying to become more aware of that side of herself. She told me how they constantly have to remember to let go, so that each can let the other person be who he or she is. She also told me how important it is to just be nice to each other! (It is so simple to do, but so easy to forget...)

INDEPENDENTLY TOGETHER Kali Carbonicum and Nux Vomica

Kali and Nux are presently both using homeopathic remedies. Kali feels that the main difference she has noticed, since they started using the remedies, is an increased level of tolerance and understanding in both of them. She shared with me a story which describes how the remedies have helped them expand further:

A couple of weeks after they started using the remedies, they stopped at a restaurant to have lunch. A young couple was sitting at a table near them. The man was continuously talking on his cell phone, and the woman was just sitting there, waiting for him to connect with her. Kali quietly thought to herself "This is just how things are!" and she surprised herself by seeing that the thought was there without any judgment. She discovered, at that moment, that her tendency to be critical and judgmental was less than usual. Later on, she mentioned the situation to Nux and asked how he had felt. Nux said he had noticed what was happening and felt how painful it must have been for the woman to just sit there and be ignored. Nux had instantly seen and understood the other person's point of view. Kali feels that the remedies are making both more tolerant and understanding of others, and she is happy about the change that is happening in both of them.

Nux and Kali have lived together now for over 10 years. The relationship hasn't always been easy, but through patience and awareness they have been able to overcome most of their differences and make the problems they have experienced into opportunities for deeper spiritual growth. This brings me to the conclusion that increased awareness is the ultimate solution to any problem in life, including relationship problems. When the relationship within yourself, between your inner male and female, has been resolved, your outer relationships with people will also reflect that change. When we are able to move beyond the duality of male and female, right and wrong, good and bad, there is no such thing as an incompatible relationship.

INTIMACY VERSUS CONFLICT
Medorrhinum and Natrum Muriaticum

This is the story of the relationship between Medorrhinum (woman) and Natrum Muriaticum (man).

Natrum was a spiritual seeker. He was trying to find his true self since he understood that there was more to life than what he had experienced so far. He had joined a group of people that he felt a certain kind of energy around. They were very alive, happy and open hearted, which really appealed to him since he came from a very strict, suppressive home environment. His parents were catholic, and they had taught him so many rules for what you should and shouldn't do that he was no longer able to tell what was his truth, and what was theirs. He felt that he needed to find out what was true for himself, and he was willing to do whatever it would take to get there. Therefore, he also joined a special therapy group where the purpose of the group was to help people like himself break through old patterns of conditioning, so they could start living their lives from a fresh space by learning to find their own paths and their own truths.

One of Natrum's issues was around sexuality. He had been very hurt in his past relationships, and he had a hard time letting go of his old pain. He realized that all his ideas of right and wrong came from his parents, and not from himself, and he had a strong need to find a better way to relate to women. He was willing to challenge his fear of getting hurt in relationships by trying new things in order to expand beyond his old conditioning. In some of the therapy groups he attended, the participants were encouraged to explore their sexuality and forget about everything they had been taught previously about right and wrong. Natrum started to really enjoy himself for the first time in his life, and since he was a good looking guy, he had no problems finding girlfriends.

By the time he met Medorrhinum, he already had 3 other girlfriends. All his girlfriends knew about each other, and nobody seemed to have a problem with the arrangement. Medorrhinum also knew about them, but she couldn't help falling in love with Natrum anyway. He was very sweet and affectionate, which appealed to her, but she wasn't happy about all his girlfriends. Medorrhinum wasn't just "playing around." She wanted love and intimacy, but with 3 other girls around, she never knew who Natrum was going to pick for the night. She just had to wait and see, while trying to get a handle on the jealousy she was experiencing.

Always being in a state of "wait and see" was driving Medorrhinum crazy. She was extremely impatient by nature, and waiting for anything felt like pure torture. In the situation that goes with Medorrhinum she is waiting for something bad to happen, and this creates terrifying anticipation anxiety. Time stops, so it feels like the waiting goes on forever, and the uncertainty becomes almost unbearable. This is exactly how Medorrhinum felt in her relationship to Natrum, always waiting, and always in a state of uncertainty. Having to compete for attention with 3 other girls did nothing for her self confidence, either. Although Medorrhinum was open minded enough to experiment with new concepts, she didn't feel comfortable in the situation at all, and she wished things could be different.

After a few months of this, Natrum was becoming very confused. Having 4 girlfriends at the same time was too much even for him, and he decided to go away on a trip so he could see more clearly what he needed to do. Medorrhinum was miserable. She didn't know when he would be back, or even if he would be back. She decided to meditate, or distract herself with her work, but nothing really helped change the creepy feeling inside of her. Finally, she thought that maybe her misery would be less if she went out and enjoyed her sexuality, too. She went to a local bar and spent the night with a guy she met there, but casual sex with a stranger did nothing to make her feel better. It just made her even more aware that all she wanted was a monogamous relationship with someone she could love, preferably Natrum.

As irony would have it, this was the night that Natrum came home from his trip. While he was away he had realized that it would be better if he only had one girlfriend at a time, and he decided that the girl he wanted to be with was Medorrhinum. He, too, had realized that playing around wasn't the same as true intimacy. He knew that Medorrhinum really loved him, and since he also loved her, she was definitely "the one."

When he came home to surprise her with his new decision and found that she wasn't there, it triggered all his fears of getting hurt again. He had a horrible night and didn't sleep at all. By going off with another man, Medorrhinum had unknowingly triggered his worst fear, the fear of being in love with someone who didn't want to be with him, and the very real possibility of getting hurt again. Maybe he had taken too long before he finally made his decision? Maybe it was already too late?

However, Natrum had no reason to worry. Medorrhinum had wanted to be with him ever since they first met, and she still felt the same way, although Natrum wasn't an easy mate to get close to. She had no intention of leaving the relationship, as long as there was still a chance that Natrum wanted to be with her, but it bothered her that she didn't really have a clue what Natrum actually wanted. She was still in love with him, but she felt so unhappy about the situation that she had decided to spend the night with someone else in an attempt to escape from her own misery. She was only trying to cheer herself up, thinking that she would feel better if she could be less attached to Natrum, but it wasn't as enjoyable as she had hoped it would be. She was still feeling miserable the next day, only now she was feeling stupid, too, after spending the night with someone she had no interest in whatsoever.

When Medorrhinum showed up for breakfast, she was surprised to find Natrum waiting for her. He looked very disturbed when he asked her if she had had a nice time the night before, and Medorrhinum truthfully answered that she hadn't enjoyed it at all, and that she would rather have spent the night with him. Natrum then told her that while he was away, he had decided to only be with her, and let the others go. Medorrhinum was overjoyed about his decision, and Natrum was relieved that she still wanted to be with him. They were finally together, just the two of them, and they both felt happy about their new arrangement, but unfortunately, this wasn't in any way the end of their troubles. There was still the issue of intimacy...

Medorrhinum wasn't afraid of intimacy. She had been hurt many times before, but she always felt that the occasional pain is just the price you pay for all the good times you experience. You just "lick your wounds", feel sorry for yourself for a while, and then you forget about it and move on. Every time Medorrhinum found herself in love again, she was totally excited and ready for new adventures, and even though she had also had many bad experiences in the past, she didn't carry any old trust issues into her new relationships.

It was different for Natrum. He was dreaming about finding true love and happiness so he never had to experience pain again, but at the same time he was holding on to so much old pain that he couldn't just let go of. He was romantic and affectionate, and he really wanted to be open to Medorrhinum, but her love of intimacy scared him more than he could handle, especially now that he couldn't escape to some other girlfriend to create the distance he needed to feel more at ease. Natrum wanted intimacy more than anything, but because he had been hurt too many times, he had built up a wall inside himself to protect his heart from experiencing more pain. This is a reaction that completely fits the Natrum remedy picture. If at anytime someone gets behind the wall of aloofness, it triggers all of Natrum's fears, and he feels that he has to do something to create a safe distance again. Natrum felt that if Medorrhinum could give him enough time, he would eventually be able to open up to her and learn

201

to trust again, but Medorrhinum didn't understand, since Natrum didn't express this to her directly (another typical Natrum trait). Medorrhinum was impatient by nature, and always enjoyed jumping into new things and "taking it to the max," so she wasn't the type to hold herself back. She wanted to be close to Natrum, the closer the better! There is nothing lukewarm about a Medorrhinum. She always tends to go to the extremes in everything she does, and she just didn't know when to pull back and give Natrum the space that he needed to feel emotionally safe. Waiting for anything just wasn't Medorrhinum's thing, and it didn't take long before the issue of intimacy again became a problem in their relationship.

Medorrhinum was open and loving towards Natrum, but she didn't understand where he was coming from. Every time she felt that they were finally coming really close, Natrum would do strange things to create distance between them. He would either start a fight about something trivial, or he would criticize Medorrhinum for some little thing and make a big deal out of it. Medorrhinum, who is naturally sensitive to any kind of reproach, was deeply affected by Natrum's criticism, especially since she didn't understand why he would be her best friend one moment and her worst enemy the next. Natrum only did this because he felt emotionally vulnerable, and he had to find a way to create some distance between them so he could cope better with his fears. Medorrhinum took his criticism very hard. Because she didn't have a strong sense of self, Natrum's attacks made her feel more and more confused, and she kept blaming herself for what was happening. She took his attacks personally, and she started wondering what, exactly, she had done to deserve his angry outbursts. The less it made sense to her, the more confused and depressed she became, and strangely enough, the more at ease Natrum seemed!

As soon as Medorrhinum became depressed and irritable, Natrum was happy because it gave him an excuse to get out of the house and get away from her. He needed more space to feel emotionally safe because the closeness was getting on his nerves. Sometimes he would even call up one of his ex-girl-friends and take her out to the local bar. Medorrhinum wasn't invited to come because she was in a bad mood, and Natrum told her he needed to have some fun again. So Natrum went out without her, and Medorrhinum found herself waiting, once again, and feeling very rejected and hurt. Her anticipation anxiety was triggered, of course, and it gave her the most horrible feeling in her stomach. The anxiety got even worse after the bar had closed, and Natrum didn't show up when she expected him to. (Medorrhinum always feels worst when a time has been set and something doesn't happen by that time). Was he going to spend the night with his old girlfriend, or was he still going to come home? Medorrhinum was pacing the room with a crazy feeling in her head and her stomach all in knots.

Natrum had a good time at the bar, and he was in no hurry to go home when the bar closed. He felt safe around his old girlfriend because he knew she was no longer going to challenge his fear of intimacy. He knew that Medorrhinum wasn't going anywhere, and he enjoyed being around someone else for a change, someone who wasn't interested in too much intimacy, so he didn't have to feel so vulnerable all the time.

However, back home, Medorrhinum was more than challenged. She was pacing around like a lion in a cage and quickly decided to hide in a closet when she finally heard him at the door. She wanted him to realize that, if he didn't treat her right, a day could come when she would no longer be there when he returned.

When Natrum came in and didn't find her, he wondered anxiously if he had destroyed the relationship once again, and Medorrhinum was happy to see that she had given him a bit of a scare. Again Natrum became afraid to lose Medorrhinum and wanted to be close to her, and again the same thing happened. This cycle of intimacy versus conflict became an ongoing issue in the relationship. As soon as Natrum let Medorrhinum get behind the wall he had created to protect himself from emotional pain, he immediately felt too vulnerable and started creating problems so he wouldn't have to be so close to her. And every time he did that, Medorrhinum became confused and tried to understand what she had done wrong. When nothing made sense to her, she ended up depressed. Why was everything going so well, and all of a sudden, there were problems out of the blue? She simply couldn't figure out why this kept happening, and taking everything personally didn't help the situation, either.

Natrum knew that Medorrhinum was having a hard time with his behavior, but he simply didn't have the courage to stay open and vulnerable in the relationship for more than a very short amount of time. The pain he was carrying from his past relationships, together with the fear of possibly experiencing more pain in the future, was too much for him to face. His ex-wife had left him for another man, and Natrum had been mad with jealousy. He had been so angry with his ex-wife that he wanted to kill her, and his friends had interfered and held him back. He wasn't proud of himself for wanting to kill her, but his intense emotions had put him into overload, and he didn't really know what he was doing until later, after he had cooled down.

Medorrhinum, who wanted a monogamous relationship, had never indicated to Natrum that she wanted to go off with anyone else, but he still couldn't get over the fear that the possibility was there. And if she ever did leave him, he needed to know that there were other women out there who would still want to be with him, just in case... Medorrhinum's independent nature didn't help him feel at ease at all. He would have probably felt safer if his girlfriend was a more needy type, or someone else who had a similar issue with intimacy, so she wouldn't get too close to him all the time. However, Medorrhinum's intensity was often too much for him, even though he did care for her.

After being together for about a year, Medorrhinum and Natrum decided to go and visit the religious group they were both associated with. They had to work to help run the place in return for staying there, and they usually didn't see each other during the day. In the afternoons they would go to the communal kitchen to have dinner, and this triggered Natrum's fears once again. If Medorrhinum got there first, she would get her food and sit down at a table and wait for Natrum to join her. If, however, someone else sat down at her table before Natrum arrived, and if that someone happened to be a man, Natrum immediately assumed that Medorrhinum had found another man. He would look at Medorrhinum with an angry look and turn around and stomp off in a different direction trying to get as far away from her as possible. Medorrhinum would get up and go over and join him. She tried to assure him that she wasn't looking for anyone else, but Natrum was crazy with jealousy and didn't believe her. His fear of being hurt was getting out of control, and he was so angry that he wanted to hurt Medorrhinum back by accusing her of things she hadn't even done. It didn't matter what Medorrhinum said or did, it just didn't make any difference to Natrum at all. His worst fears had been triggered, and he was convinced that Medorrhinum was going to betray him, if she hadn't already done it.

After several months of this, Medorrhinum was exhausted. She was tired of being accused and screamed at for no reason, and she started withdrawing from Natrum. This made Natrum even more convinced that she was planning to leave the relationship. He didn't understand how his behavior made it virtually impossible for Medorrhinum to stay with him even though she still loved him and eventually, she actually did leave. Thus Natrum proved to himself, once again, that this is always what happens in relationships.

In this case Natrum had done something that we all do; he had created the very thing he was the most afraid of. Why do we create what we fear the most? Does that make any sense? From a homeopathic point of view, it makes a lot of sense. If we go back to the story that goes with the Natrum remedy picture, Natrum feels that no matter how hard he tries, it is never enough. He thinks that he has to be perfect to be loved, but because no one is ever that perfect, Natrum deep down believes that he can never have the love that he really wants. Therefore he subconsciously sabotages all his relationships, from the start, because he basically expects them not to last. By acting as if the relationship is already on it's last legs, even though it isn't, he is trying to protect himself from being hurt when it finally does end. Thus, he is not only preparing himself for the unavoidable ending of the relationship, he is actually *creating* it. He creates what he is the most afraid of through his own actions, and when it finally happens, and he ends up feeling hurt, it confirms to him,

once again, that all relationships end in pain. This is where the issue of delusions comes into the picture.

What we believe to be real is just that, a belief, or a distorted perception
of reality. We do not see reality as it really is because we have beliefs that affect
the way we see things. Because these beliefs give us a false perception of reality,
they become delusions, in other words, they fool us. We all suffer from delusions, but we are not usually aware of them. Psychologists think that only
psychotic people have delusions, but this simply isn't true. Psychotic people may
have more obvious delusions than the rest of us do, but we all have them. Delusions are simply false beliefs about the way we perceive reality, and these
beliefs stop us from seeing the actual truth of a situation. All we can see is what
we believe the truth to be. And if we aren't aware of our underlying beliefs, we
don't even know that what we see isn't really the truth. This is why awareness
is a key to personal transformation because delusions only have power over us
when we are not aware of them. Let me use the case above as an example:

In Natrum's case, he was under the delusion that he was always going to
be hurt in his relationships with women. The delusion was so real to him that it
had literally become his reality, and every time it happened again, it would
make this belief even stronger. Normally, Natrum would involve himself in
relationships that he knew, from the very beginning, wouldn't last, so he could
protect himself emotionally from the hurt that was sure to come. He would pick
women who had no interest in intimacy because he knew that he could handle
the pain better if, or when, they decided to leave the relationship if he didn't
become too vulnerable. But the interesting question is: Why would he pick
women that were sure to leave him if that was his greatest fear? In the story
above, Natrum actually picked a woman who had no intention of leaving the
relationship, but he still ended up making it virtually impossible for her to stay
with him. Why did he do that? The answer is very simple: If you can prove to
yourself that your delusions are real, you will never become aware that the
delusions exist in the first place. If you don't know that the delusions exist, you
won't realize where the real source of your problems is! And if you don't know
where the source of your problems is, you won't have to go through the discomfort of facing your problems. You can simply blame the other instead, even
though blaming the other isn't going to make you less miserable! If you sincerely want to go beyond misery, you need to look to a deeper level, the level of
delusion, to find a more permanent solution to your problems, since understanding the delusions will make it possible to eliminate most of the problems in your
relationships. (And for the few, courageous ones, who want to go even deeper
than the level of delusions, the mind itself is the problem. Going beyond the
mind is the ultimate solution to almost every problem we encounter in this
dimension. However, we all have to start somewhere; and understanding our
delusions is a good place to start).

The issue of delusions is an issue that applies to all of us, so it is really important to understand how it all works. If for example you have the delusion that you are ugly, you will attract people into your life that will make you feel ugly, and you will focus on how mean they are, rather than on the fact that the ugliness is a feeling inside of you that is just reflected in what they are telling you. If you have the delusion that people will betray you, or steal your money, you will attract people who will betray you or steal your money, and again, you will think that they are causing the problem, and you won't be able to see that the problem is actually inside of you. Now, if you can accept that this is what we all do, you can easily see why it is very difficult to break the old patterns, because we don't easily see what the problem really is. We normally think that the problem is caused by some kind of outside influence, while the truth is; the problem is actually created within ourselves. Accepting this as a fact, can drastically change the way we deal with our problems. Instead of blaming our misery on someone else, we can rather look inside and see if we can discover what the real problem is. If we can accept that our delusions are the root of all our problems, change immediately becomes possible. With more awareness, change is always possible because when we are aware, we can also be responsible for how our lives are turning out. Without awareness, we simply become victims of circumstances. It is much easier to take a victim approach, and simply blame others for our self created misery, than to take the responsibility for the mess we are in, so that is what most of us end up doing.

Natrum was well aware that the patterns in his life were unhealthy, so he went to therapy in an effort to change, but therapy alone just wasn't enough. He was trying his very best to be true to himself, but he still couldn't break out of his old destructive patterns. Why was it so hard for him to change? Because his conscious self didn't have the power to create the reality that he really wanted. Why? Because his perception of reality was created by his unconscious beliefs (delusions that he, and his therapist, were unaware of), and these beliefs were constantly being reinforced by his past experiences, which kept proving to him that "this is what always happens!" A delusion is simply a false belief that creates an unhealthy perception of reality, and this perception affects our actions in unhealthy ways. So in a sense, delusion is sickness, and freedom from delusion is health. If Natrum truly wanted to change, he would actually have to take a leap of faith against all his past experiences, which isn't easy to do, and stop trying to constantly protect himself from some future possibility of emotional pain that isn't a reality in this moment, here and now. He would have to take a chance that his new relationship could turn out differently in spite of the fact that his past experiences didn't support this idea. Perhaps he could even become aware enough to see that his past experiences could have simply been a result of his own unconscious actions, and realize the possibility that the outcome *could have been* totally different, if only he had been more aware... A lot of courage is needed to step out of these old patterns, but the possibility of a different outcome would make it worth taking the chance!

By the time I got involved in this story, the relationship was already over, but I thought the story was so interesting that it still needed a place in my book since it really shows how these patterns keep repeating themselves in people's lives and how hard it is to change them. It is easy for anyone, who reads the story above, to see how Natrum was making it virtually impossible for Medorrhinum to stay with him, but it is not quite so easy to look at our own lives and see that this is something we all do to some extent.

My main focus, when sharing people's stories, isn't to help people stay in their relationships with each other longer, but to help deepen the understanding of what actually happens when you put two different perceptions of reality together in a relationship. Each of the partners has a delusional perception of their own reality, and because neither experience reality as it really is, they project their own perceptions onto each other instead of relating directly. You can't solve these kinds of issues through therapy alone, unless the therapist is also very aware of how people project their issues onto each other. Putting a list on the fridge of things to do together, or things to say to each other every day, isn't going to do the trick. This only teaches people how to pretend, and how to manipulate each other in more subtle ways to get their needs met. As far as I can see, more understanding and awareness of our patterns is the only key to transformation, and there are no shortcuts or psychological "tricks" that can help us avoid the discomfort of breaking through these patterns. The fact is, you won't see permanent change unless the delusions, that are the actual source of the patterns, lose their grip. Only then can we truly start perceiving reality as it is, without distortions, and only then can we stop creating so many unnecessary problems for ourselves.

In the story above, I am sure Natrum could have benefited greatly from using a homeopathic remedy in addition to the therapy he was getting. Occasional doses of Natrum Muriaticum in a high potency, over a period of time, would most likely have helped him become more aware of the patterns he was struggling with, and maybe even helped him find the courage to go against his past experiences so that a new perception of reality could become possible. A new perception, with no predetermined expectation of the outcome, and no sabotage! However, he didn't know about homeopathy until his relationship with Medorrhinum had already ended, so the best thing he can do now is to just keep becoming more and more aware of all the patterns that are keeping him tied to his past, so that eventually, he is able to just let go...

WHO'S IN CHARGE?
Medorrhinum and Silicea Terra

This is the story of the relationship between Medorrhinum (woman) and Silicea Terra (man).

Medorrhinum and Silicea fell in love at first sight. There was instant friendship, physical chemistry and a strong spiritual connection between the two, and they simply couldn't stay apart. They decided to get married 6 weeks after they met and have been together ever since.

Medorrhinum and Silicea are both idealistic and have high standards in everything. Although Medorrhinum is an animal remedy, she still loves order and can be almost as fastidious and conscientious about little things as Silicea.

Medorrhinum and Silicea love planning things together and finding ways to manifest their ideas into physical form. There are, however, certain differences between them that affect how each one of them proceeds. Silicea is a lot more cautious than Medorrhinum and never jumps into anything until every little detail has been carefully planned and he knows ahead of time exactly how well it will work. Medorrhinum is a more spontaneous, impatient type. She doesn't mind jumping into things unprepared, trusting that she will be able to deal with surprises and problems when, or if, they appear. However, that kind of approach could easily drive Silicea insane, so Medorrhinum had to learn to develop appreciation for Silicea's thoroughness and be patient with him, which is hard for someone who is always in a hurry.

Medorrhinum was happy that Silicea is what she called a "practical dreamer" and not just a talker. She likes to see concrete results and not just plans, although it is hard for her to wait while Silicea takes his time planning. He has aversion to being rushed or told what to do, and he won't take any action until he feels totally ready and properly prepared. Medorrhinum likes the fact that he is such a responsible type that she feels she can totally trust him. She knows how cautious he is, and how well he plans everything. Once he starts a project, he knows what it is going to cost, almost down to the penny, and he has the determination to follow the project through to completion. Medorrhinum doesn't have the same kind of determination that Silicea has, and tends to run out of steam halfway through things.

Silicea was also happy with his new relationship because he had found a woman who gave him freedom to do whatever he wanted with the resources that were available. Silicea was dreaming of building his own house, and Medorrhinum had the resources to do so. Medorrhinum had no problems letting Silicea be in charge of the project, and Silicea liked being in charge because he felt safe when he was in control. He wanted the house to be designed in such a way that it best served the interests and needs of the people who were going to live there, and he wanted to do it his own way, which Medorrhinum didn't mind.

Silicea liked being in charge of the project, but he didn't like being in charge of other workers. He preferred working alone. It was too much of a hassle to work with others, since people always make mistakes that he would ultimately have to go back and fix. Working alone eliminated these kinds of aggravations. By doing most of the work single handedly, he knew that there would be no surprises. With a combination of will, determination and creative genius, he found ways to do almost anything without anyone's help. He didn't even mind if the project took longer to complete, as long as everything was done correctly and perfectly, because he always felt anxious and stressed if things didn't go exactly according to his pre-made plans.

Silicea is a hard worker who doesn't spare himself in any way. He has an iron will and is unbelievably stubborn and determined, once he has decided what he wants to do. The downside is that he has a tendency to push himself to the point of total exhaustion. Although his will and determination is very strong, his energy tends to run out whenever he pushes himself too hard. This often makes him feel depressed and he can easily develop an aversion to work, so it would be helpful if he could find a better balance between work and rest. (Here, it is interesting to note that Silicea often struggles with confusion and indecision, especially if there are too many choices to make, but once he overcomes his indecision and actually makes up his mind, his decision often becomes a totally fixed idea).

Silicea likes being in control in his relationship to Medorrhinum as well. When Medorrhinum needed a new computer, Silicea searched the internet for days and read about all the computers that were available before he chose the one he thought would serve Medorrhinum's needs the best. Medorrhinum knew she couldn't do better than that since she would normally spend much less time looking around and impulsively buy whatever she thought was a good deal on the spur of the moment. She just didn't have the patience or interest in spending 3 days researching anything before making a decision, and she was more than happy to have Silicea do it for her.

The interesting thing about Silicea is that even though he liked being in charge in the relationship, he never tried to interfere with Medorrhinum's independent nature. He didn't mind at all if Medorrhinum made decisions for herself about what she wanted to do in her life, and he supported her any way he knew how whenever she felt passionate about something new. His need for control was on a different level. It was more of a need to be in control of anything that had to do with himself, or his immediate environment. For Silicea, being in control was just a way to eliminate future surprises, coping with stress, and controlling his anxiety level, and not a desire to control anyone else.

Medorrhinum liked having a mate who didn't try to restrict her freedom in any way. In the past she would often leave, if the relationship she was in became too restrictive, since independence is very important to her. In a way, she doesn't give herself totally to any relationship. She always divides her time into sections allowing a certain amount of time for her relationship and another amount of time for her creative pursuits, as both are equally important to her. She does this without any sense of guilt, which helps distinguish Medorrhinum from Natrum. She is very good at making sure that she has enough time for herself because if she has to sacrifice her needs against her will, she becomes irritable and builds up resentment. Here we can see the possibility of Medorrhinum entering a Sepia state, if circumstances require her to compromise too much, since Sepia's core issues has to do with too much compromise in relationships.

Medorrhinum and Silicea got along very well most of the time. Their values were very similar. They agreed about spiritual issues, money issues and how to raise the children and keep the house. Medorrhinum was a domestic type who took care of the children and did most of the housework, and Silicea made most of the money. This suited Silicea well, since he had no interest in vacuuming, cooking and diaper changes. They were sexually compatible, they liked spending time together, and they especially loved their spiritual connection. Medorrhinum and Silicea would often have long talks until late into the night about all kinds of wild and wonderful stuff. What one said would trigger new ideas and connections for the other. They both loved bouncing spiritual concepts around, which helped them see the bigger picture and created a deeper understanding of life itself. This was especially important to Silicea, who had a tendency to become depressed and weary of life, often questioning the purpose of everything.

The only time they experienced problems in their relationship was if their roles were reversed, that is, if Medorrhinum decided to be in charge for the day. Here we have to look at both core situations. Medorrhinum is waiting to take over a position of responsibility, even though she doesn't really feel ready because she is worried about how it will affect her independence that she loves so much. (She actually loves her independence more than she loves being in charge). However, when, or if, she feels ready to do so, she is perfectly capable. Silicea is also supposed to take over a position of power. He, too, doesn't feel ready to do so, but for a different reason than Medorrhinum. He isn't ready because he feels insecure about his ability to do so. His confidence is low and he is worried that he isn't good enough, or that he will be judged or misrepresented in some way. This is why he is so concerned about keeping up his public image.

In this relationship he doesn't mind being in charge. Medorrhinum encourages him to take this position because she knows that he is far more capable and thorough than she will ever be, and this gives him the confidence he needs to be in this position. However, if Medorrhinum decided to change the roles for the day because she didn't like what Silicea was doing, she would basically indicate to Silicea that what he was doing wasn't good enough for her. In other words, he had failed to prove himself and lost his position as a result. This is Silicea's core fear, and he would immediately feel insulted and defensive and treat Medorrhinum as if she were his worst enemy.

The first time this became a serious issue was when Medorrhinum was going to put the electrical lines in the new house they were building. She knew how to do electrical work, but Silicea had to help her make holes in the studs and do what he was told. Not only did Medorrhinum want to be in charge, but she was putting in the lines in her normal spontaneous way, not following her own plans too rigidly, and at some point even changing her plans in the middle of the job. This sent Silica "through the roof," and he became furious and verbally abusive. He was worried about whether she would make mistakes when she didn't rigidly follow the plans (fear of failure), and he could just imagine how much work it would be to rip down sheetrock and do it again later if she did make a mistake (failure=doom and ruined image, since he still felt responsible for the outcome).

Silicea had expected Medorrhinum to plan the electrical layout down to the smallest detail, like he would have done if it was his project. He wanted Medorrhinum to know exactly how many wires would go through each hole, so he could decide what size hole to make in each stud, and Medorrhinum thought this was a ridiculous request. She wanted him to just make a hole that could hold at least 3 wires, and then make more holes if needed. They both realized that they couldn't do electrical work together since Medorrhinum couldn't possibly live up to Silicea's expectations, and Silicea couldn't work under someone so "scatterbrained." Her "wait and see attitude" was like a red flag to Silicea because it triggered all his deepest fears, fear of failure and fear of not knowing what the outcome was going to be. So she asked him to go and take care of the children for a few days, instead, and completed the rest of the job with the help of his brother.

This kind of independence in a woman is often a threat to any relationship, but Silicea didn't really mind her strength. He trusted that she was capable of doing the job, but he had a problem with her vague plans and her spontaneous decision making. Her vagueness triggered his anxiety and made him want to be in charge, but since he didn't know how to do the electrical work, that was a problem. Silicea did better taking care of the children while Medorrhinum did the electrical work because it gave him something different to focus his attention on.

Silicea usually feels better when he is in charge and can rigidly follow his own plans because it makes him feel safe when he is in control, and he knows exactly what is going to happen. In the situation that goes with Silicea, he is a prince (or princess) who is worried about keeping up a proper image that proves him worthy of a future position of power that he is expected to take over some day. His best chance, of doing this, is to totally rely on himself. Having to rely on anyone else quickly triggers his anxiety and trust issues. He is not happy when anything is unpredictable because it can easily lead to possible disaster that he would be responsible for fixing. And if Medorrhinum is the one who is causing the problem, he will scold her severely. As long as Medorrhinum stops trying to take charge, Silicea and Medorrhinum are best friends and very happy together, but she has to know her place in the relationship if she wants peace and harmony.

Once in a while Silicea triggers Medorrhinum's core issues, too. This usually happens if he goes shopping without her, and he doesn't return when she thinks he is supposed to be back. Medorrhinum really suffers when she has to wait! She feels anxiety in her stomach and fears that something bad must have happened. She paces the floor and feels extremely restless. Time stops moving, she can't think, she can't remember anything, she can't eat, she can't relax. She postpones things she was supposed to do, or she'll do them in a hurry. All her neurosis disappears as soon as she hears Silicea's car in the driveway. Medorrhinum simply can't stop worrying if she has to wait, especially if a time is set, and Silicea doesn't show up on time. This situation corresponds to Medorrhinum's original situation, where she is waiting for someone to die, which basically means that she is waiting for something bad to happen. This is why any kind of waiting makes her anxious, and the waiting is always torturous, no matter what she is waiting for.

The combination of Silicea and Medorrhinum is interesting because the two situations that go with the remedies are very compatible. Silicea wants to be king, but lacks confidence and feels that he has to constantly prove that he is good enough to do the job. Medorrhinum is supposed to take over a position of power, but she doesn't feel ready for that kind of responsibility because she enjoys her independence too much. She already thinks Silicea is a great king, so he doesn't have to prove himself to her. If Silicea's mate was a natural leader type, like a Nux, Silicea wouldn't even think about being in charge since he doesn't have enough self confidence to compete with a Nux. In this case, however, Silicea feels encouraged to be in charge by Medorrhinum, and this situation works perfectly for both.

As long as Medorrhinum doesn't take charge, and Silicea doesn't make Medorrhinum wait for him, they can easily live together in peace without triggering any core issues in each other most of the time. If no core issues are triggered, they simply don't have any reason to fight over anything. So far they have lived together for almost 6 years, and they are still best friends and love each other deeply.

The story of this relationship clearly shows how relationship compatibility is greatly a matter of whether the partners are triggering core issues in each other on a regular basis, or if core issues are only triggered once in a while. If core issues are triggered every day, there isn't much chance for the relationship to survive because core issues are always very painful and difficult to overcome. If they are triggered on a regular basis, the partners may benefit from some kind of deep counseling, like primal therapy, so they can start working through their issues and eventually leave them behind. The easiest relationships are the ones where core issues don't get triggered too much. This allows the partners to experience more joy together, and less emotional pain.

THE ALMOST PERFECT
RELATIONSHIP
Natrum Muriaticum and Arsenicum Album

This is the story of the relationship between Natrum Muriaticum (woman) and Arsenicum Album (man).

Natrum's relationship with Arsenicum started out as a friendship. They knew each other for 5 years before they actually got together as a couple. They really enjoyed each other's company because they had so many things in common. Both liked sports, swimming, hiking, the news, the same kinds of food, and going to bed early and getting up early. The friendship gradually deepened and Arsenicum found himself missing Natrum when they were not together. So he picked up the phone one day and told Natrum that he felt that she was more than just a friend to him, and a few months later they moved in together.

Arsenicum told me that they had a couple's chart done by an Ayurvedic astrologer who told them that they had the most compatible combination of traits he had ever encountered in a couple. In his chart there were 36 possible combinations of compatibility, and he explained that a couple should have a score of at least 18-20 to have a decent chance of succeeding in their relationship, and Natrum and Arsenicum had a score of 30 out of 36!

Looking at the two remedy profiles, Natrum and Arsenicum do have a lot in common. Both are quiet, reserved, timid, sensitive, cheerful and affectionate. Both like being in control, but Arsenicum has better self confidence and is also more stubborn and headstrong than Natrum, so the issue of who is in charge is not a problem in the relationship since Natrum wouldn't want to challenge Arsenicum on that level. Since both are metal remedies, they both dislike chaos, and both are reliable, punctual and like things to be as perfect as possible. However, there is one major difference between the two remedies if you look into why they both want perfection, and this difference does create some problems in the relationship.

The situation that goes with the Arsenicum perception of reality is one where Arsenicum is wrongfully accused, pursued, attacked, robbed and almost killed. Somebody conspired against him. He didn't know who, he was too weak to defend himself, and almost lost his life in the attack. Arsenicum still feels that if he had been faultless, the original conspiracy and attack wouldn't have happened in the first place. This is why Arsenicum has to be perfect, to prevent anything similar from ever happening again. He is still afraid that the original situation could repeat itself, and he is still doing whatever he can to prevent it from happening. One of the ways he does this is by arguing and trying to convince people in his life that he is right and they are wrong. Arsenicum is a master communicator, and an expert at arguing his point of view. He has to have things his own way, regardless of how others feel about it, and if someone questions his "rightness," he will perceive them as "the enemy" until he can convince them that their perception is wrong. This can make Arsenicum seem to be self absorbed and controlling. However, these are vitally important issues to Arsenicum because he can only relax when he knows that nobody is misrepresenting him or misunderstanding his point of view. Therefore, he always has to be so perfect that nobody can possibly accuse him of anything because only then can he feel safe.

Natrum's reason for being perfect is very different. Natrums usually have strict, disapproving fathers, who can't be pleased no matter how hard they try to please them, leaving Natrum with a sense that she will only be loved if she is absolutely perfect. When she does her best and still doesn't receive the love or approval she craves, she feels there is something wrong with her, or that she simply isn't good enough.

The issue of perfection shows up in this relationship in many different ways. Natrum describes Arsenicum as a perfectionist, living in an imperfect world. He has a very strong inner critic and tends to think that nothing is good enough unless it is absolutely perfect. This affects everything in his life, from how his eggs look, to how his laundry is folded. He has a very strict sense of right and wrong, and a very rigid idea of how things have to be. The question is how much Natrum can measure up to Arsenicum's high ideals.

One of the issues that first showed up in this relationship was the fact that Natrum was older than Arsenicum. For Arsenicum the relationship was based more on their intellectual connection and friendship rather than on physical attraction and chemistry. He deeply appreciated and valued their friendship, but he wasn't sure about the age difference. He decided to keep the relationship secret at first, and this hurt Natrum's feelings.

Natrum wanted to be the perfect mate for Arsenicum, but she couldn't wipe out the age difference and had to accept the fact that she was less than perfect in Arsenicum's perception. We can easily imagine how this must have triggered Natrum's issues around perfection and love. She wasn't perfect, and she was living with someone who wanted absolute perfection in every aspect of his life, and there was nothing she could do about it! All she could do was to accept her position. This created a fear in her that Arsenicum would seek a younger woman, someone who was "more perfect" than she. Slowly, the thought crept into her mind that perhaps this relationship couldn't last because "How can he love me if I can't be perfect?" (The next thought waiting in line, of course, is "Uh, uh, I'm going to get my feelings hurt again!")

This mindset is very understandable since Natrums rarely receive the love they hope for in any of their relationships. The pattern totally goes with Natrum's perception of reality, in which she is hopes to find the love she is dreaming of, but it never quite turns out the way she had hoped. Arsenicum's moody, self absorbed nature doesn't do much to reassure Natrum that he really does love and appreciate her just the way she is, although she knows that Arsenicum has a big heart and that he loves her in his own way.

This brings up another difference between the two remedies, Natrum's need for emotional security versus Arsenicum's need for physical security. Natrum is hoping Arsenicum is going to give her the emotional security she needs, while Arsenicum is more concerned with issues around physical security. Emotional security is simply too vague for an Arsenicum to be concerned with, which also adds to Natrum's feeling of not being totally loved and cared for. It is not that Arsenicum doesn't love Natrum because he does love her very much. He just doesn't invest much of his energy in the area of emotional commitment because it isn't really an important part of Arsenicum's reality. He is more concerned with the issue of creating physical security for himself, which is much more important to Arsenicums in general. It is very difficult for Natrum to understand Arsenicum's lack of interest in the issue of emotional security, since it means everything to her. However, Arsenicum doesn't really get what the big deal is since that isn't what he values most.

This whole issue is completely predictable when looking at the different ways Natrum and Arsenicum perceive their realities. Arsenicum triggers Natrum's insecurity with his critical and perfectionist ways, and don't reassure her enough that he really cares. And on the other hand, Natrum already knows she can never be perfect enough for anyone. Because this is a feeling Natrum already had before she entered the relationship, Arsenicum is simply adding to her insecurity, making her fear that Arsenicum is still looking for someone better, younger or more perfect than she.

Besides the issues of perfection and lack of emotional security, Natrum is in many ways a better mate for Arsenicum than she realizes. Arsenicum described Natrum as empathetic, forgiving, understanding and flexible. He described how Natrum is always there for him, which is something he really appreciates, and he also explained how Natrum is able to voice what is upsetting to her, without making him wrong. She doesn't get hooked no matter how

THE ALMOST PERFECT RELATIONSHIP Natrum Muriaticum and Arsenicum Album

mad he gets. She simply doesn't bite, and this makes him feel safe in the relationship because it doesn't trigger any of his trust issues. This means a lot more to Arsenicum than Natrum realizes. If Natrum had been a more confronting type, who would attack Arsenicum with anger and make him wrong, it would immediately trigger all of Arsenicum's issues around being wrongfully accused of something he didn't do. When he wants to fight about something, Natrum usually doesn't fight back, and he ends up having to face his own stuff instead. Having a mate who doesn't bite makes it easy for Arsenicum to feel safe and secure. Since all Arsenicums are well aware that they don't always treat their mates as nicely as they should, they know, deep down, that there is always a possibility that their loved ones could one day decide to leave the relationship as a result. However, with Natrum, he feels totally at ease since she is an extremely loyal mate who sticks to her man through thick and thin. Arsenicum considers himself very lucky to be with her, and he told me that they have made a pact to be friends forever.

From Natrum's point of view, she feels very uncomfortable when Arsenicum wants to fight. Natrum's father was very angry, and she used to respond to his anger by shutting down and withdrawing, which is a typical Natrum response. She finds herself withdrawing from Arsenicum, too, when they are arguing, which affects her ability to open up to him and be intimate for a while after the argument (the famous Natrum wall of protection). Natrum is naturally afraid to get her feelings hurt and prefers it when they don't argue. Arsenicum actually enjoys a good fight or argument. He feels that a little argument creates healthy tension in the relationship, which he misses when Natrum doesn't fight back. Natrum prefers to be a good listener and to work things out more peacefully. The thing that most annoys Natrum is when Arsenicum leaves the room during an argument, which he does if she accuses him of anything. Once he didn't even talk to her for two days after an argument.

Again, we are dealing with issues that go with the Arsenicum remedy picture. Once Natrum accuses him of something, she becomes the enemy, and there is no way Arsenicum will admit to the enemy that he is wrong! So, if he is right, he will argue as if his life depends on it, and if he is wrong, he won't speak to her. That way he doesn't have to admit that he isn't perfect, so leaving the room and not speaking to his accuser for a couple of days is an easy solution, but not a very comfortable one for Natrum. However, if she understands his perception of reality in the situation, she won't have to take it quite so personally, although that is going to be a bit of a challenge for someone who already thinks there is something wrong with her...

The last issue that has shown up in this relationship is the issue of spontaneity when it comes to sex. Arsenicum wants Natrum to seduce him, but since Arsenicum is so spontaneous, temperamental and unpredictable by nature, Natrum never knows if she will be rejected. She already has low self confidence, which is typical for all Natrums, and if he rejects her for some reason, she will end up getting her feelings hurt. Natrums often feel devastated if they are rejected because rejection triggers their father issues about disapproval from a male. This disapproval reinforces the already existing feeling that there is something wrong with her, and it reminds her that she still isn't perfect. And since this is already such a delicate issue in her relationship with Arsenicum, she simply can't go there. Arsenicum doesn't quite understand why she can't, but by becoming more aware of the issues that go with the Natrum perception of reality, it shouldn't be too hard for him to understand her position.

In this relationship Natrum and Arsenicum trigger core issues in each other that fit the perceptions of reality that go with each remedy. There aren't any simple, practical solutions to make the relationship work better, except for each person to become more aware of the perception that goes with the other person's remedy picture, as well as their own. Through more awareness and understanding of where the other is coming from, and why the other feels or acts a certain way, they can start to consciously break through old patterns and learn to relate to each other in new ways.

Arsenicum has to learn to love and accept things for what they are, even if they are less than perfect according to his preconceived ideas. If he can see that things simply are what they are, and that nature never creates perfection according to human standards, he too, will eventually be able to relax and allow himself, as well as his partner, to be less than perfect. In addition, he also needs to understand why it is so important for Natrum to be loved unconditionally. She needs to feel that she doesn't have to be perfect to deserve love, and that he loves her for who she really is. This would make it easier for Natrum to love and accept herself more, so she can break her old pattern of thinking she has to be perfect to deserve love. Arsenicum also needs to understand why her fear of rejection is so strong. This fear is basically just an old pattern that has been constantly reinforced in her since she was a small child, and is therefore very difficult to let go of.

Natrum needs to understand why Arsenicum feels that he has to be perfect in every way to feel safe and secure, even though it makes him difficult to live with. She also has to understand how the issue of physical security sometimes takes so much of his energy that he forgets to ask how she is doing that day, but that doesn't mean he doesn't care about her. In addition to understanding where Arsenicum is coming from, Natrum also has to somehow find enough inner strength to give herself the reassurance she needs since she'll always be disappointed if she expects it to come from someone else. Anything you expect to come from somebody else usually doesn't happen, simply because you expect it!

THE ALMOST PERFECT RELATIONSHIP Natrum Muriaticum and Arsenicum Album

Maybe it helps a little to remember that the universe could have created a more perfect being than Natrum, but that is not what it did. In nature there is no perfection, so why do we feel that we have to be perfect? Have you ever seen a perfectly symmetrical tree in the forest with equal branches on all sides? Such perfection simply doesn't exist unless it is man made! So the universe created Natrum exactly the way she is, both beautiful and perfect in her own way, simply because this world wouldn't have been the same without her. And I am sure Arsenicum agrees...

DISAPPOINTED EXPECTATIONS
Natrum Muriaticum and
Lycopodium Clavatum

This is the story of the relationship between Natrum Muriaticum (woman) and Lycopodium Clavatum (man).

The combination of Natrum and Lycopodium is definitely a compatible one, since these two have already spent about 20 years together. The relationship is stable, and they are still good friends, even though they both experience a certain level of underlying friction between them. To understand what the friction is about, we have to first look at their individual backgrounds.

Natrum's parents were divorced. Her father was emotionally unavailable and sometimes abusive towards her, and all her previous relationships reflect similar issues. In true Natrum style, she would always pick men who weren't interested in commitment or emotional intimacy, and often found herself in relationships that were emotionally painful and sometimes even physically abusive. The more abusive the relationship became, the more she wanted to make the relationship work. She said she loved the abuser, and she always ended up getting emotionally hurt when the relationship eventually came to an end. She developed abandonment issues and started dreaming about "the perfect relationship" where a "princely" kind of guy would come and take care of her, and they would live happily ever after. This very romantic vision of love and relationships is similar to the story of Cinderella, where she is dealing with abusive, unloving relationships on a daily basis (evil step mom and step sisters), while dreaming about meeting a prince who would save her and make her eternally happy. This, of course, is the story that goes with the Natrum profile. Deep down Natrum feels that she will only be loved if she is perfect, so if her mate doesn't love her enough, she will obsessively work to improve herself and the relationship, hoping to eventually achieve the love she so desperately craves. Unfortunately, this rarely works and usually ends with broken relationships, disappointments and more emotional wounds.

In every Natrum's life, she will sooner or later run into a man who truly does love her and does want commitment. Interestingly enough, when this happens, she loses interest quickly; even though this is the kind of relationship she has been hoping and praying for. Natrum had previously experienced two such relationships. She said to me: "I could have had the perfect relationship with either one of these men, but it was too smothering, too intense, it wasn't what I thought it would be like, and it challenged my intimacy issues too much." This, too, is typical for Natrum. She desires love and intimacy more than anything, but when it actually happens, she can't handle the level of intimacy and emotional vulnerability it requires. It triggers so much fear in her that she has to get away. This is why she finds these kinds of relationships "smothering." She needs space to be able to calm her fear of getting hurt because that level of closeness makes her feel out of control and vulnerable. As soon as she is able to create some distance from the other, either physically or emotionally, she feels in control and emotionally safe again. However, if Natrum keeps pushing away her mate too often, constantly resisting his attempts to create more intimacy, he might eventually get tired of being rejected and start looking for someone who doesn't mind being close. He may feel that Natrum is too emotionally cold, since he usually doesn't have a clue why she keeps pushing him away. And again, Natrum often ends up in a broken relationship.

It is easy to see why this happens over and over. In an effort to protect herself from disappointment before she gets too involved in a relationship, Natrum creates the very thing she is most afraid of, simply by expecting it to happen and acting accordingly. If she could find the courage to be more open to her mate and stop blocking his efforts to be intimate, she probably wouldn't have to go through so many broken relationships. But, that would mean breaking the patterns that go with her core issues, which is never an easy thing to do. However, the Natrum woman in this story seems to have resolved many of these issues. She has done a lot of soul searching and awareness work, and this has helped her overcome many of her old relationship issues. The fact that she has been able to successfully maintain her present relationship to Lycopodium for the past 20 years is proof that Natrums don't always have to end up in broken relationships.

Lycopodium didn't tell me very much about himself, but through careful questioning I was able to get enough information to at least get an idea of what kind of person he was. As a child he was rather introverted, shy and a loner. He was an only child and didn't have a lot of experience relating to others. At school he was a straight A student who liked reading books. His mind was sharp and he had a tendency to over analyze everything. Later in life this ability became a benefit at work, where he was excellent at solving practical problems.

Lycopodium likes being in charge and hates being told what to do by others. He often becomes irritable and frustrated if people don't listen to his advice, and he has a tendency to become firm, or even dictatorial, if needed. He also suffers from a lack of confidence, anticipation anxiety and fear of failure when something new is expected of him, but he is usually perfectly capable of performing a task once he is actually doing it. (These qualities are all typical Lycopodium traits). Before he met Natrum, he used to have a high sex drive and many short term relationships since he didn't like making serious commitments to anyone. However, he explained that if, or when, he does decide to make a commitment, he always works hard to keep it.

When Natrum and Lycopodium met, Natrum felt for the first time in her life that this was the mate she had been looking for. He was gentle and definitely not abusive. He didn't even like arguments. To Natrum, Lycopodium was "magical" and "prince like" and she fell in love almost right away. Lycopodium saw in Natrum a beautiful, highly intelligent, capable woman, which was something he could easily admire. They enjoyed each other's company, and after spending some time together they decided to get married.

After living together for a while, their differences in personality started becoming quite evident. The first thing they noticed was a difference in orderliness. This is to be expected since metal remedies usually have a strong need for order, structure and discipline, while plant remedies usually have a more disorderly disposition as well as a tendency for hypersensitivity. Natrum is project oriented, busy, organized and disciplined. She gets a lot done and loves multi tasking. Her standards are high. She aims for perfection and tends to become judgmental or critical towards people who don't fulfill her expectations. Natrum likes her systems. She puts away her winter clothes when the weather warms up and her summer clothes when it gets cold. At some point she tried to involve Lycopodium in this process so he could also do the same, but she was disappointed to find that he didn't really care about upholding her systems, or keeping things in order. He was naturally scattered, messy and disorganized, and actually preferred living in chaos. She told me that he never even worried about finding things that got lost in the chaos because he would simply go out and buy a new thing if he couldn't find what he was looking for.

Natrum would often become critical, angry or emotionally intense towards Lycopodium. She has a tendency to become upset if things aren't done the way she likes them, and Lycopodium's way of doing things is very different from hers. However, when she tried to express her discontent to Lycopodium, she quickly realized that they had a serious communication problem.

Lycopodium absolutely hates confrontations of any kind. His nature is very different from Natrum's. His anger builds up slowly, and doesn't reach the level of intensity that hers does. He doesn't process emotional issues well, and often can't express how he feels, simply because he doesn't really know. He feels that she is expecting him to know how he feels, but this is hard for him because he doesn't have enough self awareness to be able to do so. He can either fight back, which usually accomplishes nothing, or he can back off and try to avoid the whole confrontation. Natrum's anger is usually much too intense for him. She comes on too strongly and doesn't always listen to what he has to say. Sometimes her facts are wrong, and she may even become irrational while confronting him, which annoys Lycopodium greatly because his logical mind can't make any sense of it. Her anger affects him so much that sometimes he withdraws from her sexually as a result.

Natrum doesn't understand why Lycopodium is having so much difficulty expressing himself. Her mind is quick and she can express herself very easily, so she often feels annoyed and irritated when he can't give her any answers. She feels hurt when he tries to escape from confrontations just because things are uncomfortable. It is important for her to express how she feels, and when she does, she expects her mate to listen and try to understand what she is saying. When Lycopodium backs off from confrontations instead, it triggers all her old abandonment issues, and this is very painful for her. If he also withdraws from her sexually, as a result of the conflict, she feels very sad, hurt, unwanted and unloved.

Lycopodium doesn't challenge Natrum's fear of intimacy, like her previous partners used to. On the contrary, he is often too cold emotionally for her taste, and she doesn't think he puts enough energy into the relationship. When Lycopodium withdraws from her because he can't deal with her level of intensity, she often feels like her needs or desires aren't being met in the relationship. Over time this has challenged her dream of ever finding the perfect relationship. Even though they have been together for a long time, and they are still good friends, this relationship didn't turn out to be all she had secretly wished for. She had wanted to find a "prince" who would make her feel really special. She still thinks the possibility of a perfect relationship exists, but she has finally realized that she may have to give up her expectations of what it should be like and learn to make herself feel special instead, while also learning to accept her mate for what he is. This is a big step for Natrum. It shows that she has achieved a level of self awareness that allows her to see that the real problem isn't her mate's lack of perfection, but her own expectations of what she thinks it should be like. Hopefully, she can now let go of all her old ideas that no longer benefit her and start enjoying her relationship to Lycopodium in a new way.

However, Natrum is not the only one with expectations in this relationship. In the last few years Lycopodium has also had some issues that are bothering him. The problem for Lycopodium is that Natrum isn't working. A few years ago she had a very well paid job. She enjoyed having a lot of responsibility and doing very challenging work, for which she got paid more than Lycopodium did in his job. But when the company she worked for suddenly closed down, she found herself in a lawsuit where the company was trying to force her to waive her rights. She felt attacked, unfairly treated and became very depressed. She had a hard time letting go and moving on, and she still hasn't decided what she wants to do next.

Lycopodium understands that the lawsuit affected her deeply, and that she needed time to regroup, but after about 3 years of waiting, his patience has come to an end. It has now become a fairness issue. In his family both parents always went to work, so the "housewife model" doesn't appeal to him. He feels that both should contribute money to the relationship, and since he isn't making very much money in his job, he often feels anxious about money matters and criticizes Natrum's spending habits. At some point he suggested that they should start a business together, but Natrum wasn't excited about it. The business idea was his idea, not hers. She didn't want to jump into anything until she felt ready, and besides, she wanted to do "her own thing."

Natrum doesn't share Lycopodium's worry about money because she knows that she can most likely find another high paying job again without too much trouble, should the need arise. It was more important for her to take time for her spiritual growth after going to court because she needed time to process what was happening. She doesn't really understand why Lycopodium is making such an issue about this, since he is still making enough money for them both to live on. She is planning to go back to work as soon as she can figure out what she wants to do, but she resents Lycopodium for putting pressure on her because she may want to do something totally different, she just doesn't know what, yet. She is thinking about the possibility of doing some kind of counseling for abused women, where she can help other women cope with issues that she has personally experienced and been able to overcome in her own life.

This is where the relationship stands today. They no longer experience too much open conflict. Natrum has realized that her intensity affects Lycopodium too much, so she has taught herself to be angry calmly, so she doesn't scare him away. Lycopodium is starting to understand how important it is that he doesn't avoid confrontations when Natrum feels the need to express herself, and he also tries to listen to her more sincerely. But there is still a definite underlying feeling of friction between them, which is caused by unfulfilled expectations on both sides.

From a homeopathic view, the combination of Natrum and Lycopodium is "mutually fulfilling" because they both play a part in each other's stories. Since we are here to learn to deal with our core issues, we always find mates who will somehow assist us in that process. In this case, Natrum has father issues, and Lycopodium can easily take on the role as the father figure in the relationship. He can be dictatorial and firm, like her own father was, and he can also be just as emotionally unavailable, since he hates confrontations and lacks the self awareness needed to articulate his feelings well. This makes him the perfect mate for Natrum because it gives her plenty of opportunities to deal with these issues. The core delusion that goes with the Natrum profile is that she can't always get what she wants, and the core feeling is that unless she is perfect, or her relationship is perfect, she won't get her needs met, or experience the love she dreams about.

Natrum can also play a role in Lycopodium's story. In the profile that goes with the Lycopodium picture, Lycopodium feels small inside and has low self confidence. He suffers from anticipation anxiety in new situations and fears that anything he undertakes might fail. At the same time, he is ambitious and wants to achieve his goals. The only way this can happen is if he is able to overcome his fears. What he finds when he does muster up the courage to do new things and take on new projects, is that he is perfectly capable of pulling things off. It is only his confidence that is lacking, not his intelligence or ability to do things.

In this case Natrum is also ambitious, which appeals to Lycopodium. Together, they can climb the ladder of success and achieve a desirable position in society. Natrum doesn't suffer from the same lack of confidence, or fear of failure, so she may have a very encouraging effect on him, since those aren't her issues. Lycopodium needs a lot of support to overcome his fear of failure, and Natrum is usually unbelievably loyal and supportive to her mate. This is exactly what Lycopodium needs and wants. However, if we consider the fact that Lycopodium was originally attracted to Natrum's ambitious and fearless nature, it is easy to see why he now has a problem with the fact that Natrum is not working. He is worried about losing the social position he has achieved without the added income she could have provided. This has triggered Lycopodium's core fear that he won't amount to anything in his life because he fears that there is a chance that he could easily lose what he has achieved unless Natrum goes back to work soon.

Looking at this relationship, we also find qualities that are very compatible in many ways. For example, Lycopodium doesn't "smother" Natrum. He usually likes a certain amount of space in his relationships to others. He likes to know that someone is in the house, so he doesn't have to feel lonely, but he isn't necessarily interested in too much face to face interaction. This suits Natrum well. She gets to keep a certain distance and doesn't feel too emotionally vulnerable around Lycopodium, although she sometimes feels that he is a bit too cold for her, or too unemotional or detached.

My feeling is that the quality of this relationship would improve if they could both let go of their expectations of each other and start appreciating the things that they do like about each other instead. This brings me to a short story that I heard a long time ago, that beautifully illustrates the problem with looking for the perfect mate.

This story is about a man who had spent his whole life looking for the perfect woman. He had extremely high expectations but was convinced that she was out there, somewhere. He just needed to find her because he knew that he couldn't settle for anything less. He traveled all over the world, looking for her everywhere, and one day he finally found her. She was absolutely perfect! She was everything he had envisioned, and more. She was beautiful, intelligent, capable, stunning in every way. He was breathless. With sweaty palms, trembling hands and a pounding heart, he somehow managed to find the courage to ask her for a date. She accepted, and they decided to meet in a local café later the same day. He didn't know how to tell her, but sometime during their conversation he was actually able to express to her that he had traveled around the world looking for the perfect woman, and that he felt that she was the one. He told her she was the only woman he could ever love, and he pulled a ring out of his pocket and asked her to marry him. As fate would have it, this woman happened to be on the same kind of quest. She had also been looking for the perfect man all her life, and unfortunately, he wasn't it!

The truth is, there is no such thing as a "perfect" relationship. There is always going to be something imperfect about the mate you have picked, but this doesn't really matter as long as you focus on the things you like about each other, instead of focusing on what you don't like. The *idea* of perfection is the problem here, not lack of perfection in your mate! So, for this couple, I can only suggest a few things: Become more aware of your core issues and preconceived ideas of how you think things should be; work on breaking the patterns that are creating friction in the relationship; and focus more on giving and loving the other rather than on getting more of your own personal needs met. A more giving approach always works better than demands, criticism, preconceived ideas and unrealistic expectations.

HOW CAN I TRUST YOU?
Natrum Muriaticum and Staphysagria

This is the story of the very short lived relationship between Natrum Muriaticum (woman) and Staphysagria (man).

Staphysagria met Natrum a few years ago when he was renting a room from her. They really liked each other and had a small fling at the time. Since then, they stayed in touch by phone and visited each other once in a while.

Staphysagria thought Natrum was the most beautiful woman he had ever met. She made such an impression on him that he wasn't able to forget her, even though he rarely got to see her after she moved to a different part of the country. He couldn't stop thinking about her, and last year he finally decided to call her.

They both enjoyed connecting by phone, and Staphysagria started calling her every day. They discovered they had several things in common, both were lonely, both wanted a relationship, both wanted to have children, and both felt it was time to settle down in a committed relationship with someone, preferably each other. They soon fell madly and passionately in love over the phone. They couldn't wait to see each other again, but as everyone knows who has ever had a long distance relationship, things are always very different when the two people actually meet in person.

Only a week after they got together, Natrum already knew that things weren't going to be what she had been hoping for. The first thing she noticed was how many things Staphysagria hadn't told her before he came to live with her. She realized that he had never been able to get over the death of his brother. He was very close to his brother, who died in a motorcycle accident about 5 years earlier. His brother was a mountain climber and a daredevil, and Staphysagria admired him greatly. He wished he could have spent more time with him before he died, and he couldn't stop missing him, nor could he let go of the grief that he felt. He had also forgotten to tell Natrum how complicated his relationship to his mother and sister was. His older sister was clever and bright and always did well at school. She was definitely his mother's favorite child, and his mother often compared the two and told him she wished he was more like her. He knew that he could never compete with his sister's ability to achieve things, so he spent a lot of time in his room, daydreaming, instead of doing his homework. He didn't really have anything in common with his sister, and he felt it was unfair that she always got whatever she wanted, and he didn't, so he didn't like her very much. He felt that his mother always kept nagging and insulting him, and he eventually started hating his mother for being so unfair. Over time, his hatred and resentment toward his mother also started affecting all his other relationships with women since he often projected his unresolved mother issues onto whomever he was with at the time.

Staphysagria told me that his mother had never been happy with him and always used to yell at him and make him feel small. She mostly yelled about his school work and about doing things around the house. Staphysagria didn't like school, and he also didn't like doing much around the house. He often left his things lying all over the place, and his mother would yell and scold him for being lazy. Staphysagria told me that he sometimes yelled back, but since he really hated any kind of conflict or unpleasantness, his main pattern was to do whatever he could to avoid it. His mother always made him feel like a failure and he felt outraged and betrayed by her for suggesting that he wasn't as good as his sister.

As far back as he could remember, Staphysagria had always had an interest in architecture, and after he graduated from high school, this is what he decided to study. He told me that architecture was an easy thing for him to do. He was artistic by nature and had an excellent eye for three dimensional details. His building designs were a harmonious blend of beauty, unusual detail and practical usefulness, which, at some point, he received an award for. At the interview he told me how it was a privilege for anyone to be able to hire him to design their house because he happened to have an extraordinary talent which, for some reason, people often didn't appreciate enough. I could see how much he desired to receive honor, respect and recognition from others, and also how small, betrayed and outraged he was feeling inside. His self confidence was so dependent on other people's recognition that it made me think of Staphysagria right away. I personally saw one of his designer house plans, and I must admit both the layout and the shape of the house were impressive. But for some reason, he felt that nobody in his life was willing to give him the level of respect he felt that an architect of his magnitude deserved.

About 6 years ago the company he was working for hired a female marketing manager who also treated him with very little respect. She was hired to help the company through some financial difficulties they were having. Her job was to increase the company's efficiency and help to better promote their services. The marketing manager didn't like Staphysagria's designs very much. She thought they were too complicated and that each one took him too long to complete. She wanted the company architects to create more standard layouts and shapes, so they could offer their clients faster service at a better price. Staphysagria didn't agree. He felt that he could be of better service to his clients if he addressed each client's individual needs, rather than just offering them a standard "cookie cutter solution," even if that meant it would take a little longer and possibly cost a little more. However, the marketing manager didn't agree, so she told the company that Staphysagria wouldn't listen to her advice or suggestions, and that he was actually costing the company money because he wasn't working efficiently. As a result of her recommendations, Staphysagria ended up getting fired from the company, which was detrimental to his self confidence.

Years later when the company started getting requests from their clients for the kinds of houses that Staphysagria used to design, the company contacted him and apologized for firing him previously. They also offered him his job back because they had finally realized that he was actually the best architect on the team. They realized that his designs had been ahead of their time, and the company just wasn't the same without him. Staphysagria turned down their offer, but he was never able to let go of the pain and humiliation that the marketing manager had inflicted upon him. This, and similar issues, had completely destroyed his ability to trust women, and Natrum started feeling an uneasy sense of cautiousness and apprehension about her newly started relationship. Staphysagria had triggered her fear of getting hurt, and she could feel herself pulling back.

In addition to his issues about women in general, there were also many other issues that showed up in the first week they were together. Natrum was living in a small primitive cabin up in the mountains. She had a wood stove and no running water. For Staphysagria, who was a "city guy," the transition was mind blowing. He had never lived under such primitive circumstances, and he really wasn't prepared to deal with such "down to earth" issues as chopping wood, making a fire in the fire place and carrying water in buckets. It didn't cross his mind that he needed to chop wood and bring it into the house when the weather was nice, so he would be prepared for bad weather. He had never done dishes in 2 gallons of water before, and he didn't realize how important it was to clean up and keep your things in order when living in a tiny space.

Natrum was not happy. She had talked to him on the phone about her living conditions before he arrived, and he didn't seem to mind it at the time, but when he actually arrived, he didn't deal with it as well as Natrum had hoped he would. One day Natrum woke up and told him it looked like a snowstorm was about to come. She asked him to bring in wood, and Staphysagria forgot to do so. The snow came, and they didn't have any dry wood, and the cabin was freezing cold. When Natrum expressed her discontent, Staphysagria felt defensive, because he didn't think it was any big deal that he forgot to bring the wood in, and he thought she should be more patient with him since he wasn't used to such primitive living conditions. Staphysagria then stepped up to the fire place and attempted to make a fire for Natrum with the few pieces of dry wood they still had in the cabin, but he didn't have any idea how to build a fire, and he didn't want any advice from Natrum. Natrum watched him for a while, and after seeing that he really didn't have a clue how to do it, she told him to move over and did it herself instead. Staphysagria felt very insulted, and immediately felt resentment towards Natrum.

Staphysagria's response in this situation was to tell her that she should show him more respect because he was such a great architect. Natrum did appreciate his ability to design houses; in fact, she was hoping he would design a house for her, since she was dreaming about building her own house some day. However, when two people are living together in a primitive cabin where daily chores need to be done, the chores need to be done regardless of the fact that one of them is a great architect. Natrum pointed out to him that his ability to design houses made no difference regarding the fact that the cabin was still ice cold because the wood was too wet to make a fire with.

Natrum's practical point of view didn't help mend Staphysagria's sense of wounded honor in the situation. He had only lived with Natrum for a few days, and she had already suggested, both by action and by criticism, that he wasn't good enough for her. All of a sudden Natrum reminded him a lot of his mother, who used to scold him for similar things. Staphysagria could have possibly put more of an effort into the situation if he didn't want Natrum to insult him so much, but since he felt that he was already bending over backwards trying to please her, he became angry, obstinate and defensive instead.

Natrum wanted to talk about the situation to see if they could work things out. She wanted to be in a relationship with him, and wanted to do whatever she could to help fix the relationship, since it seemed to be going full speed down the wrong track. She was afraid to become hurt again, and found herself on guard. She didn't think Staphysagria was putting enough of an effort into the relationship, and she could feel how difficult it was to trust him. She started withdrawing from him even more, and part of her knew that she was going to end up getting hurt, yet again.

Although things weren't going well, she was still hoping they could talk about it and somehow work things out. She felt a strong need for open communication, hoping to get the kind of reassurance and emotional support that she needed to feel safe again. Staphysagria couldn't, or wouldn't, fulfill this need. He already knew that women can't be trusted, and that it would be better for him to totally avoid any kind of uncomfortable confrontation. He felt that she was too needy, and he started feeling trapped. However, the problem with avoiding confrontation is that the issue that is avoided doesn't disappear by looking the other way. In fact, avoidance only makes the issue bigger, and the final confrontation even more hurtful, since it allows things to build up even more. The confrontations between them kept getting more and more out of control, and they were both frustrated and disappointed about the situation.

Staphysagria told me that Natrum was the bitchiest woman he had ever met, besides his own mother. He told me that he has been yelled at by women throughout his life, and that he didn't come all the way across the country just to be yelled at some more. He expressed how he even had dreams of being pursued, attacked, kicked and hit, and that he was extremely tired about the constant lack of appreciation he was always experiencing. He was so tired of this issue that he could barely take it any longer! He told me that he loves Natrum, and has loved her since the first time they met several years ago, but he had no idea how many problems they were going to have by physically living together. From Natrum's point of view, she felt that she was doing everything she possibly could to save the relationship, and she was just as frustrated as he was since all her efforts seemed to fail, no matter how hard she tried.

Staphysagria's final reaction to the continuous conflict was to stop coming home. Instead, he started going out to see his friends and often didn't come back until one am in the morning. Natrum, who had dinner ready for him, wasn't happy when he didn't show up, and he didn't even call and let her know what was happening. She was waiting up for him, ready to confront him when he finally did show up, and at that point, they both knew that their relationship could never work.

The combination of Natrum Muriaticum and Staphysagria is a challenging one. The two remedies do have many things in common, but there are also major differences. They both come from strict backgrounds where they were not encouraged to express themselves openly, they both hold on to old pain and grief, and they both become oversensitive to criticism. Both feel like they are not good enough, but they compensate for this feeling in very different ways.

Staphysagria doesn't feel good enough because he is constantly insulted, especially by women, and his response is to try to uphold his dignity by suppressing all his feelings and by trying to please the person who insults him. Staphysagria feels that he is actually greater than everyone else and he feels insulted when others can't see how great he is and give him the respect he feels entitled to. His feeling of greatness is very much dependent on other people's opinions, so when he receives insults instead of praise, he tends to feel like a complete failure, and he resents anyone who makes him feel that way. Staphysagria often reacts by totally avoiding all uncomfortable issues or simply by refusing to grow up and be responsible. These reactions are almost like a refusal to participate in the reality the women in his life are expecting him to be a part of.

HOW CAN I TRUST YOU? Natrum Muriaticum and Staphysagria

Natrum doesn't feel good enough either, but her reason for feeling unworthy is the fact that she can't please her parents, especially her father, no matter how hard she tries. Because at least one of her parents is usually emotionally cold or unavailable, she also learns to suppress her feelings and pretend everything is fine. However, her reaction to the situation is to try harder to be perfect, thinking that if she is really perfect, she will eventually receive the love she craves. When dealing with a relationship later in life, she will try harder to create the perfect relationship, always looking for another way to fix things, work things out or somehow make the relationship what she was hoping it was going to be like in the first place, still hoping to receive the love she so desperately needs.

So what happens when you put these two perceptions of reality together? The dynamics of this relationship is very simple. The more Natrum wanted to confront, the more Staphysagria wanted to avoid. Staphysagria was so outraged and insulted by Natrum's attitude, that instead of becoming more responsible, he stubbornly defied her requests and started rebelling against her in the same way he rebelled against his mother when he was still living at home. He started acting very much like a teenage boy, and Natrum naturally took on the role of his scolding mom since he wasn't taking care of things the way she wanted them done. Staphysagria needed respect, but wasn't willing to do anything to earn it, and Natrum simply couldn't give any respect to someone who wasn't willing to do more for himself.

Staphysagria tried hard to keep up his dignity in spite of her insults, but because these are the issues he needs to understand better, he often kept doing things that attracted even more insults. Staphysagria is not aware that he is actually attracting insults from people, but subconsciously he does this because it proves to him that nobody respects him, and this keeps his core delusions real.

Natrum on the other hand, has a strong need for love and reassurance from her mate, which is something she has been craving since she was a child, but Staphysagria, who basically hates women, especially if they insult him and don't give him any respect, had no interest in being emotionally available and supportive of her. He felt that he couldn't possibly give her what she wanted, anyway, and he just wanted to stay as far away from her as possible. This behavior convinced Natrum that he didn't love her, and it supported her delusion of being basically unloved, neglected and ignored.

These are the core issues that go with the two remedy pictures. Because Staphysagria can't trust women, and Natrum can't trust men, the combination of Natrum and Staphysagria in relationship is virtually impossible, unless the love between them is strong enough to, somehow, overcome obstacles of this magnitude.

At this time both parties are doing homeopathic remedies in high poten-cies, hoping it will help them ease up a bit, but the issues between them are so emotionally charged that they basically keep bringing out the worst in each other, regardless of what remedies they are taking. They even tried counseling at some point, but when you are dealing with two people, who are constantly triggering core issues in each other, even counseling doesn't help much because it is an ongoing issue which triggers too much pain in both of them.

So why do we do this "dance" through our old patterns? Why do we create situations in our lives that keep our distorted perceptions of reality intact, and why do we attract people into our lives who push our buttons and trigger our core issues? We do this so we can keep working through the same issues over and over again until, hopefully, one day we can come to some kind of completion or resolution in ourselves. We basically need to really understand what these core issues are about because the issues can only be left behind if our under-standing deepens enough that we can grow to a new level of awareness. If we can see clearly how these core issues distort our perception of reality, the distor-tion will simply dissolve by itself and will no longer be an issue in our lives. This is why I state that "time doesn't heal, understanding does!" I can even add that "understanding equals healing!"

To solve the issues in this relationship, both Natrum and Staphysagria would have to change their core beliefs about themselves, which is easier said than done. Natrum would have to come to a place in herself where she doesn't look for approval and reassurance from men, and Staphysagria would have to start making a conscious effort to earn the respect he requires and feels entitled to. Or, even better, Staphysagria could work on developing self-respect so he wouldn't need the respect to come from someone else, and Natrum could focus on finding her inner source of love, rather than expecting her boyfriend to fulfill her needs. Because two miserable people can't possibly make each other happy, the only solution is for each to drop their expectations of the other and to look within for the source of their own happiness. Once found, they will be surprised to discover that, now, their relationship problems no longer exist!

CONTROL ISSUES AND CONFLICT
Nitric Acidum and Lycopodium Clavatum

This is the story of the relationship between Nitric Acidum (woman) and Lycopodium Clavatum (man).

When Lycopodium first saw Nitric Acid, he thought she was the most beautiful woman he had ever seen. She was friendly and lively and they soon became more than friends. Lycopodium was amazed to find someone as beautiful as Nitric Acid, who actually wanted to be with him. He felt that her passion for food and sex matched his, and the attraction was mutual. The passion between them was incredible, and Nitric Acid found Lycopodium to be both caring and generous. He would buy her groceries and never ask her to pay for anything, which appealed to Nitric Acid, since it made her feel supported, loved and cared for.

Soon after they got together Nitric Acid told Lycopodium that she was dreaming about building her own house. Lycopodium immediately started looking for a suitable piece of land. After a few days he found the perfect piece, and Nitric Acid was so excited she bought it right away. Next, Lycopodium started designing a house for her. He did his best to design a house that would suit both their needs, and he worked on the computer until late at night in an effort to put his ideas on paper before showing Nitric Acid what he had in mind. When he showed her the plans the next day, she wasn't happy that he had planned everything without first asking her what she wanted. He explained that this was just a first draft, and that things could still be changed, but Nitric Acid, who wanted things her own way, felt that he had already taken over the project without even consulting her.

After arguing for a while, they were eventually able to come to an agreement about what the house was going to look like. Lycopodium then suggested that she should buy the lumber from a place where he knew they would give her a great deal. They had to travel out of state, but it was well worth it. With Lycopodium's help Nitric Acid was able to save about $7,000.00 on the deal, and Lycopodium felt very pleased with himself.

On the way home they stopped at a renaissance fair. Lycopodium had previously been involved in this festival and wanted to share with Nitric Acid all the things he loved about it, but Nitric Acid wasn't really interested. Lycopodium felt very disappointed. He realized that Nitric Acid wasn't too adventurous, and that she obviously wasn't interested in the same things he was. Nitric Acid just wanted to go home. She was in a hurry to get started on her housing project since she was hoping to get the shell enclosed before the winter. Lycopodium, however, was in no hurry to get started on the new project. He had spent all his money on the trip, and when they got back home, he was broke. He started looking for paid work since he knew he wasn't going to get paid working for Nitric Acid. Lycopodium, who tends to be full of cares, anxieties and worries, felt much better when he had some money in his pocket again, and he wasn't dependent on Nitric Acid to pay his way.

This is when Nitric Acid started feeling unhappy about the situation. She wanted Lycopodium to get to work on her house right away, because to her, a house represented stability and security. She started feeling frustrated, which is something that always happens when there are unfulfilled expectations in relationships. Nitric Acid felt that Lycopodium was talking too much and not doing enough, and she wanted to see more action. Winter was coming, and her level of frustration kept increasing while she was waiting for Lycopodium to finally get started. When autumn came and the house still hadn't even been started, her sense of urgency kept increasing as the weather was becoming cooler. She wanted her house done as quickly as possible, but Lycopodium didn't seem to mind whether it happened this year, the next, or not at all.

The newness of the relationship started wearing off sooner than she had expected. Nitric Acid discovered that there were many things she didn't even like about Lycopodium. He was too independent and didn't ask her advice when doing something. He bought a travel trailer without consulting her, and he also bought cheap Teflon cooking pots and serrated knives for the kitchen. He became very upset when Nitric Acid told him that those were not the kind of kitchen utensils she would have chosen if only she had been asked first. Lycopodium loved eating the "wrong" kinds of food, like spam, burgers and junk food, and Nitric Acid wanted him to eat healthier. He would leave messy spoons on her counters, and spill coffee without cleaning it up, and he would leave his stuff all over the place. Nitric Acid liked her place clean and neat, and she resented having to clean up after him. She started criticizing and nagging Lycopodium, which he really didn't like.

Lycopodium realized that Nitric Acid was right about his food habits. He wanted to change, not just for her, but because it would be better for him, too, but he felt that Nitric Acid was complaining way too much. He felt like he couldn't even do the dishes right without some kind of comment from her. She complained that he had the TV or the computer on too much, and she didn't like having both the TV and the computer in the bedroom. Nitric Acid was extremely sensitive to sounds, and she also disliked the music he played. She preferred absolute silence, which was hard for Lycopodium to understand, and she kept asking him to turn the music off.

Lycopodium resented being told what to do by someone else. He wanted the freedom to do as he pleased, but at the same time he also wanted Nitric Acid to be happy. He felt that he was bending over backwards, trying his very best to please her, but he had never met anyone who was consistently as unhappy as she was. It seemed to him that he couldn't do anything right, no matter how hard he tried. Lycopodium felt that Nitric Acid had such high expectations, and high standards about everything, that nothing he did was ever good enough for her. This, of course, touches on Lycopodium's core issues, where deep inside his confidence is low, and he feels that he isn't good enough just being himself. Lycopodium thinks that he is only loved through his achievements, and he only feels good about himself when he gets a lot of recognition for his efforts.

In spite of all his efforts, Lycopodium got no recognition whatsoever from Nitric Acid. He felt that there was no way he could ever please her since nothing he did seemed to make any difference. Instead of giving him recognition, she kept complaining and criticizing him, and Lycopodium found that the harder he tried to please her, unsuccessfully, the more his resentment and irritability toward her grew.

Nitric Acid didn't think she was complaining too much. She felt that her complaints and criticism were totally justified, and that Lycopodium was simply unwilling to listen. She felt that they couldn't communicate about anything without Lycopodium going into a rage, and she was profoundly affected by his anger and sharp tongue. She didn't see that Lycopodium, in his own way, was actually trying as hard as he could to please her.

Lycopodium hated the daily confrontations. He was still doing his best to make her happy, but Nitric Acid still wasn't happy. She thought that Lycopodium should have asked her what she felt was best instead of assuming he knew. She was also deeply affected by the disharmony between them. She felt that she couldn't have a relationship with someone who was so angry and insensitive to her needs all the time, so she ended up breaking off the relationship with him.

Nitric Acid had no idea how much Lycopodium had really tried to please her until after she had moved out, and she stopped back in to get something she had forgotten. He had rearranged the furniture to his liking. There were dirty dishes in the sink, clothes lying around, his favorite music was on, and the computer was running. She realized then how much she had actually asked him to change his ways when they were still together, and she finally realized that he really had tried his best to accommodate her.

From a homeopathic point of view, the combination of Nitric Acid and Lycopodium has many pitfalls and challenges. The two have several things in common, and in some ways they are almost too similar to each other. Both tend to be moody in the morning and in the afternoon, both feel vulnerable and powerless inside, and both compensate by being controlling or domineering in relationships. However, their priorities are different, and they see things in slightly different ways because there are different underlying reasons why they feel and act the way they do.

Nitric Acid feels vulnerable because she basically doesn't feel safe. She has an underlying sense of danger, and her main priority is to find ways, or situations, where she can feel safe. This explains why she felt so much urgency about getting her house built. She wasn't interested in going on adventures with Lycopodium because creating a safe living space was more important to her. She was only focused on getting her house built before the winter, and she would have liked Lycopodium to be more supportive and put more energy into the project. However, Lycopodium seemed to have other priorities in his life, and Nitric Acid felt very discontented about the situation. When she started expressing her discontent and frustration to Lycopodium, she did it in ways that triggered his underlying issues of not being good enough, which then caused a lot of disharmony between them.

Lycopodium naturally has low confidence and never really feels like he is good enough as he is. He often compensates for his inner insecurity by bragging about what he can do in an effort to impress people, and Nitric Acid was very impressed at first, but she wanted to see more action and concrete results as well. Because Lycopodium's confidence is low, he often feels some apprehension about starting new projects. In this case he was also holding back because he wasn't really sure what to do. He told me that Nitric Acid wanted everything her own way, but at the same time she had difficulties making decisions. She wasn't willing to do things on paper. She wanted to make the decisions when she was on the land, even decisions about where the doors and windows were going to be in the new house. Lycopodium needed to know ahead of time what was going to happen so he could plan things properly, and he felt that it was impossible to work for someone who was controlling on one hand, and indecisive on the other. Nitric Acid became irritable. Whose house was it anyway? She couldn't relate to "plans on paper," and she wanted the freedom to be able to change her mind if she felt like it. She expressed her discontent to Lycopodium again, and when he resisted her input, she started insulting him about his ability to even build a house. This was more than Lycopodium could handle! His confidence issues had been triggered, yet again, and he defended himself any way he knew how.

BEYOND THE VEIL OF DELUSIONS

Lycopodium needs a lot of support and appreciation from the people in his life to be able to feel good about himself. Nitric Acid's criticism and doubt in his ability to even build the house was definitely not a source of inspiration to him. Lycopodium also has "ailments from humiliation" and "ailments from rudeness of others," and he experienced Nitric Acid's comments as both hurtful and humiliating at times. In her rage she would call him names and clearly state that she had no confidence in him as a builder. Sometimes she even suggested that she would be better off hiring someone else. This made Lycopodium furious and he would often become violently angry.

Here we have to remember that we tend to attract things into our lives that trigger our core issues so that we get an opportunity to resolve them. In Lycopodium's case it has to do with a lack of self confidence that he normally tries to cover up by being ambitious, by becoming extremely competent in everything he does, and by developing an ability to achieve whatever goal he sets for himself. By constantly criticizing and doubting Lycopodium's level of competence, Nitric Acid caused his underlying lack of confidence to resurface, and he became hypersensitive and angry because of her negative attitude.

In Nitric Acid there is a sense of danger and a desire to find a way to feel safe, so she will basically attract people in her life that will trigger these issues. In this story, Lycopodium wasn't making enough progress on her house in her opinion, so she realized that her ideas about having a safe place to be wasn't going to happen, at least not before the winter hit. In addition, Lycopodium became so furiously angry toward Nitric Acid from all her criticism that she ended up feeling scared and threatened by him at times.

Here we see how they both got to face their core issues. Core issues are always difficult to deal with, and it is often easier to blame the other than to take responsibility for what is happening. In this story they both compensated by becoming more and more headstrong, domineering and dictatorial toward each other, and after many disturbing arguments, they decided it would be better to resolve the relationship.

Even after the relationship was over, Lycopodium was still thinking of ways to please Nitric Acid. Maybe he could build a house for her anyway, and charge her less than half of the going rate in the area. Maybe, if she would forgive him, he could try even harder to please her, and everything would be fine again. Lycopodium hated being alone and blamed himself for the break up. He didn't really understand why he had become so irritable and angry toward her while they were still together, and he felt really bad about himself. He knew he had said things to her that he shouldn't have said, and he wished there was a way to get Nitric Acid to forgive him.

Nitric Acid didn't understand Lycopodium at all. She liked having things her own way, and her point of view was often fixed with no room for input from others. When she realized that the relationship was beyond repair, she couldn't get away from Lycopodium fast enough. She was happy that the relationship was finally over, so she could find peace in her life again. She still felt good about herself, even after the break up. She felt that her complaints had been justified, and she didn't see any good reasons for Lycopodium's misbehavior. She was unmoved by his apologies, which is typical for Nitric Acid, and she had no interest in having any further contact with him. She moved into a small apartment, breathed a sigh of relief, and finally got stability and order back in her life. Lycopodium had created too much instability and conflict for her, which had triggered her anxiety. She realized that she couldn't live with him unless he could change his ways drastically, and although he had truly tried his best, it just wasn't enough.

In this relationship we see that both partners triggered each others core issues almost on a daily basis. If the partners in a relationship trigger each other's original issues occasionally, it really isn't a problem. If, however, they trigger each other's issues continuously, the relationship simply can't survive. If Nitric Acid had stopped criticizing Lycopodium, she would have probably had her house built by now. Lycopodium was trying very hard to make her happy, but when he received continuous criticism instead of recognition for his efforts, he became cranky, irritable, resentful and unmotivated. Since both tended to be headstrong and domineering when their needs weren't met, the relationship quickly turned into an ongoing power struggle. In the middle of a power struggle nobody listens to anyone, and when reasonable communication is not possible, it is actually better not to be together.

This relationship is another example of how the people we attract into our lives can trigger core issues in us, so we get more opportunities to resolve and complete these old issues. It is in relationships to others these issues are challenged the most, and we have our greatest potential for personal growth. However, the control issues in this relationship were obviously very difficult to overcome.

6 MONTHS LATER...

Although, this relationship was difficult for both, there was also a lot of attraction between the two. After staying apart for about 6 months, enough time had passed and they both started feeling that same attraction again. During the time they were apart, they both kept taking their homeopathic remedies in various potencies, and they both became more aware of the core patterns in their lives. They learned a lot from their first experience together, and they were both curious as to whether they could cope better if they tried living together again.

As soon as they tried again, the same patterns showed up almost instantly, but this time they were able to recognize what was happening. They knew they were dealing with old patterns, which could be broken if only they could bring enough awareness into the situation. They started looking for different options, and decided to live in two separate houses instead.

This arrangement worked very well for a while. Nitric Acid kept her own place nice and neat, and when she went to visit Lycopodium, she was less attached to how he chose to live since she didn't live there any more. Lycopodium no longer had to try so hard to please her because he could live however he choose in his own place, and if Nitric Acid wasn't happy there, she could always go back to her place. Lycopodium kept his independence and made decisions for himself without needing her approval for anything, and Nitric Acid didn't try to control him as much because he didn't live in her space. They only met and did things together when they both choose to, and they found it much easier to appreciate what they liked about each other, when they only met once in a while. This arrangement kept conflict to a minimum, but eventually they still ended up leaving each other.

This part of the story shows how hard it is to change, even with increased awareness of core patterns, an open mind, and a willingness to change. They still couldn't actually break the core patterns, but they at least had the opportunity to try to find other ways to cope, which is the first step in the process. The rest can happen when they are ready.

It is important to remember, that if there is enough love and awareness between two people, any problem can be overcome. However, the final outcome doesn't really matter, all that matters is what is learned from the experience, so that, gradually, our understanding of life itself will deepen and our consciousness will keep expanding.

FUN VERSUS ONGOING CRISIS
Phosphorus and Medorrhinum

This is the story of the relationship between Phosphorus (woman) and Medorrhinum (man).

Phosphorus and Medorrhinum were introduced to each other at a party. Phosphorus was a professional dancer. Her body was slim and graceful and her personality bubbly and cheerful. Her laughter was contagious, and Medorrhinum couldn't help feeling attracted to her. Lucky for him, the attraction was mutual. Phosphorus was happy to find that Medorrhinum also liked to dance. He was fun to be with, and she liked the fact that he was friendly and social and enjoyed being around people. Medorrhinum started visiting Phosphorus regularly, and she quickly found out how open minded and non-judgmental he was. They could talk about pretty much anything, and they often enjoyed late night conversations over a bottle of good wine (Medorrhinum's best time of day).

Medorrhinum explained to me that at the time he met Phosphorus, he felt pregnant with relationship energy. He really wanted to be in a relationship, and he was dating several different women at the time so he would have a better opportunity for making a good choice. He felt that Phosphorus was the one he got along with the best. She was always happy, present and available, and he found himself dating her more than the others. Eventually he decided that she was the one, and they got sexually involved after seeing each other for about 5 months.

Phosphorus was renting a single room in a big house, since she couldn't afford to rent a whole house on her own. The other rooms in the house were normally occupied by other renters, but at the time Medorrhinum decided he wanted to live with her, there happened to be another room available for rent in the same house. He made an agreement with Phosphorus that they would share the bedroom, and that the spare room would be used as an office, and he quickly signed a contract and started moving in.

While he was in the process of moving in, Phosphorus started feeling like she had taken on more than she could handle. He had too many possessions, much more than Phosphorus was expecting. She also realized that Medorrhinum normally lives in a state of total chaos financially, which is something they hadn't spoken about before he decided to move in. He was always on the edge, in some place of crisis, because he didn't know how to manage money or time, or how to prioritize what was important.

Medorrhinum was very happy after moving in with Phosphorus. He is extroverted by nature, and he liked living in a house with a lot of other people. Everyone had their own private rooms, but they were sharing living room, bathrooms and kitchen, and he enjoyed being around so many different people and making new friends. He felt that his relationship to Phosphorus had potential for becoming a long term relationship, which is something he had long wished for. He was buying her jewelry, and they were having fun together, although Phosphorus sometimes felt that they had more fun before they were actually living together, and before she knew about his chaotic life style. The fact that it was in his nature to live spontaneously from one moment to the next, regardless of financial consequences, started to slowly take the fun out of things for Phosphorus. She just couldn't stop being affected by it, even though it didn't have anything to do with her personally.

Medorrhinum eventually found out that he had ADD (attention deficit disorder), which explained a lot of his difficulties. Distractibility is his main symptom. If he is working on something, he can't remember what he just did, or what he is supposed to do next. He looses track of time, so he is always late for appointments. It feels like time is moving too fast, and it takes him about 4 times longer to do something than it takes others to do the same task. If he is interrupted, he forgets what he was doing and starts doing something else instead, so he has piles of incomplete tasks lying on his table. Medorrhinum finds it difficult to have commitments to other people, especially when trying to complete tasks on time according to other people's schedules or expectations. He constantly misjudges how much time he needs to complete a task, and he feels frustrated when he isn't able to accomplish what is expected of him. Sometimes he gets so frustrated that he sweeps everything off his desk and stomps on it in a rage.

Medorrhinum's inability to concentrate on one task at a time, and to cope with seemingly simple tasks, goes with the remedy picture that fits Medorrhinum (see the chapter on Medorrhinum and a New Perspective on ADD). His distractibility and inability to complete things is typical for Medorrhinums in general. There is distortion in his perception of time, and although he may be doing things slowly and inefficiently, he always has the feeling that he is in a hurry. Sometimes his feeling of urgency is so intense that he becomes high strung, irritable and even forgets to eat. Medorrhinum told me that he has a very hard time putting on weight because he never feels that he has enough time to pay attention to what his physical body needs.

Phosphorus has a difficult time dealing with these issues in her life. She can't make plans with Medorrhinum, because he is always late. He doesn't keep his word, he doesn't call, and when he finally does show up, he is full of excuses. She feels that he really isn't present, it seems like his mind is somewhere else. He is always on the edge. His car breaks down, and he doesn't even have enough credit left on his credit card to take care of it. Phosphorus feels like she has to keep rescuing him by taking on his responsibilities, and her life with Medorrhinum isn't much fun any more. In addition to living on the edge of crisis all the time, Medorrhinum can become heavy, negative, depressed, and hard to be around, and he has an extremely low tolerance for frustration. Phosphorus feels drained by the whole situation and tends to wonder what kind of relationship this is, and Medorrhinum feels bad because he can't cope any better, even when he tries hard to do his best.

Medorrhinum feels like it is almost impossible for him to please anyone. If he has an appointment with Phosphorus, he knows that she will be upset if he doesn't show up on time, but at the same time, he also knows that he will upset his clients if he doesn't complete the work he is in the middle of. He often shows up late, and if he didn't have time to complete his work, he will be thinking about it and feeling frustrated while he is supposed to be present with Phosphorus. This makes Medorrhinum appear high strung and tense. Medorrhinum simply doesn't know how to cope with this kind of problem. He becomes depressed when he feels like he is always behind on everything, and always trying to catch up with Phosphorus and live up to her expectations.

Medorrhinum's other problem is his inability to manage money. He was never taught any financial or savings skills. If Medorrhinum thinks an expense is important, he will simply pay it. He has a hard time balancing his checkbook and never knows when to expect his bills. He feels stressed when he has to make choices and try to prioritize what is most important. He deals with these kinds of issues by focusing on what is right in front of his face and not worrying about what is coming in the future (aversion to responsibility also goes with the Medorrhhinum picture). Phosphorus feels that Medorrhinum is extremely bad at any kind of decision making. She described how Medorrhinum would put a $500.00 advertisement into a magazine because he thought it was important for his business, but he forgot that his rent was also due a few days later, and there was no money left for that.

Medorrhinum explained how he has had to deal with people's judgment throughout his life. They blame him for being careless, non-caring and irresponsible, and for not trying hard enough, while in fact, he feels like he has to put enormous effort into everything he does because it is so hard for him to cope the way others cope. Medorrhinum feels that if he didn't have to do everything within a specific time frame, he would probably be able to cope much better. Right now he has a huge backlog of unfinished projects that he doesn't know if he will ever catch up on. Some of his clients haven't been billed for work that was done, but he has no records of what he did for them. Others have paid in advance, but the work hasn't been completed. Sometimes he doesn't have the time to send out invoices, and his clients won't pay unless they receive an invoice first. So, even though Medorrhinum has plenty of work, he doesn't always get paid for what he does, and people don't always get what they pay for.

Medorrhinum described how Phosphorus is good at all the things that he needs help with, but she doesn't have time to help him. He doesn't even know exactly what he needs help with, he thinks he probably needs help with everything, but since that isn't going to happen, he just tries to let go. Phosphorus has helped him with money a few times, but he really doesn't want her to have to rescue him, so he has paid her back every penny. Phosphorus feels like Medorrhinum wants everyone to take care of him and help him. She has a pattern of rescuing people in her life. It is impossible for her not to take on the dramas in Medorrhinum's life and try to rescue him because she is so sympathetic and concerned that she doesn't know how to be detached. Medorrhinum feels nurtured in her company, but she feels drained and exhausted after too much heaviness and chaos. She feels that she is constantly worrying about his situation, and she isn't getting enough attention and nurturing back. She feels that Medorrhinum is generous and loving towards her, and he supports her in her work, but she also feels like she needs someone in her life who can be more present and responsible than Medorrhinum. However, she still cares for him, and doesn't feel ready to break off the relationship.

Phosphorus eventually felt that it would be better if they lived in two different places, so she didn't have to deal so much with his personal issues. She moved out and rented a small house for herself not too far from where Medorrhinum lives. She is still seeing him, and still wants to be in relationship with him, but she feels that she needs a very different kind of relationship now. At some point she suggested to him that they should open up the relationship so they could both see other people, but he was not happy about that since it didn't fit his sense of commitment.

Medorrhinum said that he can understand how his life situation is dragging Phosphorus down. He often wishes he could totally take care of Phosphorus and pay all of her bills, but when he is behind on everything, he gets so overwhelmed that his mind shuts down, and he panics and just wants to run away. He feels like nobody understands how hard everything is for him; they just think he isn't trying hard enough. Sometimes Medorrhinum has suicidal thoughts. He feels that there is no point in being alive if he is just going to upset everyone.

After Phosphorus moved to her new house, she had a small accident as she was moving her things in. She jumped off the porch to rescue her cat from the neighbor's dog, and when she hit the ground, she hurt her right foot. She was able to walk on her foot with a limp, so she didn't think it was broken, but by evening it started looking bad, and she had to do pain medication. Over the next couple of days her ankle swelled up, and she couldn't really put any weight on it. She finally went in for an x-ray, and they found that her foot was indeed fractured somewhere near the ankle. The surgeon suggested that it should be stabilized with metal pins because professional dancers put a lot of stress on their legs, and a few metal pins would strengthen the whole area. Phosphorus was extremely upset about this, since it could possibly mean that her career as a dancer was over, and she shared her concerns with Medorrhinum.

Medorrhinum felt so worried on her behalf that Phosphorus decided she would rather go through the whole ordeal on her own. She told Medorrhinum that she didn't need his company when she went in for the surgery, but she would appreciate a call from him after the surgery was over. On the day of the surgery Medorrhinum forgot to call and ask how she was doing. Phosphorus suspected that he was too self absorbed to care, and it affected her deeply and made her feel unloved and uncared for. The feelings of not being loved or cared for always affects Phosphorus deeply since this is one of the "sore spots" that goes with the Phosphorus remedy profile.

Again, Medorrhinum's perception of the situation is very different from hers. He described how he had offered to cancel his appointments with his clients on the day she went in for her surgery, so he could drive her to the hospital and totally be there for her, but she said she didn't want him to. He was very concerned about her problem, but she didn't want him to put any "negative energy" or worry into the issue. Phosphorus usually prefers to stay light and positive in all situations if possible, but she still needs the support, attention and care from the people in her life when things are difficult. Medorrhinum misunderstood what she meant when she told him not to worry about it. He basically got so busy on the day of the surgery that he forgot about the whole thing, which Phosphorus, of course, took as a sign that he didn't care. He did care, but then again, he focused on what was in front of him and forgot everything else momentarily.

At this point in the relationship, Phosphorus seems to be withdrawing from Medorrhinum, which is a normal reaction for any Phosphorus who feels that she isn't getting enough of her needs met. Medorrhinum told me that Phosphorus doesn't even seem to be interested in sex any more. She is always too tired, and her head often hurts. He said she thinks he is too serious, and his moods are too funky. This affects Medorrhinum, since he is a very sensual person and does want to make love to her. He also feels like she doesn't show much affection towards him anymore, and he feels guilty for having burdened her with so many of his life's emergencies. He explained that Phosphorus feels like she has to take on all his problems, and he feels sorry for causing her so much worry.

Medorrhinum often feels like he is out of tune with the rest of the world. He feels enormous pressure from being so behind on everything. Sometimes he feels like he may never catch up. He feels weak physically, and gets exhausted easily from any kind of physical work. Sometimes he forgets to eat because he doesn't feel like he has time, and he doesn't take the time to exercise so he can get stronger. He feels like he is always struggling with issues in his life that he doesn't know how to overcome, no matter how hard he tries, and he often struggles with depression.

From a homeopathic point of view, this relationship is a bit tricky. There is happy, fun-loving Phosphorus living with a troubled Medorrhinum, whose life is always in chaos or on the edge of an emergency. Medorrhinum doesn't really understand why he finds everything in his life to be so much of a struggle, and why he can't cope the way others cope. His own life is so overwhelming that it becomes hard for him to find any energy left over to give to Phosphorus. The result is that Phosphorus generally doesn't get her needs met in the relationship because Medorrhinum is always too pre-occupied with his own problems. Phosphorus is sympathetic and naturally wants to help, but she easily gets drained from too much seriousness and drama, especially if the situation doesn't get better over time. Something has to change in the way they relate to each other, or Phosphorus will most probably end up leaving the relationship.

My first suggestion to both of them was to make an agreement not to share Medorrhinum's chaos with Phosphorus. Medorrhinum wasn't happy about this suggestion, because he felt that you have to share everything with your mate and not keep any secrets. The problem, with sharing his drama and chaos with Phosphorus is that she can't stop taking on all the heaviness, which takes all the fun out of her life. Since the issue isn't just temporary, it will eventually wear her down so much that she will have to get away from Medorrhinum just to recover her energy. If they can live in two different places and keep their economies separate, Phosphorus would probably feel relieved if she never again had to know about how Medorrhinum isn't coping in his life. Imagine if Medorrhinum came to see Phosphorus, and he couldn't talk about his own dramatic circumstances. He would then have to shift his focus from himself and his own life and give Phosphorus the attention she needs, and wants, instead. This would be a very welcome change for Phosphorus. Medorrhinum would then have to find the support and help he needs in his life from someone else. He could, for example, hire an office manager who could run his business and help him prioritize his daily tasks.

The other main problem in this relationship is the issue of being on time and showing up for appointments. This is something Medorrhinum simply can't do because he always ends up compromising either the completion of his work, or the time of his appointment. They can still make plans to do things together, but Phosphorus may have to let go of her expectations about the exact time something should happen. I imagine it would be possible to make plans to go out for dinner this evening, rather than making plans to meet at 7 o'clock. That way Medorrhinum could finish what he was doing without feeling bad that he was late for the date, and Phosphorus wouldn't get upset if he arrived late. She would have to trust that he would get there eventually, and she might have to eat a light meal while waiting for him if the waiting made her too hungry. This would take stress and guilt off Medorrhinum's shoulders, and he wouldn't be so absent minded and high strung when he actually did show up.

In this story, it is easy to become totally absorbed in Medorrhinum's problems and issues and forget about Phosphorus and her issues. Her issues aren't quite as dramatic as Medorrhinum's, but they still contribute to the relationship problems in the story in a very big way. The core feeling in Phosphorus has to do with feeling unloved and uncared for. She compensates for this by being friendly, cheerful, caring and helpful in order to receive love and attention in return. In fact, she expects constant reassurance that she is loved on a daily basis, and she isn't happy unless she gets it. When Phosphorus isn't happy about something to do with a lack of love and attention, she can become furious and express herself in nasty ways (like the evil queen in Snowhite), and her attitude can often be fixed and self righteous with very little room for other people's points of view.

In this story, she was often very demanding and critical of Medorrhinum because he wasn't able to fulfill her expectations about what she felt she needed from him. She wasn't really trying to understand where he was coming from, and I suspect that she didn't even totally understand herself on a deeper level. The only reason why someone thinks that they have to get all their love, affection, attention and energy from someone else is because they have lost their own connection to the Universal Source. Then they expect the people in their lives to give them what they are lacking, while in reality, they could actually have an unlimited supply of energy if they could only regain their lost connection to Source. This kind of connection can be found through deep meditation, where you move deeper and deeper inside until you connect with the center of your being. When this connection is found, a great surge of energy, love and inspiration starts flowing through you, and there won't be any need to expect the energy to come from anywhere else. Finding the lost connection to Source is what meditation is all about, so my suggestion to any Phosphorus is to learn how to meditate since this is an issue they all have in common.

This is not the kind of thing any Phosphorus would want to hear. Phosphorus has become so used to expecting love and attention to come from other people that even the suggestion, that she should drop her expectations and look for her lost connection to the Source instead, will probably trigger a response of rage, rather than increased awareness of the truth of what is being said. However, once the truth has been said, Phosphorus has the freedom to choose whether she wants to hear it, or not. It is always important to keep in mind that any story has two sides, and this is the other side of the story.

The relationship between Phosphorus and Medorrhinum did eventually end. Phosphorus was the one who ended the relationship, and Medorrhinum felt very sad at first. He went through a period of depression, soul searching and self-blame, but after a while he realized that the ending of the relationship wasn't a bad thing after all. He could see that it wasn't just Phosphorus who didn't get her needs met in the relationship, but that he also had needs that weren't met. When they were together he felt a strong need to connect with her in a deeper way. However, he often found that Phosphorus had no interest in deeper issues, and he found her lack of interest discouraging. Her tendency to focus more on seemingly superficial issues made it hard for him to even know what to talk to her about at times. He also felt that Phosphorus had been so focused on the practical difficulties he was experiencing in his life, that she didn't truly appreciate him as a person. He has now come to the conclusion that it was better that the relationship ended since they were too incompatible to have a good time together. The difference in perception between them was like a huge gap, and he couldn't bridge the gap no matter how hard he tried.

Medorrhinum has learned a lot from his experience with Phosphorus, and has finally been able to move through his depression after the break-up. He is starting to enjoy his life again, and hopes to find a more compatible mate in the future.

DESIRE FOR PEACE, LOVE AND HARMONY
Pulsatilla Pratensis and Staphysagria

This is the story of the relationship between Pulsatilla Pratensis (woman) and Staphysagria (man).

From the time Staphysagria was a child, he was always a bit of a loner. There was alcoholism in the family, and Staphysagria became an expert at avoiding confrontation. His imagination was vivid, and he often spent time daydreaming. He was naturally shy and didn't have many friends. As he grew older, he developed a great love for doing dangerous things; driving at high speeds, skiing, mountain climbing, or whatever else he could find that could give him a thrill. He described himself as being "hooked on danger," and told me that living in the moment and being right on the edge made him feel more alive. Later on he chose to work on ships where he had an opportunity to travel around the world. He loved the freedom of going places, meeting new people and not being tied down in any way. Doing "his own thing" appealed to him since he never liked responsibility very much. He totally enjoyed having freedom and independence, although part of him felt that it would probably be good to settle down and become more responsible at some point.

Pulsatilla and Staphysagria met when Pulsatilla was still married to her previous husband. Staphysagria became a friend of the family since his house was pretty close to theirs. While they were getting to know each other, he found out that Pulsatilla's marriage was on shaky ground. At the time, Staphysagria was coming and going a lot since his job required traveling, but when he heard of Pulsatilla's divorce, he felt that perhaps the time had come to finally settle down. Since they were both attracted to each other, it wasn't too long before they decided to live together, even though this was not an easy decision for Staphysagria to make.

Before he got together with Pulsatilla, he lived an adventurous life with lots of freedom and no responsibility, and he knew that all of that would have to change if he made a commitment to having a family. He was perfectly aware that his life would never be the same again! He knew that as a family man he would have to face his fear of responsibility and basically "grow up," and he also knew how much he would miss the traveling. Ideally, he would have liked to keep traveling and take Pulsatilla and her children with him, but since that was out of the question, he was forced to make a choice. We can easily imagine the conflict he must have felt within, but his love for Pulsatilla was strong enough that he was willing to make the shift.

Pulsatilla is a very sweet, nurturing, and capable woman. As a child, she didn't have the kind of connection to her mom that she would have wanted. Her mom was abusive, and her childhood was filled with a mixture of memories, some happy, and some sad and painful. Pulsatilla children naturally crave a close, loving connection with their mothers. If this doesn't happen, life can easily become quite a challenge. However, we always grow more when we are challenged, so in this case Pulsatilla ended up becoming more capable and independent than you would normally expect based on the remedy profile. Even though she is still soft spoken and mild mannered, you can sense that she is a powerful woman and that she really means it when she says something. According to Staphysagria, Pulsatilla is the "family boss." She is good with children and also understands how to manage money.

Pulsatilla was very happy to have a new partner in her life. Being a single mom is no fun, no matter what constitution you are, and for a Pulsatilla mom it must have been especially overwhelming since she naturally needs a lot of support.

One of the first things they did as a couple was to buy a mobile home that they fixed up together and sold for a large profit. After selling the mobile home, they moved to a different location, and Staphysagria found a job that didn't involve world travel, but was still exciting since it did contain an element of danger.

Staphysagria found the transition to family life quite difficult. There is always an issue when a man moves in with a woman who has children from a previous marriage. The father of the children never feels good about having another man in his children's lives (men are naturally territorial, just like animal males are), and Pulsatilla's x-husband was no exception. He didn't like Staphysagria at all and often badmouthed him to the children, and Staphysagria felt undermined and angry, since he was doing his very best to take good care of them.

Staphysagria didn't really know what to do about this situation, since he doesn't easily express his anger. He told me that he tends to explode once every 3 years, but eventually he did express his feelings to the children's father and told him to leave his house and not come back. This was a good thing, because Staphysagria felt more empowered after "drawing the line."

The other thing Staphysagria found difficult, about the transition, was the responsibility of taking care of a wife and children. He told me that he is always anxious about money and often worries about the future. There is fear around the whole issue of taking care of a family, and he is also worried about being comfortable and having enough in their old age. There is anticipation anxiety, fear of failure, fear of judgment, and a tendency to feel that he isn't good enough. At times he feels depressed and starts withdrawing and becoming uncommunicative. He sometimes experiences resentment about the responsibility he has taken on, and often misses all the traveling he used to do.

In many ways, Staphysagria and Pulsatilla fit together very well and have several things in common. Neither of them likes conflict, confrontation or disharmony, and both are mild mannered. Both can be affectionate and romantic, and both tend to suffer from irresolution. Pulsatilla feels safe being with someone who is affectionate and gentle, and Staphysagria feels good being with someone, who isn't going to insult him or challenge his fear of failure, or his feeling of not being good enough. Pulsatilla loves him dearly and admires him greatly, so the combination of Staphysagria and Pulsatilla is mutually satisfying in more ways than one. Normally, Staphysagrias tend to pick women they can work out their mother issues with, but in this case, Staphysagria doesn't have any conscious issues with his mom, so Pulsatilla doesn't have to play that role in the relationship.

One of the issues, they have had to struggle with, has to do with indecision. Since both have a hard time making decisions, it is difficult to get things done, or to move towards a common goal. This issue first became a problem when they decided to build a new house together. They both have lots of great ideas and often inspire each other, bouncing ideas around. However, having to actually make final decisions about what they wanted turned out to be very difficult. They had a hard time deciding what kind of house they wanted, or the size, or building materials to use, or what it was going to look like inside. Staphysagria, who wanted to please Pulsatilla, didn't want to make a decision Pulsatilla wouldn't be happy with, and Pulsatilla didn't really know what she wanted, so she wasn't able to help him decide. Staphysagria was also worried about how he was going to support his family and build a house at the same time (even more responsibility). For several months they were trying to figure out the details of the new house without making a lot of progress. The sense of indecision and lack of confidence about the whole project started turning into pure frustration, and they couldn't even complete the plans. One day they both agreed not to build the house after all. They honored the fact that neither of them could make the necessary decisions, and that the decision making would be much less if they just bought another fixer-upper instead. Buying a fixer-upper would allow them to reduce their debt and get a lower mortgage, which would further reduce their living expenses and the worry about money.

DESIRE FOR PEACE, LOVE AND HARMONY Pulsatilla Pratensis and Staphysagria

They both felt great relief after deciding not to go ahead with the project. They had already bought a fixer-upper previously and knew they could cope with that. Staphysagria could take his time remodeling one room at a time, without having to quit working, and Pulsatilla could decide one step at a time what she wanted, without feeling overwhelmed. They both felt a sense of relief from finally having made a decision that would make it easier for both of them.

There are also a few differences between the two constitutions, which sometimes create problems in the relationship. One such difference is the difference between Staphysagria's more cautious way of doing practical things, and Pulsatilla's more impulsive and spontaneous way. As an example, Staphysagria told me about one day when Pulsatilla all of a sudden decided she wanted a skylight in the hallway. This was at a time when he was at work, and she didn't feel like waiting for him to come home and help her. She knew exactly what she wanted and decided to do it herself. After measuring how big the hole for the skylight had to be, she simply took a saw and cut it out. Staphysagria said he came home from work and found it snowing in through the hole in the roof. Pulsatilla giggled when I told her his version of the story, and told me that there was a bit of an exaggeration in Staphysagria's version. She admitted to cutting the hole in the roof but insisted there was no snow coming in...

Another difference between the two constitutions is in their need for affection. Pulsatilla is very loving and affectionate and needs a lot of love, support and reassurance to feel safe. Staphysagria is open to affection, but he doesn't necessarily initiate any display of affection on his own. The hardest thing for Pulsatilla are the times when Staphysagria feels depressed and withdrawn and won't tell her how he feels. She can put up with it for a few days at a time, but if it lasts too long, she eventually does express her discontent, and they sometimes end up in open conflict. They both want peace, but once in a while conflict simply can't be avoided.

Staphysagria doesn't often confront Pulsatilla because he hates conflict. He doesn't feel comfortable confronting anyone unless he is confident that he is right, and usually his confidence isn't that strong. Pulsatilla will only confront Staphysagria after being upset about a situation for several days, but neither of them feels good after an argument.

Pulsatilla told me that she is probably more confrontational around Staphysagria than she normally is in relationships. This is mainly triggered by his tendency to avoid emotional issues. It bothers Pulsatilla when he becomes too emotionally evasive because when he keeps avoiding and withdrawing from her, she tends to feel forsaken, lost and unloved, which is Pulsatilla's core issue. Because she constantly needs an atmosphere of closeness and intimacy, she becomes very sad when they don't get along, or when Staphysagria withdraws. After living in an atmosphere of emotional isolation for a few days, her discomfort reaches a level where she simply has to say something, and she confronts Staphysagria, even though she hates conflict.

Staphysagria's reaction, when Pulsatilla confronts him, is to become defensive and take things too personally. His body starts shaking from anger, and he often feels so uncomfortable about the whole situation that he just wants to escape. After each argument, Staphysagria holds on to things longer than Pulsatilla since he often feels hurt and can't let go easily. Pulsatilla prefers to forgive and make up quickly to restore the feeling of peace and harmony so she can be happy again.

Staphysagria actually has a problem with depression. The responsibility of being a family man weighs him down, and he often feels very stuck. He misses traveling because, to him, it represents freedom from expectations and an opportunity for an easy, trouble free life. He told me he often dreams about the possibility of traveling again, preferably with his family this time, but Pulsatilla owns too many pets, and the children have to go to school. Every time Pulsatilla gets another pet, Staphysagria feels more and more tied down, seeing his prospects for traveling disappear in the distance. But Pulsatilla needs her pets, since her pets generously give her the unconditional love and affection she needs to feel happy.

This relationship is another interesting combination of remedies. Both partners do trigger core issues in each other, but not on a daily basis. Pulsatilla doesn't trigger any mother issues in Staphysagria because she is so sweet and gentle, and she greatly admires him. Admiration is what he needs and wants, so Pulsatilla is probably the most nurturing and encouraging mate he could have found. Normally, we pick mates that will trigger our deepest core issues, but in this case Staphysagria didn't have a bad relationship with his mom, which is unusual, so he didn't need a mate who would trigger those issues. Pulsatilla needed peace and love in her life, more than anything. Since both want peace, and both are sensitive and gentle with each other, Staphysagria is a good match for her. The relationship only triggers one major issue that is difficult for each of them to deal with: The issue of responsibility for Staphysagria, and the issue of affection and emotional support for Pulsatilla, so these are the two issues they have to try to find better ways to deal with.

The decision they made, about buying a fixer-upper instead of building a new house, was a very wise decision. It reduced the feeling of responsibility for Staphysagria to where he could cope and feel less stressed. Minimizing responsibility will always make Staphysagria feel better because although he has the skill to do whatever he wants to do, he doesn't necessarily have the confidence it requires. The more he feels pressured when he doesn't feel confident, the more he becomes anxious, depressed and withdrawn. And when he withdraws from the world, Pulsatilla feels forsaken, isolated and unloved. In this state she'll

either confront him in an effort to get her needs met, or focus her attention on
her children and pets, so she can get her needs met in other ways.

As far as I can see, the key, to making this relationship work better is to
find ways to put Staphysagria at ease. When Staphysagria is in a space where
he feels confident and able to cope without the burden of too much stress and
responsibility, he will feel happier and less withdrawn. And when he is happier,
he will also be more available to Pulsatilla, and she won't feel so forsaken or
unloved. Maybe it is important for this couple to find a house sitter to take care
of the pets so they can go traveling together during the summer. Staphysagria
feels resentful if he doesn't get to travel, and planning a trip once a year would
give him something to look forward to. If they could also find a way to go without the children, it would lift Staphysagria's sense of responsibility even more,
and their annual summer trip could become a way to rekindle their relationship.

The only other "pitfall" I can see in this relationship is the way Pulsatilla
deals with Staphysagria's tendency to withdraw. When she has had enough, she
becomes confrontational. This is a natural reaction for anyone who lives with a
Staphysagria. He attracts criticism, which provides an opportunity for him to
deal with his core issues of not feeling good enough. Looking at it this way, we
can see how this is just another subconscious pattern that needs to be broken.
Because Staphysagrias in general can't handle any level of criticism without
taking it personally and feeling hurt, it is very difficult to confront a Staphysagria without making things worse, no matter how gentle you try to be.
Staphysagria is virtually allergic to confrontation in any form. As soon as he
senses a possible confrontation coming, he will become defensive and refuse to
hear what is going to be said, even before anything has been said. This reaction
happens automatically, and it makes it very difficult for his mate to get her
point across or her needs met. I have even heard that Staphysagrias are virtually immune to any kind of psychotherapy, and this is the reason why: They
become so defensive, even before they enter the therapist's office that they can't
hear or take in anything that is being said.

The only way around this dilemma is to come from a space of understanding rather than confrontation. Staphysagria's mate needs to make an effort to
understand why he is withdrawing and feeling bad, and then they can look for
solutions together. Staphysagria likes attention when someone is trying to help
him and doesn't imply that something is wrong with him. The mate shouldn't
even mention her own needs at this point because that immediately triggers the
feeling that he isn't good enough because someone is criticizing him or expecting
something from him! The difference here is very subtle, but important to understand. Staphysagria is so hypersensitive to criticism that it is almost impossible
not to trigger his automatic defense mechanism. It takes great understanding,
sensitivity and wisdom to tread carefully enough that Staphysagria will remain

open to suggestions, but it is worth the effort because it is the only way he will hear what someone is saying. If choosing to confront him instead, his core issues are again reinforced. He will immediately feel that he isn't getting the respect or appreciation he needs because he isn't good enough in himself. If possible, this should be avoided at any cost. Staphysagria's mate needs to be mature enough to know that if she can find a solution to his problem first, he will start feeling better and be nicer to her as a consequence. This way she will eventually get her needs met, but without asking for what she needs directly. Not an easy thing to do, especially if Pulsatilla's core issues of feeling unloved and forsaken have been triggered. Yet, this is much more effective than direct confrontation, as confrontation tends to create more distance, while coming from a place of understanding will have the exact opposite effect. Why does Staphysagria get so defensive? Because of his perception that nobody truly understands or appreciates him, so understanding him is the key to smoothing out the issues, making this relationship more harmonious.

PRACTICALITY VERSUS IDEALISM
Sepia Succus and Causticum Hahnemanni

This is the story of the relationship between Sepia Succus (woman) and Causticum Hahnemanni (man).

Causticum is a very mental type who loves solving problems. Even as a child it was obvious that he had a great love for anything experimental. He was interested in science and had his own chemistry laboratory. He made a whole bunch of homemade rockets and was fascinated by science fiction, which to him was more about future possibilities than just fiction. It sparked his own imagination and probably fuelled his lifelong passion for coming up with fresh, new solutions to the problems mankind will soon be facing if things don't change. He used to read lots of books, and after growing up he often spent hours searching for information on the internet. Before he met his present wife, he worked as a computer programmer and a consultant, but when the technology left him behind, he had to find other types of work. In the interview he talked as fast as any Lachesis, and his voice was full of excitement as he described his vision for creating a better world.

Causticum never really felt like he fit in. Socially he was probably a bit too intense for people who couldn't relate to his level of passion and dedication. He was married once before, but they didn't have the kind of connection he was looking for, so they divorced after about 10 years.

At this point he felt like it was time for a change. He was tired of reading books because what he was reading was either too repetitious, or the view was too limited. He wanted to start doing something more productive. This is when he was inspired, from his spiritual quest and newfound connection to God, to create a whole new vision about a utopian future for humanity. He felt that if we didn't come up with practical, alternative solutions quickly, humanity would most probably wipe itself out. The project became his life's work, and he felt that his ideas had great potential for profit.

This is where Causticum was at when he met the woman who was going to become his future wife. The way they met was unusual, but it totally fits Causticum's busy lifestyle. He put an ad in the newspaper, and she was one of

PRACTICALITY VERSUS IDEALISM Sepia Succus and Causticum Hahnemanni

two people who answered the ad. He really liked her voice when they spoke on the phone, and they decided to meet.

Sepia had experienced both emotional and sexual abuse in the past. She carried unresolved grief and anger inside her, and at times she built up resentment against men in general. She did, however, have a close relationship with her father, whom she loved very much. After he died, she missed the loving connection they had, and when Causticum put his ad in the paper, she was already consciously looking for a life partner. She had answered several ads before she came across Causticum's ad, and she was happy when Causticum wanted to meet her.

It is part of Causticum's nature to share his vision with everyone, so Sepia was quickly introduced to the huge task Causticum was working on. What she was hearing appealed to her very much. Since Sepia and Causticum are both sympathetic types, who care about people and want to help others, they talked about possibly even working together. Nothing is more attractive to a Causticum than finding a woman who wants to help him manifest his vision, so he was very excited! Besides her interest in his vision, he was also attracted to the fact that Sepia was a spiritual person.

Sepia had always had a strong spiritual focus in her life. She had dedicated herself to the path of yoga, and for the last 16 years she was teaching yoga and helping people improve their lives through natural healing, energy work and massage. She studied Jin Shin Jyutsu for 20 years, which is a method that uses very light touch at specific energy points for the purpose of bringing someone's energy back into balance. Sepia was a happy person who lived a rich life full of all the things she loved doing. Besides yoga and healing work, she especially loved singing.

After they met, Sepia quickly realized how much she liked Causticum. She felt how loving he was and saw that he had a beautiful heart. This made her feel so good that she totally opened her heart to him, but, in the process, she lost some of her grounding. This is a common thing for all Sepias. They tend to lose themselves in the relationship because they don't have a very strong sense of self.

Causticum and Sepia enjoyed each other's company so much that Causticum proposed to Sepia after only being together for 2 weeks. She said yes, and they got married exactly 9 months after they first met. They have now been together for about 4 ½ years, and during this time, their relationship has gone through many difficult changes.

Around the time when they met, Sepia first discovered a small lump in one of her breasts. Although Causticum had a high paying job with health

262

insurance, they decided to wait until after the wedding before she went to the doctor. In the mean time there was a wedding to plan, and they also moved to a different place together. After they moved, Sepia lost most of her clients, since they lived too far away from her new residence, so she all of a sudden found herself out of work. About 4 months later they got married, and Sepia finally went to the doctor. At that time she had a negative mammogram. The gynecologist couldn't find the lump and thought perhaps it had only been a cyst.

Two months later Causticum lost his job and health insurance and started living on credit cards. This situation was so stressful for Sepia that she became very depressed and her lump started growing. Because Sepia couldn't afford to get a second opinion, she tried to heal herself by eating raw food and by using acupuncture and homeopathy. Over 1½ years later, she was diagnosed with breast cancer: stage 3.

One of her lymph nodes was affected, and she agreed to have a radical mastectomy. In the mean time, Causticum kept working on his utopian research project. He had no idea, when he started the project, that it was going to take over 10 years to complete, and his sense of stress and urgency kept increasing. He felt an incredible pressure to get his work completed, so that he could start marketing his work and turn his ideas into profit. Because his focus was on the possibility for future profit, he often didn't have enough money to pay his present bills. However, he felt that this approach was justifiable because of the expectation of monetary return at the completion of the project.

As the years went by, Sepia started growing tired of the whole project. It seemed to be taking forever, and she wished the work would come to completion some time soon. Causticum told me that Sepia's ability to put up with him has been almost super-human. She has patiently supported his need to follow his heart for many years, but now it seems that both her patience and her physical energy are becoming exhausted.

Causticum's seemingly "financially reckless" behavior is a difficult issue for Sepia. He is still more focused on the project than on earning money to pay the current bills. He believes in himself and is absolutely convinced that the finished work is going to make him a fortune. It is just a matter of time before he can completely take care of Sepia, so she can quit working all together. He feels that the debt he has accrued should only be considered research costs, which he finds acceptable based on his expectation of later profit. He only has to complete the last parts, and he is almost there...

However, Sepia isn't happy about the arrangement. After Causticum lost his high paying job, he took the opportunity to work harder on his project, instead of looking for another job, although he had promised Sepia he would look for a proper job when she went in for her operation. Because he could only find minimum wage work, he felt that it made more sense to keep working on his project instead, and they started living on credit cards. Over the next couple of years the debt quickly increased to about $100,000.00 between the two of them.

This was the financial situation Sepia had to face when she came out of the hospital after her mastectomy. She had to go back to work after just a short time of recovery even though she didn't feel strong enough to do so. Causticum eventually found a part time job that he didn't mind doing, so now they are both bringing in money, but barely enough to live on, and certainly not enough to pay their debts. They tried to juggle their debts around for a while, but the bills were totally out of control, and now they are both about to face bankruptcy.

Causticum loves Sepia very much and wishes for the day when his project is completed and he can start bringing in enough money for both of them. He feels stressed and anxious about the whole situation, but so far he hasn't found a better way of dealing with it. If he is pulled away from his work, he feels depressed and angry because this is his life's "mission." And at the same time, he knows that you can't survive in this dimension without making money. He feels that it is important to follow your heart, which is what he is doing, but finding the right balance between being a man of vision and being a provider, is not easy. By comparing the prospect of getting an insecure minimum wage job with the prospect of possibly making a huge amount of profit at the completion of the project, he decided it made more sense to keep working on his project without any further delays.

Sepia thinks Causticum should focus more on making money here and now, so she doesn't have to work so much. She suspects that Causticum is a bit selfish, and she is starting to feel resentment brewing under the surface. For 2 ½ years now, they have been living in just one room in a house since they can't afford to rent anything bigger. She knows that if he has to go to work, his progress on the project will be somewhat delayed, but in all things there has to be a balance...

Sepia is trying to stay hopeful, but sometimes she loses all hope and feels depressed, fearing things aren't going to change anytime soon. She has started withdrawing from Causticum and is doing what she can to create a different life for herself. She spends time with her friends when she needs to get out, and she has also started working on a book about her experience with breast cancer. She is a creative person who is doing what she can to make the best out of the situation, but the reality of things still weighs heavily on her shoulders. When she expresses her doubts and unhappiness to Causticum, he reacts by becoming irritable and angry, and he often feels so tense that he can't sleep very well at night. He is still optimistic and believes in himself, but something has to change because they are both suffering from the whole situation.

Causticum is totally committed to his future career possibilities, but he feels the pressure and the expectations on his shoulders. He wants the relationship to work, but he can't, and won't, delay working on his visionary project. He feels that his visionary work greatly suffers if he tries to pursue or hold down a full-time job, and he doesn't want to lose his "creative spark" since he is on a mission from God. He finds that the society we live in relies too much on money as a form of exchange. If someone has different priorities in life, they often get in trouble because money doesn't come easily when you put your focus elsewhere. However, he doesn't feel that his lack of financial pursuits in the present has anything to do with their relationship problems.

Sepia doesn't agree. She feels that his lack of concern about money matters is a constant source of conflict. His "win-win" solution is still somewhere in the future, and it doesn't take into consideration her needs in the present, and the fact that she has reached a point of exhaustion. Causticum continues to hope that things are going to change for the better very soon, but in the mean time, he still needs to consider finding the right balance between his own needs and his wife's...

The problems in this relationship are a result of the core issues associated with each remedy picture. The situation that goes with Causticum is where a group of people relies on Causticum to save them in some way. There is a sense that horrible things are going to happen. Danger is going to come from somewhere, and it is coming soon, and Causticum is the only one who can find a practical solution that can work for everyone. Since he doesn't know what the danger is, or when it is coming, or even where it is coming from, Causticum feels an almost unbearable sense of urgency. He has to find the solution before the danger appears, or he has failed his mission and let his people down.

In this case, Causticum uses the bible to predict the nature of the danger that is coming, and he has identified several possible solutions that he is almost ready to start marketing. He feels that his life is filled with meaning and purpose because he gets his inspiration from God. He also feels that no one should try to pull him away from his work because that will delay the whole process. Practical day to day concerns will have to wait because he has to keep his focus on the bigger picture. Somebody has to find new solutions, and since he hasn't found anyone else who can do it better than himself, it is his responsibility to complete the task. In addition to the possibility of saving humanity, there is also great potential for future monetarily gain. This is what he calls the "win-win" solution, win for humanity, and win for himself and his wife.

The situation that goes with Sepia's remedy picture is different. She is naturally independent and likes doing "her own thing," but when she is in a relationship, she feels very strongly the other person's needs and expectations of her. Because she wants to make her mate happy, she tends to compromise her own needs and tries to fulfill his needs instead. This is not a problem if it is only for a short period of time, but Sepias often attract people into their lives who will make them compromise over long periods of time. When this happens, Sepia starts building up resentment towards her mate. At first she will express herself through nagging and irritability, but if that doesn't work she can easily get nasty. The more resentment she builds up inside, the more she will start to separate herself from her mate. She may find that her sexual drive has disappeared, and she can no longer get turned on by her mate. She may also find that she is exhausted and simply doesn't have the energy to be close to anyone. One Sepia client expressed to me how she never even returned people's phone calls when she was in a state of exhaustion because she couldn't bear talking to anyone; it seemed like too much of an effort.

Usually when I look at people's relationship problems, I look for common ground and try to find areas where each can compromise enough to get the relationship functional again. However, when looking at these two remedies, compromise is not an option for either one of them. Causticum can't compromise because it will trigger his fear that he won't be able to complete his mission, and Sepia can't compromise because compromising in relationships is one of the core issues that go with her remedy picture. The only common ground I can see in this relationship is the fact that they both love each other, both want the relationship to work, and they both understand that compromise is not a good option. However, the fact is that Sepia is already compromising in the relationship by having to work more than she wants to when she doesn't feel good. She told me that she had a hard time taking care of herself before Causticum entered her life, and she is afraid she will have to take care of both of their needs if Causticum doesn't start contributing more. This worries her because she simply doesn't have enough energy to do so. Sepia feels that Causticum is selfish for not being more concerned with her needs, but she understands that he does have good intentions. His whole life is devoted to helping others, and one of his most sincere desires is that some day soon he will be able to take care of all of Sepia's needs so she will never have to work again. But until that happens, something has to shift between them.

After much thought, I think the biggest problem in this picture is that one of the partners has to compromise her needs continuously, and this compromise is the source of all their conflicts, as well as her failing health. If both were following their heart's desire, and both were being equally "selfish," they would understand each other better and a lot of resentment and stress could possibly be eliminated. The only way I can think of eliminating this problem is if they can have two separate economies. They don't necessarily have to live in two separate houses because that will be too expensive and probably too painful emotionally, but perhaps they can open two different bank accounts. Whenever a bill comes, Sepia can write a check for half of the bill, and Causticum will have to write a check for the other half. If he doesn't have the money, he has to find a way to make what is needed, and it is important that Sepia doesn't pay more than her half to fill the gap. The same applies to food shopping. She can tell Causticum to give her money or sign a blank check before she goes shopping, and each pay for half of the food.

This very simple approach has many advantages. Sepia doesn't have to nag Causticum about not making enough money. It will be obvious to him if he can't write a check for his own half, and he doesn't need anyone to tell him. And Sepia won't feel like she has to take care of both of their needs. She can work enough to take care of her own needs plus half of the bills and food, and Causticum will have to adjust his work hours enough to get his bills and food needs taken care of as well. This way he doesn't have to feel guilty and pressured about having to work more than he wants to as long as his basic needs are covered, and Sepia won't have to pay for more than her own half.

It would be healthy for Sepia to stop taking care of Causticum's financial needs because she would stop compromising for the first time in her life, which is an issue all Sepias are here to learn about and hopefully resolve. And Causticum would probably be more than happy with a practical solution to the problem that is not requiring too much of an adjustment on his part. In a way, Sepia is lucky to have a "selfish" mate like Causticum since she can learn from his behavior how to stand up for herself and get more in touch with her inner strength. This would be a good thing for her to learn, and I am sure Causticum won't mind her new independence if it means that she will become both happier and healthier in the process. If Sepia could find her happiness again, that alone would reduce the stress and pressure Causticum is feeling, which would instantly change the dynamics of the relationship.

Sometimes the simplest solutions are the hardest ones to discover, but the solution doesn't have to be complicated to make a difference. What I have suggested above is practical, easy, and possible to do, and it is a true win/win solution for both partners.

CAUSTICUM'S RESPONSE TO MY SOLUTIONS...

Just before I sent the story to this couple for review, Causticum had upset his present boss and got himself fired from his part time job, so when he saw my suggestion for a solution he was furious. He feels that he is so close to being able to market his ideas for a possible profit that he resents having to put any energy whatsoever into daily concerns. He felt that my "out of context proposal" did nothing but delay the moment of truth in regard to his future career. My solution gave his wife yet another excuse to turn away from issues of faith and pressure him into finding work, and he told me that my proposal to end his wife's current "small compromise," could easily become the source of a much bigger compromise by delaying his mission from God. He also told me that the faith of a woman in her husband's work is one of the most potent sources of hope and miracles in the world, and the lack of such faith, one of the most enduring curses.

My suggestion may have "delayed the moment of truth" in regard to Causticum's career, but it certainly didn't delay the moment of truth to his wife. She thanked me for making things so clear to her, and she told me she will stick to her demands that he has to pay for half of the bills because she will no longer compromise and sacrifice her life and needs for someone else's.

Causticum's reaction is exactly what one could expect, considering the mental symptoms that fit the remedy picture. Some of these are: Rigid, unmoving, inflexible, religious, fanatical, critical, faultfinding and self righteous. He uses quotes from the bible, both to criticize my suggestions and to justify his actions to his wife. If she still isn't convinced, she obviously has faith issues that she needs to work through! (Here it is interesting to note that she is a Buddhist and he is a Christian, and Buddhism isn't concerned with faith issues, but Christianity is. Again, he is imposing his own view on hers...). His idealism seems to have become so fanatical that he is willing to totally disregard his wife's needs in favor of his own goals. He didn't appreciate my any of my suggestions because he wasn't willing to make any personal adjustments in his life whatsoever. Even my simple suggestion of having two different economies where each pays only half of the bills was totally unacceptable to him. He also resented my efforts in the story to compare him with the Causticum remedy profile because his personality doesn't fit into any fixed "archetype," and he doesn't like being "pinned down." In short, he hated everything I had written in the story above.

Causticum still cares about Sepia and obviously wants to have a relationship with her, but at the same time he demands total control over her. On one hand he is extremely controlling, and at the same time he is also deeply sympathetic and wants to help humanity's chances of future survival, especially if he gets paid well for his efforts, so he actually does care in his own way. However, his mind rationalizes everything in such a way that he misses the obvious, which is the fact that you can't ignore what is needed here and now while preparing for the future. Sacrificing the present for the future is a sure way to waste your life because the future never comes. Do we ever live in the future? No, we always live in the NOW because now is all there is. We can make plans for the future, and we can have a general direction in our lives, but even the future becomes NOW once we get there, so it is important never to disregard the value of the present moment. Sepia once told me on the phone: "Oh, how I wish he could hear what you are saying!" But for someone who lives his whole life preparing for the future, nothing I can say about living in the present is going to appeal to him. The present is a gift that should be treasured, that is why it is called "the Present," but right now Causticum can't, or won't, see the value of living in the NOW. However, we have to keep in mind that we are all here to walk our own paths and learn the lessons of life in our own time, and that all paths ultimately lead to the same goal.

STUBBORNESS VERSUS SPONTANEITY
Silicea Terra and Nux Vomica

This is the story of the relationship between Silicea Terra (woman) and Nux Vomica (man).

Nux and Silicea met at a wedding when both were 22. During their first conversation they discovered that they had both gone to the same school and that they lived only a short distance apart, so it was pretty strange that they had never even seen each other before the wedding. However, when they finally did meet, there was mutual attraction between them right away. Nux thought Silicea was a very good looking woman, and she seemed like she was easy going, too. Silicea felt that Nux had what she described as "solid strength." He had loving eyes, and when they hugged, he was warm and she felt right at home. The connection between them was so strong that they didn't even have to talk much. They just felt very comfortable together, and they moved in with each other a month later.

During the first year they were together, Silicea noticed that Nux had a tendency to be very moody. Sometimes he was brooding and didn't want to talk about it. Silicea said that is how she deals with things, too, so she didn't really mind. But, after the first year, things changed a bit. They moved to a different place, and Nux started feeling angry a lot. He also started expressing his anger towards Silicea, which she wasn't happy about. Little things aggravated Nux, like when Silicea bought a laundry detergent that didn't have an easy pour spout (unpractical), or when she left the toilet seat up or the house was too messy when Nux came home from work. He was angry, irritable and critical, and this was hard for Silicea, who didn't like conflict.

Nux has high standards and likes to have order in his life. He is picky about little things, especially around the house. Because he is a practical type, he likes the house to be clean and tidy so he doesn't have to waste any time looking for things. He is often demanding about how he wants specific things to be done, and if things aren't done right, he becomes confrontational. This is a problem for Silicea, especially if she is too busy or too tired to live up to his expectations. She takes care of their little baby during the daytime, and she isn't as concerned as Nux about how the house looks at the end of the day.

Silicea's natural tendency, when a fight is about to happen, is to escape, walk away, avoid, tell him that she doesn't want to talk about it, or tell him that his timing is wrong. She feels that the timing and circumstances have to be just right before they can discuss something unpleasant. She also feels that she needs time to prepare herself for what is coming, and she doesn't like it when he springs things on her. If Silicea refuses to blow up or even talk about it, Nux goes back to brooding again and instead tries to work things out for himself. It is very hard for Nux if Silicea doesn't want to work things out with him because he becomes tense and uneasy if he doesn't quickly get to the bottom of things. However, if he comes on too strongly, Silicea feels intimidated and doesn't know how to deal with it, and she withdraws and "puts a wall up" to avoid the confrontation.

When Nux feels angry, he raises his voice, and Silicea hates it. She feels attacked, scared and victimized, and she shuts down and becomes defensive. She feels that he will just keep going and there is nothing she can do about it except to totally agree with him. But it doesn't feel right to have to agree with him all the time, either. Silicea is mild mannered and doesn't like raising her voice. She tries to reason with Nux in a calm way, but that doesn't normally work, either. She feels like Nux just wants to fight, and that he pushes until he gets a reaction from her.

Nux is naturally impatient and has a fiery temper, which makes it very hard for him to wait for the right time before he can discuss a problem. Silicea, who is naturally patient and mild tempered, doesn't understand why he is in such a hurry, or even why he has to confront her in the first place, and this creates an ongoing issue in their relationship.

One reason why Nux and Silicea have such different ways of dealing with issues is the fact that they come from very different family backgrounds. Nux grew up in an outspoken family where they all expressed their feelings until the issues were properly resolved. There were a lot of anger issues in his family because his dad was an alcoholic who would sometimes get angry enough to punch holes in the walls. But there were never any issues of timing. Whenever an issue would come up, it would be dealt with immediately to get it out of the way, and Nux would feel better as soon as the problem had been resolved.

Nux explained that he feels extremely tense when there is unresolved anger in the air. To him, the tension is worse than any confrontation. It builds up inside him if he doesn't get to let it out, and he feels that the tension must be released somehow. If the problem isn't resolved, he will remain tense, irritable and angry until the time when the problem has been dealt with.

Silicea's family background was very different. She grew up in a family where they mostly avoided any kind of confrontation. Her family didn't feel comfortable with a display of strong emotions, so emotional issues were carefully avoided to preserve peace in the family.

Whenever issues of anger show up in relationships, there are often sexual issues as well, since the energy of anger and sex is closely related. Because Nux is so different from Silicea, they are not always compatible sexually. Silicea feels like Nux can easily have sex all the time, and he sometimes gets upset when she isn't up to it. She wishes Nux would tell her ahead of time if he wants to make love to her, but this doesn't fit Nux's spontaneous nature at all. Nux feels like he can't possibly decide, hours before, that he will want to make love to Silicea later that evening, and at the same time Silicea feels like she needs time to mentally prepare herself before she can be open to his advances.

A third issue in this relationship is the issue of spontaneity and risk taking versus caution. Nux often tends to get himself into trouble when he makes business decisions without first consulting with Silicea, especially if they are risky business decisions. This also reflects traits that go with each remedy profile. Nux behaves as if he were continuously on a battle field - he has to make decisions quickly without consulting with anyone, and he has to take risks if he wants to survive. Silicea is a princess who is trying to keep up her princess image. She isn't willing to risk ruining her image, or losing her position (standard of living). She is afraid of failure and doesn't like anything that looks like it could go wrong. When Nux wants to start a new business on the spur of the moment, it triggers all of Silicea's fears. But if Nux doesn't get to be adventurous in his life, he will feel trapped and stagnant because he is too adventurous by nature to play things safe.

We can easily see how very different these two people are. Nux is impatient, and Silicea is patient. Nux takes risks; Silicea doesn't. Nux needs to express what he feels and actually thrives on confrontation, especially if the issue ends up being resolved, while Silicea is timid and mild mannered and doesn't like any kind of confrontation. Nux is spontaneous and needs to act here and now, regardless of timing or circumstances, while Silicea is not spontaneous and wants the timing and circumstances to be just right, so she can be prepared for what is coming.

Whenever a person is attracted to a mate who is their exact opposite, I believe they are supposed to learn a lot from each other, so they can develop more wholeness within. The key, to developing more harmony in this relationship, is to look for common ground. In this case, the most obvious thing they have in common is the love they feel for each other, and their commitment to the relationship. As long as there is love and both are willing to become more aware, anything is possible. So let's step back and look at one issue at a time.

The first issue is the way they each deal with confrontation. We can't change Silicea's feeling of discomfort about conflict, but she may be willing to address the conflict, instead of avoiding it, if Nux is willing to discuss the issue when the time is right for her. Waiting for anything is hard for Nux, especially if he is feeling tense, so we have to also find a way for Nux to be able to reduce the tension he feels while he is waiting for the right time to discuss the problem with Silicea. Nux also told me that he has a strong need to be heard when he is trying to express his feelings, and if Silicea doesn't want to hear what he is saying, he will naturally keep going, and keep pushing harder, continuously repeating himself, until he feels that Silicea has really heard him. Silicea feels annoyed when he repeats himself, but she doesn't quite know how to get him to stop.

The reason why Nux keeps repeating himself is the fact that he doesn't know if Silicea has actually heard him. He doesn't feel assured when she keeps trying to avoid the confrontation instead of acknowledging that she has heard what he is saying. So, we have to look for a way to assure Nux that Silicea has heard and understood him. By avoiding confrontations that are important to Nux, Silicea's lack of response actually makes them worse (this is similar to what happens when you argue with an Arsenicum – he also needs to know that he has been heard). On the other hand, Silicea hates being put on the spot, so we have to look for a solution that can fulfill both their needs, somehow.

After much thought, I came up with a few simple solutions that can make a difference to both of them. Because Nux is impatient and feels tense if he doesn't get to speak when something is bothering him, he should be allowed to express his feelings right away, but without expecting Silicea to respond at that time. After expressing his concerns, they can agree on a time to deal with this issue later the same day.

There are several advantages to dealing with conflict this way. First of all, Nux gets to express his feelings right away, which will possibly reduce some of his tension since he "got it off his chest." Silicea won't feel pressured or put on the spot because she can pick a time when they can discuss this issue later. She can think about it and prepare herself for what she wants to say at that time without feeling rushed or pressured. Nux will have a hard time waiting for the pre-determined time, although it may be worth waiting for, since there is less of a chance that Silicea will avoid the issue if she has had enough time to prepare herself first. In return, Silicea would have to agree not to avoid the confrontation, if she gets to choose the time and place, because she needs to understand how important it is for Nux to resolve the issues that are bothering him.

When the time comes to discuss the issues, Silicea should start by repeating Nux's complaint, so that he knows that she has really heard him, before they start the discussion. That way he doesn't have to be pushy or keep repeating himself. Once they have agreed that Silicea has understood Nux's concerns, they can hopefully discuss the issue calmly since Nux has already had time to cool down before the discussion. If Nux can be calm during the discussion, Silicea won't feel so intimidated, and she might be more open to hearing what he has to say. This solution covers both their needs, and should help bring more harmony into their relationship.

When it comes to this couple's sexual issues, we have to start looking for more common ground again since a possible solution also has to take both people's needs into consideration. One suggestion could be to agree on certain days when it is fine for Nux to approach Silicea sexually. This would allow Silicea to relax on the days that are "off limit," and she could prepare herself for the possibility of making love on the days that they have already agreed on. This way Nux wouldn't have to make an arrangement ahead of time before making love to her, and he would know ahead of time that every Friday (or some other pre-determined day), it would be fine for him to approach Silicea spontaneously, if he happened to feel like it. In return, Silicea would then have to agree not to turn him down on those days, regardless of whether she feels like having sex, or not. I know that nobody likes to compromise when it comes to sexual issues, but because these two people are so different by nature, it is necessary for both to compromise a little, even in this area, for the purpose of making the relationship work better. If they aren't willing to compromise in a way where both get some of their needs met, the one who doesn't get any needs met will eventually build up resentment towards the other, and as soon as that happens, they won't be very happy together.

When it comes to the issues of risk-taking versus caution, there is still more room for possible suggestions. One solution could be for Silicea to let Nux pursue his new ideas as long as he is willing to consider Silicea's fears and concerns first. Nux would then have to promise to plan his new projects well, carry them out carefully and keep the risk factor as low as possible. Silicea needs to be consulted, even if it is against Nux's nature to consult with anyone, because otherwise, she will withdraw her affection from him, or "put a wall up" and stop communicating altogether. This would have a negative effect on the relationship, so Nux is better off consulting with her. He has to understand that the main reason why he has to consult with Silicea is not because he needs her advice, but because she needs to know what is happening, and her feelings and opinions about it need to be heard and considered. Nux's need for adventurous projects also needs to be understood, because he is adventurous by nature, and he needs a certain level of excitement in his life. The key here is to consider each other's needs and fears and to keep looking for solutions that cover both their different needs.

By learning to honor each other's differences in such a way that both have to let go of something, and both get some of their needs met, they can change the dynamics of the relationship and experience less conflicts and more joy together. As long as there is love and friendliness between them, anything is possible; it will just take some re-adjustment on both parts to make it work better.

After focusing on their obvious differences, it is also important to look for areas of compatibility between the two. In some ways, the combination between Nux and Silicea is very good. They have a strong connection, and they feel really comfortable with each other. Nux has so much strength that Silicea feels safe with him, and Silicea is a very good mother to their child. She is the princess who wants to be taken care of by a strong man, who can provide the standard of living that she likes, and Nux doesn't mind taking care of her and her needs. He likes making the money and providing well for his family, so Silicea doesn't have to go out and work. Nux also likes being in the limelight, which suits Silicea well, since she doesn't feel comfortable with too much public attention. So, in many ways, they are actually very compatible. It is important to bring the main focus back to the things they like about each other, and to remember that the discomforts they are currently experiencing in their relationship can be overcome. By becoming more aware of the old patterns they are both stuck in, they will have a greater chance of changing what is happening. For real change to happen there also has to be a willingness to look for more creative solutions to their problems as well as openness to new ways of relating.

PART FOUR
THE BIGGER PICTURE
Conclusions and Reflections

CHANGING CONSTITUTIONS
A Controversial Subject

Here is another controversial issue, the issue of whether people's constitutions can change. Some homeopaths don't seem to think that that is possible. Constitutions may look as if they can change, but perhaps it only looks that way because we aren't able to perceive to the very deepest layer when first taking the case. Other homeopaths believe that we come in with many predispositions, and that the one we develop is the one that serves our survival best at a given moment. Let's step back for a moment and explore this issue some more. Why would we be born with different pre-dispositions for constitutions? Are the different pre-dispositions layers or just possibilities?

Remember the basic concept that I introduced earlier in the book, where someone experienced a situation that simply couldn't be resolved, and that the trauma from this situation was stored in his cellular memory and passed down to his offspring? What if his girlfriend or wife also had experienced something traumatic that was stored in her cellular memory? Naturally, their children would inherit this kind of information from both their parents. So which one of these core situations will end up becoming the child's main perception of reality, or in other words, his constitution? The one that manifests is the one which serves him best in his particular situation. So what if he grows up, and his life changes in such a way that acting out the other situation would serve him better? Since he has inherited both, it would be in his best interest to change his perception, since life always tries to preserve itself, and his best interest is always a matter of survival. Taking this one step further, their children could find mates who perceived reality in different ways than they did, and their children's children could also do the same. A few hundred years later, the children born would have a predisposition for a vast number of constitutions. The one that manifests at any given moment is always the one that serves the child's survival best in his present situation, but because life does whatever it takes to preserve itself, it is easy to see how a person's perception has to change if the issue of survival requires it.

I have seen many examples of this in my clinic. Usually the client responds very well to a particular remedy and can totally relate to the psychological issues that go with this remedy, until I start going to high, or very high, potencies, and all of a sudden something shifts in the person and a completely new picture emerges.

I saw this very clearly in one of my Alumina clients. She may have been originally Natrum Muriaticum, but because of her extreme childhood conditions she had to become as invisible as possible just to survive. Her father left when she was very young, and her mother was unable to take care of her for some reason, so she put her up for adoption. She was adopted by a woman who was an alcoholic, and because her step mother was very unhappy, looking for any excuse to create conflict, Alumina's survival depended upon her being invisible so she wouldn't create any waves. Because nobody paid attention to her, she had no sense of self. She was even invisible in her dreams where she would be in a room full of people, and nobody would see her. She felt nothing inside, and when I started working with her, she had a hard time even feeling a pin prick on her skin. In fact, she didn't even want to have feelings because feelings always hurt so much that she felt safer being totally numb. She felt like her brain had stopped functioning properly, her thinking was fragmented, and she kept hurrying all the time, yet never really got anything done. She knew something was very wrong when she experienced an almost irresistible urge to kill her boyfriend with a kitchen knife, and she came to me for help because she was afraid she was going crazy.

She responded really well to Alumina. Her mind became clearer, the urge to kill disappeared, and she was able to start feeling again, both emotionally and physically. She stopped behaving as if she was invisible, and her boyfriend wasn't sure if he liked the way she was changing. He had gotten used to her being so easy going that he didn't have to consider her feelings at all. When she became more in touch with herself, she wanted him to consider her feelings, too, and she started expressing herself more. She would no longer accept him treating her as if she didn't exist, and she even had a dream where he was complaining about her being too real! This shows how Alumina had attracted a mate who fit her perception of reality. She felt that she didn't exist, so she had found a mate who treated her as if she didn't exist. When she started becoming more real, she wanted a relationship that reflected her newfound sense of "realness," and her mate had to choose whether he wanted to be part of that reality or not. Because her mate had an aversion to commitment of any kind, he simply floated away without even telling Alumina if he was actually coming or going. She waited for months, hoping that her non-existent relationship was going to become real one day, while continuing to use Alumina in different potencies whenever the numbness, or desire to kill, returned.

After using Alumina 10M for a while, the symptoms started shifting. First, she became furiously angry. She was angry about the way her mate had treated her. She was angry about how her last mate had treated her, too. In fact, she was angry with her father for having left her while she was still a baby, and she realized how much resentment she was actually holding inside. Now there was no question of numbness anymore. She could feel everything, and it hurt! She felt betrayed and angry, and she started expressing herself to the people she was angry with. Expressing herself was still very difficult for her since she had never really done it before. She had to consciously deal with people that she had dysfunctional relationships with and try to be clear for the first time, and she had to find a lot of courage to do so. The people in her life had obviously been attracted to her "invisibility" because of issues in their own remedy profiles, and it is interesting to note that when she changed, most of them didn't take the transition well, and many of them left her life. This triggered the grief that was underlying her anger, and she started responding well to homeopathic Natrum Muriaticum. At that point, totally different kinds of issues showed up in her life, issues that were a reflection of the Natrum Muriaticum remedy profile, and her old Alumina issues seemed to have mysteriously disappeared.

I have also seen similar changes in other clients after using high, or very high, potencies. One Calcarea Carbonica client, who was obsessed about wanting someone to build her a house, became more and more dissatisfied about everything in her life. She thought that getting her house built would make a huge difference in her life until I pointed out to her that she wasn't happy the last time she had a house, either. She realized then that maybe the house wasn't the real issue after all. The truth was that she couldn't think of anything that would truly make her happy, in fact she didn't really feel like being in this dimension at all. Everything in the third dimension seemed to require a huge effort, and she was feeling too fragile to even be here. She told me how people would offer her hugs and then squeeze her too hard. She became oversensitive both to touch and to people's energy, and she felt that people were too rough and insensitive for her. She told me how she couldn't wait to move on to other dimensions, and she became more interested in psychic realms. Her depression no longer responded to Calcarea Carbonica, so I retook her case and came up with Thuja for her new state. Homeopathic Thuja lifted her depression quickly, and within weeks she found a new job she liked and a better place to live.

So, which one is the constitutional remedy? Was Alumina born a Natrum with an Alumina disposition, or was she born Alumina with a Natrum disposition? Does Thuja represent a deeper layer than Calcarea and is therefore the "real constitution," or is Calcarea Carbonica her constitution that she will eventually revert back to? The picture is complicated, and there isn't really any way to know for sure what the true answer is. It does, however, explain why there are so many different opinions about this issue among homeopaths.

Just to add an interesting angle to this chapter, I would like to remind everyone that the whole system of homeopathy is based on natural law, which means that anything we are trying to understand or explain about homeopathy must also be based on our understanding of natural law. The main natural law, which applies to everything in the universe, is the law of balance. The law of balance simply states that everything in the universe will strive to be in a state of balance, simply because a balanced state is a state of stability. If something isn't balanced, the system is unstable and will immediately attempt to readjust itself until another state of balance is achieved. (In homeopathy, we use remedies to help bring the body back into a state of balance because imbalance equals sickness or disease). When trying to understand the law of balance, it is very important to understand that balance is never a fixed state, it always changes. Just think of a tight rope walker – always leaning a little bit this way and then a little bit the other way, constantly adjusting and readjusting. This state of balance is never fixed; it is always in a state of flux, always changing and flowing. This is the natural way. Understanding this, we can easily see why change is always happening, in fact, it is the only thing in the universe we can always count on. Change is life, change is creation, and anything fixed and stuck represents death. As an example of this, think of a tree. As long as the tree is changing, growing and stretching its branches towards the sky, it is alive, but the moment it stops changing or growing, it is dead. Therefore, my own feeling is that even constitutions can change because nothing in life is ever fixed, and therefore, nothing can always be the same.

Whether you agree with the way I see things, or not, doesn't really matter because knowing the true answer to this question is not a requirement for being a good homeopath. The main requirement for being a good homeopath is the ability to carefully listen and observe the picture that is presented when taking someone's case, to be open to the possibility that the symptoms may start shifting at some point, and when that happens, for whatever reason, to be willing to retake the case and possibly change the remedy. Whether the remedy we pick is the person's true constitutional remedy, or not, doesn't really matter, as long as we pick a remedy based on what we can see in the case at the time. And, because life is always in a state of change, we, as homeopaths, must also be open minded enough to change our opinions about what remedy someone might need, regardless of what we think their constitution may be.

THE MYSTERY OF ATTRACTION
Personal Reflection

As I was writing these stories, my mind went through its own journey of discovery, and many things began to fall into place. After writing the story of Nux and Silicea, and Nux and Kali, it struck me how very different these people are from each other, and I kept wondering why such different beings would feel so drawn to each other. One morning when I woke up full of inspiration, I could see exactly why. The answer lies in the stories that fit each remedy picture. Because we are replaying these stories as if they were still happening, the stories are affecting our perceptions of reality, and this perception affects everything we do in our lives, including who we are attracted to. Let's step back for a moment and see if this makes any sense.

Nux is the warrior who fights for a cause where he has to conquer some kind of dangerous or evil enemy in the process. He is usually trying to save someone, or something, whether it is a person, a people, a country, or a way of life. Whatever it is, it is something he is willing to risk his life for. If we look at the situation that goes with Silicea, she is the princess who needs someone to save her and take care of her. In the fairytales the princess is usually trapped in a tower, guarded by a terrifying dragon. You would almost have to be a Nux to be able to overcome the dangers and obstacles it would take to free her. Freeing the damsel in distress, or fighting for someone who can't fight for themselves, is what gives Nux purpose in life. He is the only one who has what it takes to overcome the challenges. If he didn't have anyone, or anything, to fight for, his life would quickly become meaningless, and he could easily lose his sense of purpose. If we look at the situation that goes with the Kali Carbonica picture, we see a situation where a group of people were attacked and couldn't defend themselves successfully. They felt weak and vulnerable and tried to stick together as a group, but many still got killed in the attack. Imagine how happy and relieved they would have been if a Nux had suddenly showed up to defend the helpless! A Nux who was strong, brave, fearless, and intelligent, who could defeat their enemy and help restore peace to their people! Nux would be the hero, and any young woman in the group would love to be his mate. This is something that appeals to Nux, since he doesn't mind a little glory and admiration for his heroic efforts.

I saw a similar example when watching the last movie of "The Lord of the Rings · The Return of the King." This is the final battle between good and evil, and Aragon, the future king, is fighting a losing battle. Then the message comes that the fairy princess, whom he loves, has chosen a mortal life, and she is dying because the evil is draining her energy. Now he *has to* win the battle, because if he doesn't, evil will win and the fairy princess will die. A superhuman effort is needed since the odds are not in their favor, so he summons all the dead people who dwell in the mountain, and together, they are able to overcome the enemy.

The interesting part of this story is the fact that there are two women who love him, but he only feels attracted to one of them because only one fits the story associated with his remedy picture. The fairy princess is the one who fits his story. She is incredibly beautiful, and she is so fragile that she is dying from just the energy of evil. Aragon is the only one who can save her because no one else can take on a battle of that magnitude. As a mortal, she is helpless, and she needs him to save her life and take care of her.

The other woman, who loves him, is also very beautiful. She has long, blonde hair and is also a princess, but she doesn't need Aragon to save her or take care of her. She is strong willed and independent and she even has enough strength and courage to go into battle and fight by his side. In many ways she is a better mate for Aragon than the fairy princess since she can actually help him in his cause, but because she doesn't need him to save her or fight for her; she can never give his life the sense of purpose that he needs. She loves him more than anything, but he doesn't even see her because the fairy princess needs his help. But even if he didn't already love the fairy princess, he still wouldn't have been attracted to her. She simply doesn't fit the story that Nux is acting out, where he is the great hero who saves the princess and lives happily ever after. She doesn't need to be saved, so she can't be part of the picture.

It is also interesting how all the fairytales stop right there. The great warrior, or the prince, marries the princess, and they live happily ever after... Or, so the story goes. Obviously, Nux is "mentally programmed" to pick the girl who fits the story, which isn't necessarily the most compatible companion he could have picked. And, because nobody wants to ruin a good story, no fairytale ever talks about the differences they experienced in their relationship after the honeymoon was over. (The relationship between Prince Charles and Diana is a good example. Prince Charles was far from charming, he didn't take good care of Diana, and they certainly didn't live happily ever after).

This also explains why Natrum Muriaticum is attracted to unavailable men because in the story that goes with the Natrum picture, she is not getting her needs met by the man in her life. The first man in her life is her emotionally or physically unavailable father, and later on she will be looking for another man to play the same role. Arsenicum will look for someone who can take care of him, if he should ever need it, because deep inside he feels weak and unloved and he is worried that something bad is going to happen to him. Or, he will attract someone who will betray him, steal his money or leave him at a time when he really needs them. Staphysagria, who hates his mother, is looking for a mother figure he can hate, so he often picks someone who reminds him of his mother. Causticum wants a mate who can help him save humanity or make the world a better place; Calcarea Carbonica wants a mate who can provide for her and make her feel safe; Phosphorus wants a mate who will love her forever and think she is eternally beautiful; Pulsatilla wants a mate who will never leave or die; Carcinosin will often end up with someone they can take care of to the point where they completely lose their sense of self, and Medorrhinum is looking for someone who can be "the king" of the relationship, so she doesn't have to take on the responsibility of being in charge. This also explains why we usually end up repeating the same kinds of relationships over and over, always ending up with the same type of person, time and time again. When two people have stories that match, they feel helplessly and irresistibly drawn to each other and often end up in relationships where each can keep acting out his or her own situation until it is resolved, or the relationship falls apart. And if the relationship falls apart before the issues have been resolved, or the lessons have been learned, they have to find a similar mate who can provide the same opportunity to learn the same lessons. This is why the patterns in our relationships always seem to repeat themselves. What a strange arrangement! But it does make sense...

So, what about freedom of choice? Is there no such thing? Yes, there is freedom of choice, but only through increased awareness and understanding. The more awareness we have, the more we'll be able to understand why we do the things we do, and the more understanding we have, the more freedom we have to break through the old patterns that keep us in bondage. Once we free ourselves from these old patterns, we can consciously create positive change and stop living our lives in a state of stuckness and predictability.

MEDITATION AND RELATIONSHIPS

The story of Kali Carbonica and Nux Vomica describes how this couple learned to overcome their differences through their daily meditation practices. For anyone who might be interested, but doesn't know exactly what meditation is, I have tried to clarify below what it is and why it is so important for creating harmony in relationships, as well as for your individual spiritual growth.

Meditation is a state of peacefulness and tranquility, beyond the mind, that can sometimes happen through the use of meditation techniques. (This state, beyond the mind, where no thoughts exist, is often called a state of "no-mind," or Mind with a capital M, which is what the Buddhists like to call it. Both concepts refer to the same state). It is, however, important to understand that the technique itself is not meditation, although people often misleadingly describe it as such. Meditation isn't just the chanting of a mantra so that you can create prosperity in your life or cope better with your daily tasks. Neither is it something you can do for just an hour a day as a spiritual practice because, eventually, your whole life needs to become meditative. The meditation technique is only a device that can help bring you to a state where "no mind" can happen, spontaneously.

Living a meditative life requires a complete shift in focus. Instead of constantly looking outside yourself for fulfillment, you have to start looking inside for a deeper, more permanent kind of fulfillment, a fulfillment that can only be found by going beyond the mind. This way of life becomes an inner journey to the center of your being. Through this journey, you consciously try to reestablish (or, more accurately, remember) your lost connection to source so that you no longer have to walk through life feeling lost, separate or incomplete in yourself. When you are able to feel your connection to source again, your whole perception of reality will slowly start changing. More and more, you will be able to see how everything that happens in your life is only a part of a much bigger picture. Over time, the ability to see the bigger picture eventually creates deeper wisdom and understanding of life in general. In this state, worldly concerns seem to disappear, or they simply become irrelevant. Your connection to source increases your ability to see what is essential in life, and what is not, and this also makes it easier to get your daily priorities straight.

In a relationship, the priorities are simple: Each person needs to focus on his or her own spiritual journey. We are here to remember our connection to source so that we can achieve our highest potential, which, to the spiritual seeker, is the state of Enlightenment, or Ultimate Oneness with Source. The problems we experience in our relationships should simply be seen as opportunities for further spiritual growth. When both partners focus on their own connection to source, they are also nurturing their connection to each other, because spiritually, we are all connected to the same source. This works much better than what people normally do in relationships. Instead of focusing on all the things they don't like about each other and constantly trying to convince the other to change, they will eventually realize that the only person they can truly change is themselves. This perception can then turn the relationship from being a battle of egos (selfishness and separation) into a place of love, nurturing and compassion (togetherness and oneness).

When the focus is on each person's spiritual expansion, instead of the state of their relationship, many more things become possible. Negative patterns become easier to drop because there won't be a need for anyone to be defensive. As you keep going deeper within, little by little, you also start discovering that the feeling of separation is simply another delusion, a delusion of separation, which is another name for ego, or separate, selfish self. You'll eventually understand that remembering your connection to source is the only permanent solution to resolving all your feelings of unhappiness and misery. You'll also understand that the solution can never come from other people in your life because nobody else can make you happy. You have to find out how to make yourself happy, and the easiest way is by simply going within. However, going within may not always be as easy as we would like it to be.

What usually happens is that instead of looking within, we start looking outside ourselves for a mate who can become our "better half," so we can start feeling whole again. The only problem is that the "better half" concept doesn't work! There is no way that two people, who are not feeling complete in themselves, are going to feel more complete together! Unfortunately, what we actually find, through repeated trial and error, is that no one else can ever fill the sensation of inner emptiness; in fact, no other can ever give us the feeling of wholeness that we are looking for. It simply cannot happen because what we tend to attract is a partner who has also forgotten his, or her, connection to source, and as a result, we end up with two people who are lost together. This doesn't make anyone feel more fulfilled, or more whole, rather it multiplies the misery and the inner sense of emptiness. The relationship becomes a great disappointment to both because both expected the other to make them feel fulfilled. This is not possible because only YOU can make yourself whole again, by finding you inner connection to source. If you are not aware of your connection to source, the fact is, you have nothing but misery to offer to the other, and this is the main reason why relationships generally tend to become so mutually unfulfilling.

In the relationship between Kali and Nux, both partners are focusing on becoming more spiritually whole. When two whole people come together in a relationship, some alchemy happens where the two together become more than they were when they were single. They become fellow travelers, both moving on a spiritual path, both trying to reach their highest potential, both seeking to find the deepest possible levels of truth. Their spiritual connection becomes the main thing they have in common, and this connection is more important than any of their worldly differences. If both can find their own connection to source, the energy from source inspires their creative potential and strengthens their sense of purpose in life. This helps them grow and expand, which can also ultimately have a positive effect on their relationship.

Because we are here to grow and expand, finding a spiritual path becomes very important. Our whole journey here is about finding a way to reconnect, and eventually become one with, the Ultimate Source, and everything we experience, including relationship problems, are only stepping stones in the process of continued spiritual expansion. All it takes, to be able to see everything in a whole new perspective, is just a small shift in perception!

GIVE AND TAKE IN RELATIONSHIPS

Have you ever heard the expression "there has to be both give and take if a relationship is to work?" Let's look at this statement a little deeper because this issue is not as self-evident as it may seem. Harville Hendrix's book "Getting the love you want" became a best seller because the title reflects an issue a lot of people are interested in. I am not even going to question the content of the book because Harville Hendrix has good intentions and wants to help people, and I honor that. But, the title itself is worth looking at. Why would a title like "Getting the love you want" become a best seller? Why did he not call it "Giving the love you want?" The truth is, his title appeals to people simply because people are naturally takers. They live in a state of lack where nothing is ever enough, and they always want to *get* more than what they have. I am not just talking about physical assets or money. This also applies in a very big way to people's relationships in the form of getting love, getting attention, getting your needs met, and so on.

When first starting a relationship with someone, things usually start out in a very different way. Have you ever thought about why everyone loves the honeymoon so much? Love and energy is overflowing from within, and both are in a place where they just want to give and share with the other. At this point there isn't even a question of whether you are getting your needs met, or not, because giving and sharing, generously, is such a joy in itself. But, unfortunately, this state of mutual giving doesn't usually last very long, at the most a few months, and then the pendulum swings to the other side of the coin, and selfishness begins. The newness and excitement of newfound love fades a lot quicker than you would want it to, and you are left with only a vague memory of how incredible it was.

What happens next is interesting. Stinginess creeps into the relationship; stinginess about giving and loving. Subconsciously, people start keeping scores. Every time we do something nice for the other, we expect the other to also do something nice for us, to keep things even and fair. If one cooks, the other should do the dishes or take the trash out. If one contributes anything to the relationship, the other is expected to do something similar in return to keep it balanced. If the expectation isn't met, frustration sets in. Both start thinking the other is either too selfish or too controlling. The focus shifts from being giving and loving, to being stingy and wanting more from the other. The big problem here has to do with duality. Anytime you choose one side of duality, you are always going to create an unbalanced state. To illustrate this, we can use a simple thing like breathing as an example. As long as we breathe in and out, there is no problem, but if we choose to only breathe out, we'll be dead very soon. Any choice between polar opposites will have a similar effect, because both sides of duality are needed to create a state of balance.

To give you an example of how this issue may manifest in relationships, imagine that something happens in your life where you find yourself in trouble, and you really need someone to help you. You reach out to one of your friends for help, but for some reason she isn't able or willing to do what you want her to do. Something may be happening in her life that makes it difficult for her to deal with your problems in addition to her own. Your feelings are hurt. If she were a real friend, she would have dropped everything in her own life, just to help you! You would have done that for her, so she has all of a sudden proven herself to be less of a friend than you had hoped for. In your disappointment you decide to withdraw from this so called "friend." She has shown "her true colors," and now you will show her yours!

What happens next is very interesting. You may find that you have stopped liking this person because she is too selfish. Your reaction to her selfishness is that you will stop giving and sharing with her. You may even start behaving hostile towards her because you are so upset that you want to hurt her feelings, like she has hurt yours. You are angry because she acted selfishly, so you may try to get even by acting selfishly back. Giving her back her own medicine is obviously the only thing she understands! Serves her right, doesn't it? Maybe it does, or maybe it doesn't... Does selfishness ever serve anyone right? How can something, that is totally one sided, serve anyone right? The acts of just giving, or just taking, are both extremes, and extremes are always states of some kind of imbalance. The key here is to not get stuck in any fixed ideas about how things are supposed to be, in other words, not to choose only one side of duality. However, since we happen to live in a dimension of duality, it is very tempting to pick only one point of view and stick to it, stubbornly, so this is an issue that applies to pretty much everyone.

You may have noticed that all the relationship problems begin as soon as the honeymoon is over, and selfishness has entered the relationship. (This is a sure sign that the self, or the ego, is back!) When the focus changes from an attitude of giving to an attitude of getting, the unfortunate thing is that love simply dies. The other may, or may not, learn the lessons you so generously are imposing, but something very bad happens in the process, not just to your relationship, but to you, too. You also become selfish! You become the quality you hate so much in the other because you are trying to fight selfishness with selfishness, and that makes you selfish, too! And when you become selfish, you stop giving freely, and when you stop giving freely, your heart closes up. This is why getting even by acting selfishly, to teach someone a lesson, never works.

The problem with having your heart closed is that you can no longer give or receive love from anyone. Instead, you feel dead and cold inside. You may not understand what has happened to you and why you can't feel love any more, and you may wish you could change it back to the way it was before, but you don't know how. Once your heart is closed, love simply disappears from your life, and your relationship either turns emotionally ice cold or hellish. You may even find that the love of your life has turned into the most annoying creature imaginable. A man may find that he likes his girlfriend less and less, and he might even start questioning why he ever felt attracted to her in the first place. Instead of seeing that the real problem is not in the relationship, but lies within himself, as lack of love and compassion in his heart, he starts projecting all his problems onto his mate. "If only I could rid myself of this albatross once and for all and start over with somebody nice!" he might secretly think to himself, and before he knows it, divorce is on his doorstep. The funny thing here is that instead of trying to teach his mate a lesson, he should have taught himself the lesson instead! Even if he does start over again with someone nice, someone who is able to melt his frozen heart and allow the energy of love to warm him again, the newfound feelings of love are still only going to be temporary. As soon as he discovers any signs of selfishness in his new mate, the same reaction is triggered again, and again, the pendulum swings from one side of duality to the other. And since people are more or less selfish by nature, the new mate will also disappoint him, eventually, just like his last mate did, and he will disappoint her as well. This is what happens when people don't learn from their mistakes.

However, things don't have to be quite so bleak. There is another option that is much more beneficial to everyone involved, but it takes more awareness, understanding and effort to achieve. This approach is based on understanding and compassion, rather than criticism and desire for revenge. The key here is to stop choosing one side of the coin, and simply start living in a loose and natural way without any preconceived or fixed ideas of how things should be. What happens when you become loose and natural? You naturally give, when that feels right, and you naturally take, when that feels right. Then, how is this any different to what normally happens in relationships? There, too, there is sometimes giving and sometimes taking, so what is the difference? The main difference is in the attitude of each person. Someone, who is loose and natural, has no fixed ideas about how things are supposed to be and, therefore, has no expectations of the other. Since the cause of all relationship problems has to do with expectations and fixed ideas, relationship problems will simply disappear if you drop expectations. So, how do you create this shift so you can start living a life of no expectations? You simply have to stop choosing only one side of duality in a fixed way, and as you become more aware, you will find a natural balance between giving and taking arising within yourself. This approach will ultimately transform both you, and your life, in addition to improving your relationship.

One of the most important things that has to happen, if you want spiritual growth as well as a better approach to relating, is to stop keeping score. Drop the whole idea of what is fair and what is not. (Remember, fair and unfair are also part of duality, so don't compare, and don't choose...). The solution is to give whatsoever you can, freely and naturally, when it feels right, without focusing on whether an equal amount is given in return, and take, just as freely and naturally, when that feels right. By giving and taking in a loose and natural way, resentment will drop, effortlessly, and loving energy will naturally start flowing through your heart again. When your heart is open and energy is overflowing from within, you start feeling happy and fulfilled for no reason whatsoever, regardless of outside circumstances. You may not be able to "get even" with somebody who isn't giving equally in return, but you wouldn't even want to. Keeping your heart open is reward enough in itself, and a much better reward than any revenge. Not only are you nurturing others with your love, you are also nurturing yourself. If your heart is closed and you feel empty and cold inside, you hope and expect that someone else will fill up your inner emptiness, which of course, will never happen. But if you are full of love, overflowing from within, you don't need fulfillment to come from somebody else. Once you are in touch with the loving energy emerging from within yourself, there is always more where that came from, and you are no longer in a state of lack. This is when you realize that true love has nothing to do with relationships. True love is something that happens inside you when your heart is open and energy is flowing through it. It can be shared with anything or anybody because it is a state of overflow and abundance from within, and this state is also very attractive to any possible future mate. So, first, look inside and find "true love" within, and then, you can easily find a mate to share it with. To do it the other way around unfortunately never works.

One of the problems, about living in a dimension of duality, is that most people will choose only one side of the coin. Therefore, it can sometimes be difficult to have a giving attitude in a place where everyone else has a taking attitude. As soon as people discover your giving nature, they will often do what they can to take advantage of you. This doesn't happen because they are mean, but because they don't have enough awareness to see that there are better options, and they also haven't found their own inner source of love yet. Each has to learn this in their own time, when they are ready. Here, we also need to look a little deeper into the concept of "giving freely," which means that you only have to give what feels right to you. If someone asks for more than you wish to give, you are no longer "giving freely," you are "giving with effort," or giving out of duty, because someone is expecting you to, which is basically a drain of energy. So, anytime you feel drained, remember this: A gift is something that is given, not taken. When someone gives a gift to you, you don't turn around and say: "This isn't enough, I was expecting more!" The same applies to gifts of love and caring. Giving freely doesn't mean being a doormat. If someone takes advantage of your giving attitude, and you start feeling drained, you need to draw the line and make the other aware that they are draining your energy with their expectations and lack of will to take responsibility for their own issues. Drawing this line can be difficult, and you may lose your so called "friends" in the process, but if you don't draw the line, you'll start building up resentment, which in turn will close your heart and make you hateful instead of loving, and you'll eventually end up becoming selfish, too. Everything in life is about finding the right balance.

Reading this book you will see that the issue of give and take plays a part in all the stories. This issue applies to everyone because we are all basically selfish beings. In many of the stories I suggest solutions that involve compromises. A compromise is a willingness to give a little, to become a little less selfish, for the purpose of improving the relationship and also for the purpose of becoming more balanced in ourselves. My suggestions are an effort to show that both end up benefiting if they can only learn to give a little more and expect a little less from each other. But, ideally, the best attitude for two people to have in a relationship is if both give and take in a loose, natural way, without any expectations of whether the other is reciprocating. When you find your inner balance between giving and taking, the whole issue of "getting" simply becomes irrelevant.

In one of the relationship stories in this book, the story of Causticum and Sepia, Causticum is being selfish and Sepia is giving too much, which basically creates a state of imbalance between them, as well as within each of them. Sepia has been on a spiritual path for a long time and has learned how to give, but she tends to give too much. Causticum is also on a spiritual path, but because he is on a "mission from God," his view is fixed and clouded and he can't see that Sepia is becoming drained from putting out more energy than she has to spare. He rationalizes that what he is doing is God's will, which, of course, no one can question since there is no way to prove, or disprove, what God's will actually is. And because he can only see his own point of view, his ideas are fixed and he is basically acting selfishly.

Sepia is on a very different path. She is giving, her heart is open, and she is a very loving person. But she hasn't learned how to draw the line between giving freely and being taken advantage of. When she started drawing that line, Causticum became extremely angry, both with her and with me, for suggesting such a thing. Unfortunately, the attitude of selfishness isn't easy to change, once it has taken hold of someone because we get used to keeping things the way we like things to be, and we generally don't want anything to change. Change requires both awareness and a willingness to do what it takes to break the patterns that no longer benefit us, and we often experience emotional pain in the process. However, the emotional pain of transformation should only be looked at as "labor pains," since you are actually in the process of giving birth to your true self.

When looking at relationship dynamics with great honesty, it is easy to see that the root of all conflict in relationships is fixed ideas about how things have to be. Fixed ideas and lack of willingness to change are actually the main causes of the patterns and delusions that create our reality. Hahnemann, the founder of homeopathy, mentions that our susceptibility to disease started with evil thought. Evil thought preceded all the miasms, which is basically an inherent weakness that gives us a pre-disposition for sickness. First there was evil thought, and then evil thought led to evil action, and evil action often led to serious diseases, such as gonorrhea or syphilis. But, it all started with evil thought. So, what exactly is evil? Evil is vicious, mean and uncaring. Uncaring is selfish and fixed. Selfish doesn't share. Selfish doesn't care. Selfish doesn't love. And therefore, changing from a selfish, fixed point of view to a more loving, loose and natural state, by simply dropping fixed ideas and preconceived expectations is the ultimate key to self-transformation and also to solving all conflicts between people. Whether you want to do this is a different matter; but once you can see clearly what the problem is, it's up to you if you want to keep expanding, or if you choose to remain in stuckness, misery and bondage...

ADAM AND EVE
A True Story

This is a modern version of the story of Adam and Eve. I couldn't possibly write a book about relationship issues without also looking at the very first relationship that ever existed in this dimension - the story of Adam and Eve. We tend to read these old stories as if they were stories that happened to somebody else, long ago, and we like to believe that they no longer apply to us. Unfortunately, the story of Adam and Eve still applies to all of us. The issues they experienced have now become part of our deepest emotional heritage, simply because they were never resolved, and it is up to each one of us to find resolution and completion within ourselves. Therefore it doesn't matter what constitutions the two people in this story are, because in this case, the homeopathic point of view is irrelevant. It doesn't even matter how much time has passed since the original story happened because time in itself never heals; only understanding does. I have therefore chosen to call the people in this story Adam and Eve, too, since nothing much has changed, and they are still dealing with the same issues.

Adam, in our modern version of this story, had always had a questioning, critical nature. Whether he experienced success or failure in his life, there was always an underlying feeling that "there must be more to life than this!" His quest for meaning led him to try many things, but no matter what he achieved in his external life, there was still this nagging feeling of inner emptiness and meaninglessness. He eventually decided to sell everything he owned and go on a long journey, not even knowing what he was really looking for. He hopped on an airplane, stayed in a hotel for a while and eventually bought a motor home to travel in. Traveling without any idea where he was going, his life became an adventure. Things that were happening, and people he was meeting on the way, became pieces in a bigger picture. Everything started falling into place and clarity was coming. His awareness and trust was growing. There were no goals, no problems, no distractions, no ambitions and no responsibilities to worry about. In fact, all his worries were completely gone. He was learning how to go with the flow, and he was becoming more and more connected to the Universal Source of All, or, as some people call it, God. The energy from the Source started flowing through him. It blew his heart wide open, and for the first time, he felt love arising from within for no reason at all. He almost couldn't stop smiling.

ADAM AND EVE A True Story

This was a kind of love that was totally unrelated to any kind of relationship. It was overflowing on it's own accord. It was coming from a source beyond anything he had ever experienced before. It was flowing through him and radiating outwards, shining on everyone he came into contact with. He felt at one with everything and everybody, and there was so much happiness and love within him that he simply had to share.

This is when he met Eve. Eve had also been on a spiritual path since she was a child, always questioning everything in her life. She decided early on to live an unconventional life where her quest for truth became the main priority in her life. She dropped her university studies to become a disciple of an enlightened master, and she lived in a spiritual commune for a while. She went through many relationships with men and none of them were easy. However, her attitude towards life always remained the same, no matter what she was experiencing: She had a commitment to learn from everything that happened to her, so that she would continue to grow spiritually.

A while before she met Adam, she had just been through a divorce. She had custody of a small child, and she had no idea what to do next, or even how to make a living and take care of her child at the same time. She knew that the most important thing she could do for herself at that point was to connect herself to the Universal Source. She spent every spare moment meditating. She was going deeper and deeper within, with an attitude of surrender and trust. Pretty soon she could feel the energy of the whole, pulsating through her being, and she became more and more joyful every day. At this point she wasn't even looking for another partner in her life. She felt so much love arising inside her for no reason at all, that she felt more fulfilled than anything she had previously experienced in an actual relationship.

It was around this time that Adam and Eve started becoming aware of each other's presence. She could feel Adam's love radiating, and it made her heart jump an extra beat every time she looked into his eyes. The feeling was mutual, and within a very short time, they were living together and making wedding plans. A while after the wedding, Eve became pregnant, and they were both overjoyed about having created a "love child" together. It felt like they had finally entered Paradise, but as we all know, from the story of Adam and Eve, their time in Paradise was to be very short. In the original story Adam and Eve lost their connection to God and had to leave Paradise, and they have been looking for a way to get back ever since.

To get back to the modern version of this story, Eve didn't eat of the fruit of knowledge. She did something else instead, something very insignificant that she wasn't even aware of at the time, but it had the same effect on Adam. One day when they were shopping together, she wasn't feeling too good. She was pregnant and very tired. She may have even felt nauseated, and in that state, she became selfish. She told Adam that she was too tired to go to any other stores. They had done everything she wanted to do, and when it was time to do what he wanted, she told him she was too tired. Adam had opened his heart so much that he was feeling extremely fragile, sensitive and vulnerable emotionally, and when she told him that she didn't want to do what he wanted, without any regards for his feelings, it felt like he had just been hit with a sledge hammer. His newfound connection to source was so fragile that one insensitive comment was all it took to shatter it. In a split second it felt like something had broken inside of him, like shattered glass, and he knew instantly that he had lost his connection to source. He looked at Eve and didn't know what to do, or even how to express what had just happened. Because his connection to source had been shattered, no apology could possibly reverse what had happened, so there wasn't even any sense in saying something about it at the time. Here was the woman he loved, carrying his baby, and through a moment of unconscious selfishness she had basically destroyed his first and only experience of Paradise and connection to God. He was devastated and did the only thing that made sense to him at the time. He kept giving her the love he still felt in his heart until he had given her everything he had left, and then he was faced with utter emptiness for himself. He knew that he had lost his connection to Source, and he knew that his heart had closed up, but he didn't have a clue how to open up again. He found himself, little by little, blaming and resenting Eve for having destroyed his inner source of love and bliss.

Eve had no idea what had happened to Adam. She didn't even realize that she had said or done anything that would upset him, although, she could feel a difference in their relationship. Adam wasn't as warm and loving as he used to be. Sometimes he became extremely moody, depressed and introverted. She tried to understand, but she couldn't really, since even Adam didn't totally understand what had happened, either. She wondered why he no longer showed any affection towards her, and when she asked him about it, he wouldn't answer and became even more resentful. All he knew was that he had lost something that he couldn't find again, because of something she had said that had shattered his connection to source. He felt dead inside and eventually became totally indifferent to everything and everyone. He no longer loved anyone, not even himself or his own life. Suicidal thoughts started coming, and also thoughts of leaving his wife. Maybe he could find another woman who would spark the energy of love in him again! Maybe someone else could inspire him to find his lost connection! His resentment towards Eve grew into total indifference and even hatred at times. He could no longer see her or appreciate anything she was doing for him. Even his perception of her had changed. Now she only looked old and ugly to him.

Eve understood what was happening. She had committed herself to living a life of truth, and she could see, with no denial, what was happening in her relationship with Adam. When she asked him about it, Adam told her the truth. He told her that he had been considering divorce, and that he had been thinking about other women. He told her that whatever she said at that time, long ago, had shattered his connection to source, and that he couldn't stop blaming her for what had happened. Forgiving her wouldn't make any difference, since he still didn't know how to find his connection again. He had found something, so unbelievably precious, that he simply couldn't get over the fact that it had been lost. He wanted to leave Eve so badly that it was driving him mad, and at the same time, his inner guidance kept telling him not to leave the relationship because there was more to come. "This isn't all there is to it, stay, stay, hang in there and you will see..."

Eve could see clearly where things were going. Adam had told her a while back that one of her biggest problems was that she was doing whatever she could to keep the relationship alive. "What is wrong with that?" she asked, not understanding what he was talking about. He answered: "You found the love of your life, and now you want to make it last forever, even after the love is gone." She understood and told him he could leave if he wanted to. He told her he didn't intend to leave, which confused her. She didn't understand why he would want to stay, if he no longer loved her, and he couldn't explain it to her, because he didn't really understand it either. However, at this point, Eve decided to do the only thing she could think of, she surrendered. She surrendered to the situation she was in, accepting what was happening, without any clue what was going to happen next. She surrendered to the will of the divine, and accepted the fact that life is full of mysteries and uncertainties, and that these uncertainties have their own wisdom as part of a bigger picture. She focused on letting go, as totally as she could, while accepting the pain, which she was already feeling in her heart. She knew well that pain is the price we pay for the joy that we experience in our lives. She knew that life always comes in opposites, and that pain and pleasure are just two sides of the same coin. You can't have one without the other in a dimension of duality, and she was willing to face her pain without denial or resistance.

What happened next is nothing less than a miracle. One night they started having a conversation about the state of things and their relationship in general. It first started out like a normal relationship argument, both blaming each other for this and that, both unhappy with the situation. Eve felt hurt and started crying. She wanted to run to her room and close the door so she could lie down under her covers and cry in self pity, but something made her stay where she was. Her inner guidance told her to stay and listen, even though her feelings were hurt. Adam finally remembered exactly what it was, that she had said to him so many years ago, that had shattered his connection to source.

When Adam told her what had actually happened, Eve was instantly reminded of the original story of Adam and Eve. She realized that a very similar thing had happened to them. In the original story, Eve had caused Adam to lose his connection to God because she had eaten from the tree of knowledge and made him eat, too, and he blamed her for what happened, even though he had also played his part. They were thrown out of Paradise into a world of duality and separation, which, of course, caused them nothing but misery. Adam didn't know how to find his way back to Paradise, and his whole journey here on earth became an effort to overcome separation and duality so he again could find oneness with God. This is what the journey of enlightenment is all about, transcending duality and finding the way back to Oneness (paradise).

Adam looked at her for what seemed like an eternity, as things started expanding inside of him. He could see that what had happened was a replay of the oldest relationship story since the beginning of man - the story of Adam and Eve! He remembered that man is here on earth to find his way back to God, which won't happen unless he can also to overcome his resentment towards Eve. Before they were thrown out of Paradise there was no separation from God, or even between the two of them. They were one with each other, and one with God, so there wasn't really a question of blame. They were all just playing different parts in the story. Even God was playing a part, by pointing out which tree they shouldn't eat from, or by even creating the tree in the first place.

In the modern version of this story, Adam could finally see that Eve had only played her part, and that he was actually meant to experience being disconnected as part of his spiritual journey. In the beginning of his relationship to Eve, Adam first experienced the bliss of love. It was as if he had found his inner Paradise. Then Eve destroyed the connection he had found so that he was thrown out of his newfound Paradise into misery and despair. Since then, his biggest challenge in life became how to find his lost connection to source again. He could finally see that Eve, by playing her part, had actually brought him to this new place of understanding. The deeper truth of the situation was slowly starting to dawn on him. Looking with newfound awareness, he could see that all the things that happen in life actually help the spiritual journey. At the same time, he also realized that there are no victims. We may feel like victims at times, but that only happens if we forget that we can learn something from everything that happens, no matter what it is! Transcending victim consciousness is only a matter of a shift in perception since there is always more to life that what we can see. We just have to stop focusing on what it looks like, and try seeing the bigger picture instead.

Adam finally understood that Eve didn't mean to be horrible to him. She didn't mean to destroy his connection to God. It was only a part that she had to play, to help him come to this new level of understanding. Adam was able to see that the reason his connection to God had been so fragile, was the fact that he had basically stumbled upon it during his journey into the unknown. Unless the connection has been found through personal experience, maturity and wisdom, it can only be a momentary experience by it's very nature.

When Adam first experienced this connection, he didn't yet have the depth of understanding that was needed to keep the connection open. He hadn't walked enough of his path to have earned a more permanent connection at that point. After he fell from bliss, he had to walk through the valleys of despair and darkness for a long time. He had to experience "the dark night of the soul," where he was face to face with all his fears and inner demons. He had to see for himself how selfish and separate he really was. He had to understand how it was his own ego that kept him in a state of "stuckness," bondage and separation, and that this stuckness had nothing to do with Eve and her selfishness, because the truth is, they were both selfish at times.

After walking this long, arduous path, feeling completely alone the whole time, he started realizing how much effort it takes to truly be on a spiritual path. There are no shortcuts, and nothing is easy. Spiritual growth can only happen through having a deep commitment to walking the path, as well as persistence and discipline when facing pain and despair. Once you have been able to reach a deep enough level of understanding and wisdom, you can again rediscover your lost connection to source, only this time, your connection is not nearly as fragile as the first glimpses of bliss were. The first connection Adam experienced had been more like a glimpse of the other side of misery, in the form of happiness beyond belief. Now, after walking his spiritual path with much difficulty, he was finally able to see that the way back to God was through transcending duality altogether. He could finally see that the love that he had felt for Eve had to first be changed into misery so that he could learn more about the dimension of duality. He needed to see that both pain and happiness were part of the same duality, and that his goal was to transcend both. He could finally see that the two of them had been re-experiencing the oldest relationship archetype since the beginning of man - the story of how Adam and Eve had lost their connection to God (and to each other).

Eve was listening to Adam, as he was able to see and express one thing after another. His consciousness kept expanding, and things started falling into place. Everything was slowly beginning to make sense. While listening to Adam, she could feel a transformation happening in herself as well. It was the strangest thing. She could feel the pain of their lost love in her heart and, at the same time, be happy for the new depth of understanding that was happening. Tears of joy and sadness were running down her face, and she couldn't even tell if she was happy or sad. It felt more like both were happening at once.

Something was starting to melt inside of Adam. When Eve looked at him, she saw the transformation in his eyes, and she could also feel the same thing happening inside herself. Her understanding of what had happened was deepening, and the deeper it went, the more she could see how every moment was exactly as it should be. She could see how everything is an opportunity to deepen the understanding of the workings of the Universal Source, and a deep relaxation started happening inside her.

They looked at each other with a new softness in their eyes. Adam told her that she looked young again. They embraced with great tenderness and love. He said to her softly: "My friend, my love, we have walked a long and difficult path together. I can see now that it was all a necessary part of the paths we had to walk." The honesty made them feel closer to each other than they had felt for years. There was no more blame, resentment or defensiveness, no more expectation, and no more separation. Both could feel a new surge of love arising within them, as well as a deep wave of gratefulness towards each other. Two beings, each one on their own spiritual path, together and separate at the same time, both moving towards the light, both knowing that deep, down there is no separation. Beyond the veil of delusions, we are one with each other and with all that there is.

INDEX

INDEX

L

lack of confidence, 66, 73, 83, 84, 85, 113, 145, 158, 222, 226, 241, 255

lazy, 50, 52, 97, 117, 142, 160, 173, 174, 175, 230

leader type, 3, 103, 126, 139, 162, 214

lighthearted, 130

logical, 2, 3, 65, 66, 67, 70, 71

loner, 60, 147

love of power, 75

low self confidence, 108, 158, 219, 226

loyal, 218, 226

Lycopodium Clavatum, 73, 221, 237

M

malicious, 41, 49, 68, 77, 122, 131, 151

mania, 26, 58, 64, 123, 139

manic, 55, 117, 142, 161

Maya, 9

meditation, 194, 195, 251, 287

meditative, 129, 149

Medorrhinum, 12, 19, 85, 86, 87, 88, 89, 90, 91, 92, 93, 94, 95, 96, 97, 98, 199, 200, 201, 202, 203, 204, 207, 209, 210, 211, 212, 213, 214, 245, 246, 247, 248, 249, 250, 251, 252, 285

melancholic, 78, 87

mental dullness, 67

mental instability, 26

mental type, 64, 70, 158

mentally unstable, 25

methodical, 64, 75, 83

mild, 187, 193, 196, 254, 255, 272, 273

mild mannered, 25, 53, 66, 73, 101, 113, 115, 129, 144, 145, 149, 157, 158, 179

mischievous, 49, 90

miserable, 200, 201, 205

mistakes in speaking, 67, 87, 150, 168

mistakes while speaking, 25, 125

mistrustful, 54, 150

money issues, 1, 49, 61, 160, 211

moods alternate, 26

moody, 88, 217, 240, 271, 299

mortified, 25

mother issues, 230, 255, 257

N

Natrum Muriaticum, 1, 12, 19, 88, 101, 104, 155, 199, 207, 215, 221, 229, 233, 280, 281, 284

natural leader, 84, 121, 126

need for physical security, 63

needy, 189, 203, 232

nervous, 18, 32, 160

INDEX

INDEX